A WALK WITH GOD

*Life-transforming
strategies for the
important issues
men face today*

Jack Hayford

THOMAS NELSON PUBLISHERS
Nashville • Atlanta • London • Vancouver

TABLE OF CONTENTS

CHAPTER ONE:

THE POWER OF ALTARS–
HEART-TO-HEART
ENCOUNTERS WITH GOD

I could take you to the very spot where it happened.

I doubt that it would strike you as a particularly holy place. In fact, by appearance alone most anyone would call it "common" or "mundane."

I'm talking about a special point on Interstate 405, north-bound, near the Victory Boulevard offramp. That's where it took place.

That's where I'll always remember it.

That's where God met me in a unique way.

That's where He spoke words to my heart--highly significant words regarding my future; words which turned out to impact both my own and the future of God's purpose for a church congregation. It's the same one I've now served for nearly 25 years since that moment, so the importance of the encounter is obvious.

That section of freeway will always remind me of that divine encounter.

For me, that stretch of pavement is an altar.

Not Just the Wooden Railing

If we look at godly men of old and observe their encounters with the Most High God, and observe those places where God intersected their lives; in pivoting the course of their destinies into a new direction, one thing stands out.

Altars.

At the point of their encounter, it's there that you'll find an altar--a clear milestone erected in one form or another.

Say "altar" and most people picture furniture. But I'm not talking about furniture in an ancient tabernacle, an area in a cathedral, or a wooden prayer rail in front of a church platform. I'm actually not even yet speaking about a physical stone pile, as with the case of our text which relates to Abraham's altars. Please understand--all the above *are* legitimate expressions of an altar, but at the mere human plane. None of these sites or symbols alone by themselves has the intrinsic power to:

- Alter the direction of a human life,
- Change the fabric of a person's character,
- Shape the realization of someone's destiny.

I have no problem with wooden railings or high altars in churches, nor qualms about other devoted sanctuaries of human consecration. Altars, as a means to worship and prayer, are sometimes imperative and often revitalizing. However, I *do* have a problem, as I'm sure you do, with religious artifacts--places or practices--that lose their original power and significance because mechanical routines have replaced spiritual vitality with human traditions.

Many of us have past experiences in church where kneeling at an altar was something you always "just do." I've been in churches where a Sunday service couldn't conclude without the leader proclaiming, "Now everybody, let's all come down to the altar in front." Sometimes it was dynamic, but other times it was merely a habit; a weekly re-verification of something no one seemed quite sure of. And often, after about two minutes, most of those who "came forward" were already up and gone. In five minutes, the whole place was empty.

Such habits usually hark back to a time when the power of God *did* visit people; when contrite, seeking souls came and were on their knees before the Living God at those altars for *hours*. But "glory eras" pass, or new seasons come, and each one calls for its own refreshing, lest we merely exercise routine habits devoid of wholeheartedness, diligence, or understanding.

Altars.

To some, the word may only sound religious. Uninteresting. Conjuring images of candles, incense, and genuflection. Yet altars have time and again been the very threshold for the power of God to pour forth on earth to people who have met God at one. They've met the *Living* God, in *living* faith, and entered a *living* relationship, and realized *living* experiences. These *altar experiences* frame the context in which Heaven's power invades hellish dominions; the setting in which God's Spirit penetrates earth's heartaches. Altars have set the conditions and met the moment in ways which have resulted in Christ's Lordship being expanded through human vessels. They have become thresholds of glory; glory which has poured forth into believers' lives as they are shaped under God's hand . . . at an altar.

Altars *are* thresholds--the footings of a doorway--because Heaven's power does not pour forth from a giant garden hose in the clouds. It opens its grace and pours forth over this planet through people like you and me who will find a place to meet God, and then *kneel* there and *knock*. Altar experiences with the Lord create within us new capacities; we become *wider* apertures, *larger* channels of grace, more *generous* and *powerful* conduits of the Holy Spirit. At the doorway of Heaven we find the doors of our being swung open to God, private quarters unveiled, heart secrets revealed, and God's life-power released to us. None of us can experience that without altars.

God's Word shows Abraham as a *prototype*--a first-of-a-kind person, who models through his own learning process what it means to walk by faith. Abraham's fruitfulness in life clearly came forth through a succession of "altars"--through dynamic encounters with God. He learned a walk with God that can teach every one of us today as well; but we will find one inescapable fundamental: *The unalterable need of an altar.*

At the core of a man's walk with God is each man's readiness to meet God *personally:*

• To answer the summons on your soul when He deals with you, rather than to subvert or rationalize His dealings and attempt an escape from His direct points of correction, instruction, or conviction.

• To be ready to submit to the Holy Spirit, whose relentless operations in our life are always to bring more and more of the likeness of Christ into our living through His faithful disallowance of things we would excuse, and His regular call to principles our flesh seeks to escape.

This pathway of walking with God has a distinct individuality to it. No one can walk this way as your proxy or substitute. In a way, it might be said that it's the ultimate *true* path of rugged individualism, in the most spiritual of terms. It's the place a man "gets to know God for himself," and where God truly "gets the man for Himself."

But before we probe further along this very biblical pathway of "spiritual rugged individualism," let me establish an imperative point of balance.

Anyone familiar with my ministry knows that I put great emphasis on the practice of people getting together and praying with and for one another. It's scriptural. It's powerful. Its benefits have been proven unerringly. However, truth out of balance becomes error.

So in keeping wise checks and balances in place on this issue of a man's walk with God, let me be clear. I would not want for one second to deter anyone from the valid and proper place of regularly going to another brother or group of fellow Christians and saying, "Will you pray with me?" Nor does the path we're probing avoid the honesty and humility in acknowledging to peers, "I'm facing something tough; could we get together and talk about it?" I wouldn't want to seem to dissuade anyone from seeking godly counsel within the Body of Christ to obtain help in a difficult time.

In fact, I *encourage* that practice. However, I find that today this is an increasing substitute for personal encounters with God, and bearing each other's burden was never meant to lead to a dependency. I think that we need to perceive the difference and learn the place of both--prayer's fellowship, partnering with others; and prayer's partnership, fellowshiping with God alone.

Actually, it is plain wisdom to seek the strength of brothers and sisters. You'll likely die spiritually without it. But when that becomes a habit or substitute for a growing private walk with God, something within your spiritual life either never develops or will begin to atrophy. If I don't learn to draw on His well-spring of life within myself, I'll not learn the resource that will enable me to be His hand of strength to others. If I find I've become only a consumer and not a supplier by God's grace in me, it's probably due to the fact that I haven't been meeting the Lord often enough at my own altar.

Further, many of today's Christians need to learn most of their problems simply aren't going to be solved in a counseling office or in an effort at a quick-fix session of interaction with another believer. As valuable as such practices and spiritual human resources are, *most* of my life-problems and need for life-answers will only be solved on my knees before Jesus Himself! Coming into the presence of the Lord and finding an encounter with Him, from which point you go away *never the same again* with regard to that particular problem in your life, is an indispensable practice. His presence is the place where our hearts are *"altared"*--i.e., *put on the altar,* and as a result our whole lives will be *altered.* [Note the spelling difference: we're al*tar*ed to be al*ter*ed!]

These pages are not aimed at learning a ritual piling up of stones, kneeling at wooden railings, or sticking markers on the landscape. But there is a quest to build altars. And the goal is to facilitate a walk according to God's Word, pressing all of us into a liberating and life-changing understanding of altars as meeting places with God. Because we are dealing with issues of the heart and its intimate responses to God, an altar can range anywhere from a fireplace hearth, to a spot on the beach or in a field, to a profound encounter when you were alone with the Lord at a booth in a donut shop. God is everywhere and some of His most *altering* dealings with us happen in surprising settings, and sometimes when we weren't expecting it at all. That message is seen clearly in the life of Abraham.

As with you, dear brother, the Word of the Lord came to this man to reveal to him his divinely-appointed destiny. That Abraham learned to believe God, and to continue to hear God speak, is because Abraham learned to continue to build altars--to respond to God and to submit to His dealings with his soul. The very fulfillment of a man's *destiny* is contingent on his own *heart* being progressively changed, steadily being expanded to receive and embrace God's unfolding purpose in his life.

So it was with each altar Abraham built to the Lord. As his heart was altered--shaped and grown--his full destiny was being received from the hand of an eternal God and brought into reality in this temporal world. It's a prototypical case of a man learning to walk with God.

TALK ABOUT IT! Chapter questions to discuss with a friend.

1) Even though you might not have realized they were "altar experiences" at the time, share an example of when you *knew* the Lord divinely directed your course in life and *how* you knew it was the Lord (examples: where to go to college or what to study; whom to marry; what profession to enter or a career change; priorities with your family; etc.).

2) Discuss why it is so important that we continue to build altars throughout our lives.

CHAPTER TWO:

THE PURPOSE OF ALTARS–
MILESTONES OF
GOD'S DEALINGS

Every altar has its own application, its own story, its own purpose in God. And most dramatically, every altar has its own potential of a power-encounter to change one's life. That's the reason I'd like to ask you to walk with me through an examination of eight "altars" in Abraham's life. A few of them do not recite the word "altar" but they are all, nonetheless, very significant and strategic intersections of God's dealing in his life. Each of them speak pointedly to the process and the unique values of "altars" in a man's life, and to the way they build and advance his walk with God. While we'll study these eight altars over the course of the following chapters, let's first get a panoramic view of the altars Abraham built to God.

The essential elements of the life of Abraham, "the father of the faithful" can be read in a matter of minutes. In most Bibles, the whole of his biography occupies little more than a dozen pages. Let me encourage you to read it all at once--perhaps this evening. In about 30 minutes you'll have reviewed the primary details of a very ordinary, sometimes fearful, always faithful man--who learned to walk with God. Beginning at Genesis 11:27, read through Chapter 22. *

As you read, note these eight "altar" occasions:

Altar 1: Genesis 12:7** - This occurs when Abraham first comes into the land of the Canaanites, after God issues His call to him.

Altar 2: Genesis 12:8 - Though immediately approximate to the preceding altar in the text, there would have been a time-lapse between the two occasions.

Altar 3: Genesis 13:4 - Abraham returns from the confusing trip to Egypt, and now reestablishes the altar he earlier built.

Altar 4: Genesis 13:18 - Again, no measured passage of time is given, but sufficient time had elapsed to occasion the growth of his flocks (vs. 6). God is now giving a more explicit perspective on the earlier promise of "the land."

---

* Other details continue through Genesis 25, but they are not primary to Abraham's lifelong pursuit of God's will.

** Though he is first called Abram, we will consistently refer to Abraham by the fuller name God eventually gave him (see Genesis 17:5).

Altar 5: Genesis 14:18-24 - No altar is specified, but in his saying, "I have lifted my hand to the Lord," describing his worship at Melchizedek's direction, Abraham references an encounter with God that has long-term implications.

Altar 6: Genesis 15:1-21 - Verses 9-10 specifically describe the sacrifices offered, so although the word "altar" doesn't appear, it is clear that one was employed. Again, we are probably looking at a time passage of at least months, if not years, between these "altar" encounters.

Altar 7: Genesis 17:1-27 - In the establishing of the covenant of circumcision, Abraham's encounter does not report a stone or earthen altar being built, but his own body becomes marked by the will to worship and sacrifice to God.

Altar 8: Genesis 22:1-19 - This event, probably 35-40 years into Abraham's advancing walk with God, occasions the highest "altar" of his lifetime because of the powerful prophetic picture it gives of Christ, and because of the glorious seal it provides to Abraham's faith-walk.

With this summary in mind, we're about to look at the power-principles for a growing walk with God as demonstrated in Abraham's life. But before we do, let me make three encompassing statements. For as surely as Abraham's life teaches us POINTS of power, there is something of vast importance to be learned about the PRO-CESS of God's power in a man's life. Please note:

• THE PRINCIPLE OF TIME: Abraham's encounters with God as they appear in the altar experiences noted in the Scriptures covered a period of at least 40 years. This is not suggesting that "every five years" God met him on an appointment basis, since eight incidents are in focus. But it should help us to see that a maturing walk with God involves God-given time for growth.

• THE PROBLEM OF FEAR: Abraham's arrangement with Sarah, that she lie about their relationship whenever they were in a hostile setting that might threaten Abraham's life, is certainly unbecoming. Yet the patience of God with a fearful man should be noted. In short, the Bible makes clear that God's ability to build a man of faith is *not* removed because at earlier points in his walk with Him the man has struggles with fear.

• THE PRIORITY OF RESPONSIVE-NESS: Abraham's faith is the product of his readiness to respond to God. Though he is called the "father of faith," he did not arrive at that title by reason of a grand exercise of mighty spirituality. All he does is simply answer when God calls. Even though he is sometimes apparently fearful and even though his development takes decades within his lifetime, the essence of his faith is in the fact that he *responds* to God, rather than hides from His call.

Let these three factors weld themselves into your soul, dear friend.

You are clearly interested in becoming a man with a growing, effective walk with God. That interest is a strong beginning. But the above insights will prove, I've learned, *very* essential to maintaining patience and perspective. So, with that foundational counsel in place, let us begin looking at the individual altar-encounters of Abraham--as we learn from these milestones of God's dealings with a man.

A Man's Altar of Promise

How does God whisper *promise* to a man's life?

There are many ways, but the most common is a direct utterance from His Word--The Bible. You're reading one day, and a phrase, a text, an incident in the Scriptures JUMPS OUT AT YOU! Suddenly, it's in strobe lights: your heart leaps, or is warmed, and you KNOW--it's not simply "biblical," but it has suddenly become *personal*.

It may have been in a service as the Word of God was being taught. Or the text of His Word may have become electrically alive as the Holy Spirit breathed a "word" of prophecy, and the exhortation underscored a *truth; your* truth from *His* Truth--The

Word alive, for *you.*

This is God's way; something He delights to do--to make His Word a promise of purpose, power, and destiny to *you.* As surely as He first wants to make His Son ours as personal Savior, He wants to build our walk with Him at a personal level as He applies His word--*personally!*

God isn't in the generalizing business. He gets specific, and His Word is filled with promises He wants to press into a place in our hearts so that we will each know for certain: His promises not only are *true,* they're for *me!*

Abraham's experience was exactly like this, with but one exception. At the time he lived there was no written Word of God. Still, the Lord spoke to him, and in Genesis 12:1-7, we're given the beginning of His doing so: the setting, the promise, and Abraham's response.

Now the Lord had said to Abram: "Get out of your country, from your family and from your father's house, to a land that I will show you. I will make you a great nation; I will bless you and make your name great; and you shall be a blessing. I will bless those who bless you, and I will curse him who curses you; and in you all the families of the earth shall be blessed." So Abram departed as the Lord had spoken to him, and Lot went with him. And Abram was seventy-five years old when he departed from Haran. Then

Abram took Sarai his wife and Lot his brother's son, and all their possessions that they had gathered, and the people whom they had acquired in Haran, and they departed to go to the land of Canaan. So they came to the land of Canaan. Abram passed through the land to the place of Shechem, as far as the terebinth tree of Moreh. And the Canaanites were then in the land. Then the Lord appeared to Abram and said, "To your descendants I will give this land." And there he built an altar to the Lord, who had appeared to him.   *Genesis 12:1-7*

It's essential in learning a man's walk with God that we grasp two important things from the onset. First, there is *promise* seeded in the call God gives in inviting you and me to that walk. Second, there is *purpose* for each of our lives which is waiting to unfold.

Listen to God's words to Abraham, and inherent within them I'm asking you to hear His voice to you as well. From the text of Scripture quoted above, take a pen and fill in the phrase from His words to Abraham, and apply them to yourself.

• God's promise is to BLESS you (12:2a).

_____

• God's promise is to do something GREAT with you (12:2b,c).

_____

• God's promise is to MULTIPLY you (12:3).

• God's promise is to give you a PLACE in His purpose (12:7).

I can't urge you strongly enough to lay hold of this first principle: GOD WANTS TO BRING YOU TO A PLACE OF PROMISE, AND SEAL THAT PROMISE AT AN ALTAR OF ENCOUNTER WITH HIM! In other words, He wants you to be so confident that He *means* to bless, multiply, and bring you to largeness of purpose in His will, that you will let this become a covenanted matter with Him.

That's what constitutes the milestones of a man's walk with God. It is staked out by the altars--the places, times, and moments when you *hear* God speak to your heart about His purpose for you, and you *agree:* you *receive* and *seal* that covenant in an altar-like encounter. Let me illustrate.

Earlier, I mentioned a moment in time on the 405 Freeway in the San Fernando Valley area of Los Angeles, and an "altar" encounter I had with God there.

It was a crystal clear afternoon, two weeks after that Wednesday in March over two decades ago, when my wife and I had accepted a short, interim pastorate of a small church in Van Nuys. As I drove northward, having left the print shop where I'd placed a small order for church bulletins (we only had about 20 people in the congregation), I had little on my mind other than a comfortable drive back to my office.

Suddenly, without any premeditated thought on my own mind, other than that my eyes had scanned the "bowl" formed by the surrounding mountains hemming this portion of Los Angeles, the Holy Spirit whispered: " This is your valley." The impression was clear and the meaning was obvious, though I could fathom no way to apply it. "Your valley" meant "The place of your assignment, and the intended location of God for your ministry."

As I said above, *I thought* I was on an interim, temporary deputation assignment to oversee a small congregation for a six-month span of time. Little did I know God had charted the course of my destiny for this place, and for many years to come.

My response?

It was very, very limited--as limited as my understanding at that moment. And because of my limited point of view, all I did was take the words to heart--accept them for whatever God meant them to be, because I certainly didn't understand them myself.

As it has turned out, God has done remarkable and mighty things in making that small congregation into a global ministry center which serves the entire San Fernando Valley as well. But that day, all I knew to do was *receive,* to let my heart (which had other plans than this valley) keep open to God's purpose.

And I tell this simple story because it's a practical testimony.

1. It illustrates one man's "walk" in opening to a forward step with God, even though he doesn't know where the path will lead. (That's what Abraham did--Hebrews 11:8.)

2. It illustrates the way that God's promise doesn't need to be understood in its fullness in order to be received at its beginning. [Abraham at first was told he would become "a nation" (12:2), then "like the stars" (15:5), and even later "a father of many nations" (17:4).]

3. It illustrates the fact that a simple "present yourself at the altar of openness" is all that's needed. From that point, the heart has released God to bring about His higher purposes in the man to whom He has spoken.

When God said to Abraham, " To your descendants I will give this land," the next words we read are: *"And there he built an altar."* To build an altar is to agree with God:

• Accepting His promise for your future, and committing to walk forward with Him toward its fulfillment.

• Laying your life in openness before

Him as the Lord of your life's issues and as the Master of your destiny.

Listen, dear brother in Christ! This is crucial to a man's beginning a faith-walk with God. Let me share it with you just as I spoke it at one of our men's gatherings.

*   *   *   *   *

Now, men, notice God says, " To your descendants I will give this land (vs. 7). . . Go to a land that I will show you" (vs.1).

Do you see that?

God gave him a *promise*. He promised him greatness, significance; that He was going to do something with his life to bring him to an appointed destiny.

Does that sound familiar? It should because that's exactly what the Lord says to you and me. He says, 'I call you to come out and follow Me. I'm going to make you amount to something. I'm going to bless you. I'm going to bless people through you. And I'm going to bring you to an appointed place--a destiny that I have fashioned for you."

That's God's promise to you and me throughout Scripture, since God's Word speaks of us as the spiritual offspring of Abraham. In Romans 4:11-13 we're referred to as the spiritual progeny of Abraham, and he's a kind of prototype of all of us . . . the people of faith.

Now, in our text (12:7) Abraham arrives at the *place* of his destiny and God says, "Abraham, this is the place! I'm going to do something with you here; *even though it hasn't happened yet, this is the place!*" God makes His promise firm. It's tagged to a specific point. And when Abraham might later feel the temptation to doubt, he can look at that stone altar baking in the noon-day sun or towering in the moonlight; stones which could whisper, "Remember the day I was built? God spoke to you. And what He promised *will* happen!"

Brother, what has God said to you? Let's apply it.

Build a Milestone of Remembrance

Rather than stones, take up pen and paper. Abraham didn't have the convenience of a computer or a stationery store down the street, but we do. And I would urge every disciple of Jesus Christ to benefit from keeping a spiritual journal. Men who walk with God have always done this: Martin Luther, John Wesley, Hudson Taylor, Jonathan Edwards--the list goes on and on. Such men kept notes on God's dealing with them.

Words from the Lord to your own heart, as edifying as they may be, can easily lose their power and sustaining grace in your life if they are not set in place--written down. It's like placing the stones of an altar. Such pragmatics can be intensely spiritual and powerful in daily life.

Listen, when God speaks to you, you can be sure the Adversary of your soul will be quick to sow seeds of doubt each time the Lord gives you His word. "Has God said?" is a famous line from hell--one which even Jesus had thrown at Him by the devil. But when the record of God's personal dealings with you is in ink, it's much easier for you to point to the journal, and reply to hell's host or your own doubts:

   • "Yeah? Look right here--page 15!"
Or,

   • "I was standing right under the oak tree at my uncle's house reading the Bible!"
Or,

   • "It was March 19--That's when that scripture came alive--right out of the Word for *me* that day. I *knew* it and I *know* it!"

Hell has to back off in the face of that kind of confidence at such "altar" moments. So, establish that wisdom, brother. As a man committed to a walk with God, secure the wisdom of keeping a spiritual diary, recording things the Lord has shown to you or promised you. These texts show it to be both practical and scriptural:

Then the Lord answered me and said: "Write the vision and make it plain on tablets, that he may run who reads it. For the vision is yet for an appointed

28

*time; but at the end it will speak, and it
will not lie. Though it tarries, wait for it;
because it will surely come, it will not
tarry."*   *Habakkuk 2:2-3*

*I will remember the works of the Lord;
surely I will remember Your wonders of
old.*   *Psalm 77:11*

*Remember His marvelous works which
He has done, His wonders, and the judgments of His mouth . . .*
        Psalm 105:5

A Man's Altar of Prayer

The second altar Abraham erected secured another principle in his life. It was a
principal key as he learned a man's walk
with God.

*And he moved from there to the mountain
east of Bethel, and he pitched his tent
with Bethel on the west and Ai on the
east; there he built an altar to the Lord
and called on the name of the Lord.*
        Genesis 12:8

Abraham *called on the name of the Lord.*
That's the *first* time we have direct reference
to Abraham's calling on the Lord by His
personal name. The significance of this is
that his prayer enters a new dimension of

intimacy in his knowledge of the Lord.

The language of that time contained names for the Lord that focused on His role as Creator-God and as The Almighty One. But here is the personal Redeemer-God-- Yahweh--the One who will become mankind's Savior. In a real and powerful sense, Abraham is getting to know God in a new, deeper way; perceiving more of His character and Person.

Coming to know more of God's way as you walk with Him is born of coming to know more of God Himself! Psalm 25:14 says, "The secret of the Lord is with those who fear Him, and He will show them His covenant." This, too, is a call to altar-building; but it isn't a one-time encounter. It's a progressive discovery of coming to more of a "first name" relationship with the God who has called you, who has promised to work His purpose and power in your life.

Further, will you notice, Abraham "moved . . . " (12:8). Make no mistake, Sir. A man's walk with God doesn't stagnate. The issue isn't geographical movement, but *forward* movement--advancing in the knowledge of God's Son, His ways, His heart, and His Spirit. Hear the Apostle Paul say, after having walked with Lord for nearly 20 years, *"That I may know Him!!"* Listen to those words, because they echo the sound of the man who has found the *way* of beginning with God, but who wants to move unto the *wealth* of knowing Him-- MORE!

How is this altar erected? Probably the simplest specifications are in the answer, "morning by morning."

Try an experiment. This is not a law, nor a legal requirement for true spirituality. It's an experiment. And the goal of the experiment is to prove in your own experience the faithfulness of James 4:8 which says, "Draw near to God and He will draw near to you." Here it is:

Set your alarm clock 30 minutes earlier than usual--60 if you dare. Begin to spend a newly devoted block of time weekday mornings--worshiping, meeting, talking with the Lord . . . just "drawing close" to Him. I say that risking the danger that someone will interpret this as a legalistic demand for true spirituality, or as if providing a magic span of time will achieve familiarity with the Almighty. But my guess is that the Lord has already been dealing with your heart about spending even *more* time before Him. If He's telling you to expand to 15 minutes, honor that. If it's weekly, daily, or three times a week, just do what He says. In any case, cut new ground.

Pursue the Lord. Set your new regimen for a three-month target. Then, at the end of that time, see if that altar of prayer hasn't shaken loose something of the "old life" and, in exchange, fostered a fresh invasion of holy intimacy you've never known with the Lord before!

I issue this bold challenge, trusting that you will understand my point: the issue is a dynamic pursuit of the Lord, not a legal edict mandating a time-span. I want to urge you, brother: ask the Lord how *He* would have *you* pursue Him at the altar of prayer. Then build it--and expect Him to meet you there.

A Man's Altar of Permanence

We're told exactly why Abraham went south to Egypt: "There was a famine in the land" (12:10); but there is one highly important *missing* piece of information. Nowhere does it say, " The Lord *said,* 'Go to Egypt.' "

There is a common feature to most of our personal biographies: *we wander without wisdom.* It doesn't happen all the time. It doesn't happen because of an indifference toward walking with God. But it does happen, and it is usually because we come to circumstances where our *survival* seems at risk and our *seeking* is sacrificed. Let me share a testimony of a "near miss" I had along this line.

My wife, Anna, became pregnant with our first child just seven months after we entered the ministry. It wasn't a very opportune time, seeing as our salary was very slim and our tiny congregation hardly established at all. As the early months of her pregnancy went by, we hoped we might be able to save for the costs of the baby's birth, because there was no insurance resource available at that time. Then, with only six weeks left until the due date, I became restless.

"Honey," I said, "I'm going to get a part-time job on the side. I know it will remove time from my studies and pastoral responsibilities, but we need the money."

I was also concerned that I not be a bad example by appearing to the other families in our small flock to be slothful. I reasoned, "If I don't do something to see these costs covered, some of the men--especially new believers--will think 'faith is irresponsible.'" And I remember how it was in this mood that I took the morning newspaper in hand that wintry morning, to look for a job.

Equally clear is the memory of the inner pressure as I began to search the paper for job opportunities. It was a clear tug on my heart which made me extremely uncomfortable. No words were spoken to me, but a heaviness came upon my soul that only lifted when I prayed, "Lord, I think I understand what You're doing. You're *stopping* me from launching out on a path of my own wisdom, and You're calling me to trust You with this matter."

Though it's been years since that day, it's a well-defined moment when I was called to build an altar of *permanence*--to establish the fact by faith that I was called to do one thing in the will of God, and that probing other pathways was not His plan-- no matter *how* "good" the motive or purpose seemed. I have no idea what distraction or confusion I may have avoided, but I do know the marvel of the miracles of God's provisions that eventuated, for when our first child arrived--a sweet little girl!-- we had enough to (1) pay off the doctor and hospital completely, (2) buy basic supplies for setting up a home with "new baby equipment," and (3) provide 6 weeks of the special canned formula prescribed by the doctor for feeding our child. It was thrilling!! And it was an early lesson in "walking with God" and avoiding "wandering into Egypt."

Abraham's trip to Egypt wasn't without a logical reason, but when we study the whole text, we find his venture leads to manipulation and compromise. Read the story.

Now there was a famine in the land, and Abram went down to Egypt to dwell there, for the famine was severe in the land. And it came to pass, when he was close to entering Egypt, that he said to Sarai his wife, "Indeed I know that you are a woman of beautiful countenance. Therefore it will happen, when the Egyp-

tians see you, that they will say, 'This is his wife'; and they will kill me, but they will let you live. Please say you are my sister, that it may be well with me for your sake, and that I may live because of you." So it was, when Abram came into Egypt, that the Egyptians saw the woman, that she was very beautiful. The princes of Pharaoh also saw her and commended her to Pharaoh. And the woman was taken to Pharaoh's house. He treated Abram well for her sake. He had sheep, oxen, male donkeys, male and female servants, female donkeys, and camels. But the Lord plagued Pharaoh and his house with great plagues because of Sarai, Abram's wife. And Pharaoh called Abram and said, "What is this you have done to me? Why did you not tell me that she was your wife? Why did you say, 'She is my sister'? I might have taken her as my wife. Now therefore, here is your wife; take her and go your way." So Pharaoh commanded his men concerning him; and they sent him away, with his wife and all that he had.

Then Abram went up from Egypt, he and his wife and all that he had, and Lot with him, to the South. Abram was very rich in livestock, in silver, and in gold. And he went on his journey from the South as far as Bethel, to the place where his tent had been at the beginning, between Bethel

*and Ai, to the place of the altar which he
had made there at first. And there Abram
called on the name of the Lord.*
Genesis 12:10 -13:4

There are two lessons this "return-to-
the-altar" experience of Abraham teaches
us: (1) *Don't* wander via human wisdom,
but *do* walk in God's (12:10-20)! (2) *If*
you've wandered in presumption, ignorance, or confusion, you *can* return to the
altar of God for reestablishment (13:1-4)!

Learning to walk with God calls us to
learn to heed the inner signals of His
dealing, to expect progressive calls to new
levels of sensible, biblical faith. The altar of
permanence doesn't need to be built *after* a
trip to Egypt. You can build your altar of
permanence *before* drifting into confusion
and compromise through not trying to solve
your problems by journeying according to
your own map.

"But," someone says, "it appears that
Abraham returned *richer* as a result of his
Egyptian junket, even though he stumbled
into compromise!" And the truth of the
matter is that it *does* seem he did. But we'll
miss the grander points of the text if we
presume that God's prospering was a sign
of pleasure, when in fact it was a signal of
His incredible mercy.

There seems to be a principle of God's
dealings with all of us who choose to walk

with Him. If we *will* to walk in self-willed paths, we insure unfruitfulness. But if we *stumble* onto dead-end streets in the learning process, God doesn't approve of the detour, but He will mercifully bring us out-- and we'll profit from the lesson. And, by the way, as to Abraham's increased wealth from his time in Egypt (12:16, 20; 13:2), please remember that God didn't need Egypt's help to provide for Abraham's well-being!! Just as I learned long ago through the incident of being "stopped before Egypt" as the baby's arrival drew near: God-Our-Provider is capable to meet needs and abound *without* the assistance of human wisdom's enterprise!

Listen, dear brother. There is someone reading this page right now who has fumbled and slipped into Abraham-like patterns of compromise and confusion. You wonder how a man like you who wanted a walk with God got in a place like this; also wondering if there is a way you can return to a compromise-free, unencumbered-by-Egypt walk.

The answer is YES! And the place where you've met God at the altar *before* simply waits for you to come and rebuild the altar *now*. Never let the Adversary of your soul tell you otherwise!

Dave had returned from Viet Nam, and when I saw his face in the service that night I could read his thoughts like a book. His guilty face seemed to say: "I've been gone so long. Failed so foolishly while overseas:

37

compromised my commitment. I'd love to return to the fullness of the Lord's way, but I don't deserve to do so." It was as though he felt he needed to earn his way back to God.

When my message was concluded, most everyone in the room had knelt at their seat to enter into the regular prayer-meeting format for this midweek night. But I went down from the platform to where Dave was seated, head buried in his hands. I simply whispered, as I leaned over to his side:

"Dave, it's not a mile or a thousand steps to come back, it's only *one*--one step from where you are to where Jesus is--right now."

He looked up, his eyes flashed with hope, and he stood and took one step--into my arms, and then both of us went to the altar to pray.

Today, Dave is a gifted Christian counsellor, his home a center of vital joy and life in Christ, for that night he *came back*--and built an altar of permanence.

It can be built *before,* by hearing God's wisdom.

It can be built *after,* even though you've wandered.

And the earnest, humble heart wanting to walk with God will be profited by His abundance of grace and mercy!

**TALK ABOUT IT! Chapter
questions to discuss with a friend.**

1) What *realistic* goal do you
feel the Lord leading you to make for
spending time with Him in prayer
over the next three months? Be
specific: decide when, where, how
long, how often, etc.; and write down
your commitment below. Remember, this may be different for each
person--there is no *right* answer;
the key is to commit to *expanding*
your present prayer pattern.

2) Discuss the benefits of keeping a spiritual journal. Commit to
devote part of the prayer time above
in writing down your thoughts,
prayer requests and answers, Holy
Spirit-given insights, and even questions about situations or circumstances you don't yet understand.

CHAPTER THREE:
THE PRACTICALITY OF ALTARS--
FACE-TO-FACE WITH DEITY

I could reel off the names of half a dozen teachers I've had and another half dozen authors, who have dramatically touched my life at significant times. I could also talk about many individuals whose personal lives, counsel, teaching, example, or ministry has been a great blessing to me; people whose words greatly helped, at moments when God used them to speak a phrase or reach with a touch that proved to be a point of great personal release and encouragement. Without question, there is a place for *people* teaching and strengthening one another.

But I want to also tell you that the major points in my life--the moments to which I return and say, "*That* is the point at which there came a turning; *that* is the time when my life moved into a whole new realm; *that's* the occasion when solid things were anchored in my soul" ... *those* are usually times when I have been *alone with the Lord*.

He is the Central Personality for us all-- the One ready to progressively shape life under His touch when He can find a person--a *man*--who will walk with Him from altar to altar. There aren't short cuts. There are simply some things that the Lord is just jealous enough to not let anyone else get in on. He wants to have the hand in the establishing and firming up of some things in our lives that will happen no other way.

• We won't get it by running to another meeting;

• It won't come by listening to another tape;

• You won't get it by going to another counselor;

• I'm not going to find it by any device, regardless of how positive or beneficial that resource may be.

But you and I will find that our "next step with God" at such times is by one means--*alone*: Coming to the Living God and building an altar!

A Man's Altar of Possession

Let's read Abraham's fourth altar experience:

The Lord said to Abram, after Lot had separated from him: Lift your eyes now and look from the place where you are; northward, southward, eastward, and westward; for all the land which you see I give to you and your descendants forever. And I will make your descendants as the dust of the earth; so that if a man could number the dust of the earth, then

your descendants also could be num-
bered. Arise, walk in the land through
its length and its width, for I give it to
you. Then Abram moved his tent, and
went and dwelt by the terebinth trees of
Mamre, which are in Hebron, and built
an altar there to the Lord.

Genesis 13:14-18

Abraham--a man learning to walk with
God--is a man whose life is increasingly
being marked by a trail of altars. Similar to
a string of lights etching the outline of an
airport runway at night, his altar fires
served as a holy means by which God
escorted him into the destiny to which He
had called him.

Each altar testifies as a monument to
something the Lord is speaking or doing in
his life. At key moments altars are built and
become witnesses that God has spoken. In
this fourth case, the altar becomes direction in his life to move him another step
toward possessing his destiny. This altar,
in a very real sense, becomes a weapon of
warfare.

The striking thing about this altar encounter in Abraham's evolving walk with
God is that the altar so very inescapably
links God's *promise* of the land (13:14) with
a call to *prophetic action:* "Arise, walk in the
land through its length and its width, for I
give it to you" (13:17).

"Prophetic action" is action taken in the physical, visible realm because of something we believe about the spiritual, invisible realm. Abraham was told a promise of future possession--*now* he *acts* as the possessor, and he builds an altar to commemorate the act.

Such action moves beyond the *idea* of God's promise to the actual conviction that His promise is in action--*NOW!* It's wise to see the practical, nonsuperstitious nature of such action. Both passivity and unbelief scoff at such actions as Abraham's: "Walk through the land?! What difference does it make? If God's going to give it to him, He's going to do it anyway!" But God isn't wasting words or playing games. He's moving Abraham from ethereal, intangible notions, to solid, faith-securing convictions.

There's a good deal of innocuous, indecisive religious habit today. Maybe a degree of sincerity rests at the roots of such spiritual passiveness, but too many believers don't know or don't think it important to anchor promises to a firm foundation of action; to *possessing* the promise by faith's participative act. And seldom do they learn to tack down their experiences in meeting God by building altars. Consequently, the revelation/memory of that moment where God intersected their lives, in a way they should never forget, dissipates. If an altar isn't built at such times, we yield that moment to a potential void of forgottenness.

Just as with words drawn in thin air by a skywriting plane, as time passes and the winds of adversity blow, the clarity of the message fades away. So we too easily lose *possession* of the promise and conviction wanes.

Imagine asking Abraham, "Has God promised you that you would possess this land?"

"Yes, He has."

"How do you know? Was it one day when suddenly you felt impressed that way?"

"No," he would say, "Come and I'll show you where it was." And he would lead you to a place and announce, "See that-- right there . . . that pile of stones? That's where I was. It happened about 25 years ago. God dealt with my heart, and I said, 'Okay, Lord. I receive Your promise.' " He could answer you as to how promise of God's purpose was nailed down in his own personal experience again and again.

You continue your interview: "Abraham, you seem to know the Lord pretty well. How'd it come about?" His answer begins as he leads the way to another site.

"See that place there?" He points across a valley, "There, between Bethel and Ai? That's where the Lord deepened my understanding of Him; where I began to know Him more intimately--by His name, if you will." He pauses, then continues: "I already knew that God was promising me *something*, but that altar is where I really came to know *Him*--the Living God, as He manifested Himself to me by *His name*."

"But Abraham, how come you've never gone home again--back to Haran, to your family there?"

"Simply because God told me, *'This* is my land!' "

"Don't you ever get homesick?"

"I have, just as anyone longs for things past. But God has called me *here*, and *here* I'll live. He told me this is where I was to stay--in His purpose."

"How did you make up your mind?"

Again, the patriarch answers: "God dealt with me. See, there's another pile of stones there. They testify to that fact! When that was 'nailed down,' as you say, it was done!"

"Abraham, even though you don't *have* it yet, you seem to really believe you're going to possess this land."

"Possess it? I've walked over the whole thing. God told me wherever my foot went, it was becoming mine! I believe that-- though it is mostly yet to be seen, I've 'seen' it with His eyes. It's coming!"

"So you have a good spiritual feeling about it?"

"No, feelings have little to do with it. But there *is* something to see--there's a pile of rocks right there. There's where I sealed and settled it with God--according to His Word and promise, which never fails!"

Listen to that conversation, Sir. And look at that line of altars. They've become milestones in the life of a man, marking his walk with God. And they become something else, too.

If a man wants to find out *where he's going*--how God's leading him--all he has to do to look into the future is to stop a minute, turn around, and see the trail of altars behind--the points of God's dealing with him until now. They indicate direction--because God isn't zig-zagging us through life in an arbitrary Keystone Cop chase. He's bringing each of us along a divinely-scheduled pathway . . . if we'll walk with Him. And if we'll "nail down" actual experiences by building altars, with time we can turn around at any point and check: "Is where I'm going in line with where He's been taking me?" And believe me, it always *will* be. Even though the Lord does do new things in our lives--"great and mighty things which we know not"--His dealings will always have roots in things He's done years ago; consistently in harmony with His past dealings and always in alignment with His Word.

This is the way to a solid sense of direction. It beats just flying along on whatever happens to be the current ear-tickling teaching or the latest point of social or religious excitement or some giddy exhilaration in your life. Altars built in your life become granite anchors. Abraham had them. And he became the prototype of how a man walks with God.

A Man's Altar of Priority

This altar of Abraham's was not a conventional arrangement of stones. But the purposed determination in Abraham's life in Genesis 14:16-18--as he is approached by two kings--focuses an altar-type encounter with God's representative.

The battle against the coalition of five hostile kings has been won by Abraham. His nephew, Lot, who had been kidnapped, has now been recovered. The story proceeds in the wake of this victory.

So he (Abraham) brought back all the goods, and also brought back his brother Lot and his goods, as well as the women and the people. And the King of Sodom went out to meet him at the Valley of Shaveh (that is, the King's Valley), after his return from the defeat of Chedorlaomer and the kings who were with him. Then Melchizedek King of Salem brought out bread and wine; he was the priest of God Most High. And he blessed him and said: "Blessed be Abram of God Most High, Possessor of heaven

and earth; and blessed be God Most
High, who has delivered your enemies
into your hand." And he gave him a tithe
of all.   *Genesis 14:16-20*

There's a strikingly interesting con-
trasting study in the two kings Abraham
meets, and strong instruction is in it for any
man.

First, the King of Sodom is a perfect
depiction of Satan--the king of hell. "Sodom" literally means "burnt or scorched."
This king was the leader of a hell-bent city,
destined to be destroyed by divine judgment. Second, and in contrast, Melchizedek,
the King of Salem, ruled over the ancient
city of Salem (Jerusalem). This righteous
king is shown in the book of Hebrews as a
type of Jesus, a priest both preceding and
exceeding the Aaronic and Levitical priesthood. Melchizedek's name means "Prince
of Peace," a startling prophetic picture to
say the least. And now both kings come out
to meet Abraham.

You might say that, on one hand, Abraham is virtually approached by Satan
himself, and on the other, he is virtually
encountered by Jesus--the Priest of the
Most High God, our Great High Priest.

Abraham's confrontation by these two
kings teaches a great principle. Neither
you nor I will ever gain a spiritual victory
but that shortly thereafter we'll face a new

choice as to our priorities. There's something heady about spiritual triumph that begets an unusual vulnerability in the finest man, a vulnerability to distraction or deception. Remember, the surrounding text notes Abraham's warfare and rescue of Lot. Now this confrontation: This man's walk with God is going to face a real and practical decision. Where are his priorities when it comes to his devotion and his resources? It would be very easy for Abraham to make himself an independent prince who worships at his own shrine and only finances his own interests, but something else happens.

It's our wisdom to carefully tune to the message the Holy Spirit has for us in this episode. Our lesson is real: gain a spiritual victory, and you'll face a practical decision. Such situations have a way of *sealing* our priorities. They teach us that no degree of attainment bypasses the need for our faithfulness to the basics.

In Abraham's case--and in our study!--worship and giving are shown to be inescapably important. Abraham doesn't play with them. He kept these priorities clear.

The subtlety of approach by the King of Sodom is almost demonic. He says, "Look, you can have all the plunder, just give us the people." That's Satan's way: "I'll give you anything, just let me control souls."

In contrast, Abraham had just secured

priorities with Melchizedek, who had come to him with bread and wine. Think of it! Our text is 2200 years before Christ, and precious principles still alive today are seen already speaking prophetically.

See Melchizedek, a picture of Christ Jesus Himself, bringing bread and wine to Abraham. Here's a perfect picture of our Lord calling us to worship, as we do when we commemorate the Lord's Supper and testify to His death on the Cross.

Abraham worships!

He faces down the King of Sodom with the words, "I've made my choice. I've lifted up my hand to the Most High God, Creator of heaven and earth." Then, Abraham rejects Sodom's king as he proposes making him rich on his terms. Next,

Abraham tithes!

Read it clearly; verse 20 says it all: "Abraham gave (Melchizedek) a tithe of all."

Brother, this is so powerfully significant in understanding a man's walk with God. Once we enter the pathway of discipleship, the only biblical response from an economic standpoint is the priority of our serving God with our money. The tithe is timeless as a testimony of this priority being fixed in a man's heart and life. *Everything is God's:* And my tithe indicates that all I have is His!!

When the King of Sodom says, "You can take everything, Abraham," Abraham's reply is, "I don't want anything that's got the smell of your life on it." The altar is in place. Heaven is exalted--hell is defeated!

TALK ABOUT IT! Chapter questions to discuss with a friend.

1) We are all grateful to the Lord for the many pastors, teachers, authors, and counselors who have helped shape our lives, but explain why it is those times *alone* with the Lord that make the biggest impact in changing our thinking and lifestyle. Share such an experience you've had alone with the Lord and its resulting benefits.

2) Society and modern-day media can make us think the word "destiny" refers to fairy tales or something that only happens to people who "live happily ever after." Yet, it is a wonderful truth that God has a destiny for each one of us to possess! Describe what the Lord has spoken to you about your own destiny.

CHAPTER FOUR:
THE PROCESS OF ALTARS—
THE CONSUMING OF FLESH

A Man's Altar of Perception

Have you ever faced dark times and wondered what God was doing with your life?

One of the most trying times of my earlier walk with God took place following one of the most glorious seasons of fruitfulness I'd ever known. Things had been "comin' up roses," as we say; but suddenly--in a matter of weeks--the forward movement and sense of blessing, which three years of labor had abounded, was now sunk in the doldrums of uncertainty and discouragement.

Officials holding office above me seemed doubtful about my efforts at serving. All momentum related to anything I was involved in was dragging to a halt. When I prayed, it seemed nothing happened. I didn't feel God had forsaken me, but I did have the feeling that I was either "washed up" or a "washout."

But during that season, I turned to the Word of God. I had no emotion whatsoever, but I would daily turn to the Scriptures and simply open God's Book to see if He might speak. And even though there were no explosive moments, as week followed week certain passages began to become impressed upon my heart as being "for me."

Slowly, I began to fix these things in my heart--like the stones set in place in the formation of an altar--and an entirely new perspective on my future began to come about.

I would later realize what was happening. God was creating a hiatus--an in-between-break--to differentiate between what had gone before and what He was getting ready to do. The whole season of seemingly slogging along--*but doing so as a measured walk with Him, however blind I was to His presence*--resulted in:

(1) Finding a new perspective on what He *was* doing and *intended* to do; and

(2) Discovering a pathway through the dark, and that He was always there even though I couldn't see Him.

This is very much what Abraham's experience teaches us. We're about to meet him as he comes to another altar encounter--one which brings perspective on God's long-term *purpose* for him, and God's constant *presence* with Him.

And he said, "Lord God, how shall I know that I will inherit it?" So He said to him, "Bring Me a three-year-old heifer, a three-year-old female goat, a three-year-old ram, a turtledove, and a young pigeon." Then he brought all these to Him and cut them in two, down the middle, and placed each piece opposite the other; but he did not cut the birds

53

in two. And when the vultures came down on the carcasses, Abraham drove them away. Now when the sun was going down, a deep sleep fell upon Abraham; and behold, horror and great darkness fell upon him. Then He said to Abraham: "Know certainly that your descendants will be strangers in a land that is not theirs, and will serve them, and they will afflict them four hundred years. And also the nation whom they serve I will judge; afterward they shall come out with great possessions. Now as for you, you shall go to your fathers in peace; you shall be buried at a good old age."   *Genesis 15:8-15*

Notice, Abraham's quest for perspective--for insight on God's timing and assurance. "How shall I know that I shall inherit the land?" He already had the *promise* secured in hand, but he also had a *problem*--a problem with seeing what he thought God was going to do actually take place as he expected.

See this, please, Abraham believes God; he isn't saying, "Lord, I don't believe You--Your promise is a dud!" But he's saying, "Lord, in some way, I need to know more what's happening. Please show me how all this comes about." The Lord's answer shouldn't surprise us. "Build an altar, Abraham. Offer sacrifice."

Now it seems a corner is about to be

turned.

I won't be dogmatic about this, but even though altars had been built, not before this is there mention of Abraham offering a blood sacrifice. Because he had raised altars several times, I suppose most would preclude that he presented blood sacrifices there. But all the preceding times he raises an altar, each seems to be more of a monument to the Lord and a memorial to His dealing with Abraham. These towers of testimony had been places of worship, prayer, and fellowship. But now it seems Abraham is about to learn quite literally the role of "blood, sweat, and tears" when a man finds the fullest stages of divine purposes being worked out in his walk with God.

The revelation of God's blood covenant is manifest here. Abraham is about to gain deeper perspective; receiving a lesson in the fact that *God's ultimate means for possessing all promises* is through slain flesh and blood.

How does God fulfill these promises today?

To begin, He fulfills them all--every promise, every possibility--through Calvary; through the provisions inherent in the finished work of Christ on the Cross. The "slain flesh and blood" I just mentioned, which Abraham will only see as an early prophetic type, is an accomplished fact today. We are now recipients of provisions full and finally paid for through Jesus' death. The flesh slain is His, as the Son of God, and the blood shed is His as God's Lamb.

But let me say something, brother. As foundational as the work of Christ is, still-- ultimately--any outworking of God's fullest purposes in you and me will at one point or another start cutting into our own flesh as well. That's what Jesus means when He calls us to " Take up your cross and follow Me" (Mark 10:21). This doesn't mean the Lord is leading us to a means of *earning* through suffering, agony, and misery, as though we would accomplish something by *works*. But rather, He calls us to *learn* (not earn) the power of His *grace* (not our works) to move through the darkness to discover new light!

The Lord is summoning all of us to discipleship: "Follow Me--to Calvary!" He'll be there to lead and teach us, but the only way to learn what Paul calls "the fellowship of His suffering" (Phil. 3:10) is to learn the kind of violent perseverance Abraham demonstrates here.

We need to grasp the dynamic lesson Genesis 15:11 unfolds.

After Abraham's sacrifice is made, wild birds begin to assail the carcasses sacri- ficed on the altar. Darkness is settling on the same. The sun has gone down and a deep sleep is shortly to fall on Abraham. There are two principles that distill here; things which are not uncommon when God is teaching men like you and me what it means to walk with Him on the pathway of the Cross.

First, just as the vultures attacked Abraham's sacrifice, in the same way our Adversary the devil will sweep in to attempt everything possible to prevent us from presenting our full sacrifice to God.

Second, like the darkening sun and the deep sleep, you'll experience some order of "blackout"--an inability to see what God is doing. The question rises: Where did God go?

You've had such blackout moments, haven't you? Times when you, like Abraham's "How shall I know," have said, "Lord, I want to know more about what You're doing--I don't understand." We affirm, "Lord, I believe You, so that's settled. Now can we move on with fulfilling the promise--soon?" But then it's as though the Lord replies, "You really want to learn? Okay, here we go."

Then, it's sacrifice.

Then discipleship deepens.

Then you find Him involving you in dealings which "cut flesh," removing carnality.

And hardly has this new discipling begun, when the next thing you know the Adversary is circling like a devouring vulture. He will do anything possible to block, stop, or swallow up our learning Christ's pathway of seeing the Cross applied to our lives in its promise-releasing power.

Certain New Testament parables use fowls to illustrate the workings of the powers of darkness; how Satan seeks to come and "eat up"--to remove what you or I have opened of ourselves and exposed to the Lord in sacrifice. But see Abraham beat those birds away, and remember his style when Satan tests your commitment.

Once you expose your full self to God, expect the Adversary to sweep down and say, "Heh, man, I've controlled this flesh of yours 'til now! This is my turf. I've got a right to snatch this away. God can have the 'spiritual' you, but I own the 'practical, daily duty, work and business' you! None of this 'everything under Jesus' Lordship' stuff! Besides, you're not worthy of this sacrifice anyway."

But when Satan comes, rise up, brother! Resist the devil, and he'll flee from you!! See Abraham drive the vultures back, protecting the sacrifice; and that, my dear friend, is our responsibility, too.

How tempting to say, "Well, I did my part. I made my sacrifice, and since then the devil's just been giving me a horrible time."

Listen, I *know* people are often plagued by the devil. But I would *love* to hear a lot more people say, "Yessir, the devil *has* been plaguing me, *but I've decided to plague him back!!* I'm gonna stand in spiritual warfare! I'm asking God to make those demons wish they had never touched me!"

I'm not minimizing our Adversary. But, my brother, I'm also persuaded that if we would rise up in the Name of Jesus;

- to stand straight, taking the Blood of the Cross,
- to move forward, singing--"in his face"--of the Blood of Jesus,

we would find Satan is not an unconquerable opponent. So, get on your feet! Begin to attack! And those "birds" will scatter.

Hallelujah!

Let's both rise and defend the sacrifice of discipleship which we've made!

Let God arise, let His enemies be scattered; let those also who hate Him flee before Him. As smoke is driven away, so drive them away; as wax melts before the fire, so let the wicked perish at the presence of God. But let the righteous be glad; let them rejoice before God; yes, let them rejoice exceedingly.

Psalm 68:1-3

Walking in the Dark

Then, the darkness came.

Sir, dark, black times come for us all. There are times in a man's walk with God that you can't see God at all! You feel like the Lord has gone to the far side of the Universe, leaving you sitting in a personal crisis of some kind. But my brother, when you face those times, as I have too, you'll do well to remember the wisdom of Psalm 18.

And He (the Lord) rode upon a cherub, and flew; He flew upon the wings of the wind. He made darkness His secret place; His canopy around Him was dark waters and thick clouds of the skies.
Psalm 18:10-11

Listen to it! God *dwells* in the darkness! We serve a God who works in the dark. He did so at Creation. He did it at Israel's deliverance from Egypt. He did so at the Cross. And just as at those times, so He still will work creatively, redemptively, and victoriously in our dark times. Remember,

• When we can't see *anything,* He sees *everything.*

• When we are most vulnerable, He is most powerful.

• The darkness that makes you feel He's at the *greatest distance* is the time when He is the *most near.*

This psalm says that God puts on darkness as a coat; stepping inside your darkness, He will wear it like a garment. *He is in there with you!!*

A horror of great darkness came on Abraham, but it was then and there that the Lord began to speak to him. It's in the middle of his darkness that God is, in effect, saying: "Now, I'm going to explain my timing, Abraham. I'm going to keep My promise to you, but it's not going to be on your schedule or work out the way you thought."

Have you ever had God say something like that to you? Sure you have. And it shouldn't ever disappoint us, because God isn't being contrary or capricious, or opposing our ways just to prove He's the Boss. But He is working in ways transcending ours; embracing purposes far more expansive than our life and circumstance alone.

This text introduces us to a grand concept. Abraham is beginning to see the reason God is taking longer in his program of fulfillment, and it's because what He's doing in Abraham involves God's purposes with many other peoples.

Can you capture this truth? God is using us *amid* His purposes, not *apart* from them!

This is extremely profound. And profoundly important.

God's dealings with Abraham were not just for Abraham's sake, though he was certainly large on God's agenda and much on God's heart. But God's dealings with Abraham were not just for him and his family, or even for the nation of Israel--as central as that nation was and is to God's purposes. The Lord enlarges Abraham's perspective, showing him how he fits in with things God is doing which encompass nations and span centuries.

Think of it! See how God's dealings with this one man take into account the future of God's seeking to bring entire *nations* to repentance! The phrase from Genesis 15:16, "The iniquity of the Amorites is not yet complete," not only reflects God's longsuffering with an entire nation--His gift of opportunity for their repentance; but this reveals His synchronous, multi-layered dealings with all humanity through a cause-and-effect circuit that could blow our human minds' capacity to comprehend!

Sir, we're instruments in the hands of a redeeming God who wants to use us--each one--to impact far more than we could ever dream! Just as God says, "Abraham, My dealing with you incorporates the flow of My dealings with nations and peoples yet to come," so, my brother, none of us lives or dies to himself.

Most of us have seen the delightful old film, *It's a Wonderful Life*; a kind, humanistic parable involving a man who in the midst of being driven to the brink of suicide is intercepted by an angel. The theology of the dramatization isn't quite biblical, but the central concept of the movie certainly is: the lives of multitudes would have been tragically different if he had never been born. So it is, a man's walk with God is not for his own sake alone, but to impact entire communities, peoples, nations. That's why we need to trust the Lord's timing when promised fulfillment sometimes seems slow. It's often simply because of larger issues than your or my personal circumstance alone--issues involving great interweavings of things He's doing in your life as it eventually intersects other lives.

So, don't let yourself be pinched into a pigeon-hole-box way of thinking about the Lord's working in you, toward you, or through you. As God said to Abraham, "I will make your name *great.*" Remember--He wants you and me to hear Him, because He's saying the same thing to us: "I have great purposes for you."

This is absolutely biblical! Make no mistake, God is up to great things in our lives! Listen to the Apostle Paul's prayerful appeal: *"The eyes of your understanding being enlightened; that you may know . . . the exceeding greatness of His power toward us"* (Eph. 1:18-19).

Further, the same passage says that it's going to take "the ages to come" for God to bring us to fully see "the exceeding riches of His grace" (Eph. 2:7). Yes, Sir, God *is* up to something with men who choose to walk with Him. He has big things He's doing with us.

God: "Abraham, look, it's like the stars . . . You can't count them all, but what

I'm doing is BIG" (Gen. 15:5).

Abraham: "But God, when, how?" (Gen. 15:8).

God: "This is the way, Abraham. It's a pathway to the stars, but it moves through the blood of sacrifice, the battle against the birds, and via a way of darkness--a way of learning time elements that you don't understand.

"But when it's all over," the Lord teaches Abraham, "I'm going to fulfill the huge dimensions of purpose I've promised and measured to you. I am your shield, your exceedingly great reward--your Defender and your Fulfiller."

Listen to those words as they address us.

And let's be consumed by God's way of thinking, learning through the darkness to see His perspective. It's *all* and *always* working together for good for men who choose to walk with Him!

TALK ABOUT IT! Chapter
questions to discuss with a friend.

1) Have you ever gone through a "dark time" of discouragement or personal crisis when you felt like God was nowhere in sight--a time when, despite your efforts to follow God's way, the Adversary seemed to swarm around you like flies? Share something the "Lord Who Works in the Dark" taught you through one of these darkness experiences.

2) Like the vultures which sought to attack Abraham's sacrifice, Satan will test the commitment you've just made to spend more time in His presence. Let's be prepared for his attack and have our battle weapons ready! (James 4:7; Eph. 6:10-18). Share some of your victories in scattering the devil's "vultures" in your life.

CHAPTER FIVE:
A MAN'S WALK . . .
UNTO SETTLED TRUST

A clearly marked trail of six altars in Abraham's life is now in place, and the *process of progress* cannot help but encourage you and me as men seeking a walk with God. We are tracing the way to liveable, practical, faith-filled, and dynamic life in Christ--and we haven't hit a "religious" snag yet. Contrary to the suppositions of many unbelievers, as well as contrary to the legalistic formulas of many Christians, spirituality is neither "otherworldly," nor is it a rigid, mechanical lifestyle. As we follow Abraham's footsteps, exactly as we're taught to view his human modeling of warm-blooded holiness (Rom. 4:12), all the pieces begin to fit together.

• An ordinary man can become God's "extraordinary";

• A fearful man can find God's dynamic;

• A stumbling man can find sure footing;

• A growing man can learn God's priorities;

• A questioning man can learn holy certainty; and now we'll see--

• An imperfect man can be formed through God's perfecting!

A Man's Altar of Perfecting

Now, there are two altars which bring us to the conclusion of our study of Abraham's pathway of progress in God's grace, and I'm calling them "A Man's Altars of Perfecting." Foremost in our approach to these incidents, with which God puts completing touches on Abraham's understanding of his covenant with Him, is that we not be intimidated by the word "perfecting."

Various translations of the Bible have intermittently used this word, not to describe accomplished perfection but to describe the advancing path of maturity--the "I'm-gonna-keep-on-growing-in-Christ-for-a-lifetime" pathway. The settling factors which establish a man's walk on such a path are finally rooted in two giant truths. These are "cutting edge" truths--both which literally bring us "under the knife of divine surgery." And even though the usual figure of exploratory or major "surgery" has a way of striking us as negative, *corrective surgery* shouldn't.

Think of the difference.

In one procedure--the kind we fear--the body is cut, organs or limbs removed, and then--as tragically is often the case--the patient still doesn't survive. But *corrective* surgery results in new *capacities* being realized, originally intended *efficiency* released, and new *dimensions* for joyous living opened up.

This is the concept of "perfecting" as we examine Abraham's learning of lessons for our own growth in God's way. These altars bring us to understanding that the essence of His program of "perfection" is *not* so much in accomplishment, attainment, or verified excellence, as it is in our settled, certain *direction*--at all times.

Remember that, my brother. Let these words be fixed in your soul for your lifetime in Christ: *God is not so interested in my perfection as He is in my direction!* What happened with Abraham at these last two altar encounters became the capstone on his earlier life of learning God's way, and secured his movement in God's will for the rest of his earthly walk.

"Perfecting": Step One

It's an interesting fact that, chronologically, these two altar encounters (which are separated by only a few years) are early enough in Abraham's life that more than a full one-third of his years follow without any question or bewilderment. In short: There *is* a place in Christ where life-patterns become fixed, faith becomes settled, but the adventure of ongoing advancement in God never becomes boring, disinteresting, or dull. So it *is* possible, brother. You and I *can* learn a walk with God that becomes "perfected" unto solidity--and joy!

Let's read together the first of these last two "perfecting" encounters:

When Abram was ninety-nine years old, the Lord appeared to Abram and said to him, "I am Almighty God; walk before Me and be blameless. And I will make My covenant between Me and you, and will multiply you exceedingly."

Then Abram fell on his face, and God talked with him, saying: "As for Me, behold, My covenant is with you, and you shall be a father of many nations. No longer shall your name be called Abram, but your name shall be Abraham; for I have made you a father of many nations. I will make you exceedingly fruitful; and I will make nations of you, and kings shall come from you. And I will establish My covenant between Me and you and your descendants after you in their generations, for an everlasting covenant, to be God to you and your descendants after you. Also I give to you and your descendants after you the land in which you are a stranger, all the land of Canaan, as an everlasting possession; and I will be their God."

And God said to Abraham: "As for you, you shall keep My covenant, you and your descendants after you throughout their generations. This is My covenant which you shall keep, between Me and

you and your descendants after you:
Every male child among you shall be
circumcised; and you shall be circum-
cised in the flesh of your foreskins, and
it shall be a sign of the covenant be-
tween Me and you." Genesis 17:1-11

I want to literally "cut" to the core of the
message this "altar" of Abraham's contains. The profundity of the implications
involved in the ancient rite of circumcision
is too grand to elaborate here. In fact, one
of our future books in this series for men
will be given in entirety to discussing the
power-principles hidden in the Old Testament covenant practice of circumcision,
which was religiously observed until New
Testament times. But at the heart of this
practice is God's call that we surrender to
the cutting away of our flesh; that we
submit to the sword of His Word which calls
us away from carnal indulgence and fleshly
mindedness, and permits the Holy Spirit to
excise the unnecessary.

Just as the removing of the fleshly
foreskin of the body in no way inhibits
future reproductivity, God only calls for us
to submit to the removal of habits, ways of
thought, modes of behavior, and bent atti-
tudes--any one of which (and certainly *all*
together)--will reduce our fruitfulness, block
our progress or hinder our potential for
effectiveness in our lives and living.

Of course we always have a choice. You can back off and say, "I don't want to have any of that 'cutting' in my heart!" But remember, if we do, we'll have to live with the consequences of bypassing that "altar" call. We'll find in time the undesirability of the excess baggage, the bondage, and the burdens of flesh. Instead, let the circumcision of your heart reveal the power of the Holy Spirit, who brings instead His fruit, His love, His joy, His peace, and so much more. So Abraham's "altar" of circumcision is the picture of the power of God's Word through the Holy Spirit's ministry to carve away the unnecessary, the carnal, the unproductive.

And with that seventh altar, we come to the eighth and last altar we'll study in Abraham's life. It's the second of two "altars of perfecting," but this one became at one and the same time the greatest test and the greatest victory of Abraham's faith.

Now it came to pass after these things that God tested Abraham, and said to him, "Abraham!" And he said, "Here I am." Then He said, "Take now your son, your only son Isaac, whom you love, and go to the land of Moriah, and offer him there as a burnt offering on one of the mountains of which I shall tell you." So Abraham rose early in the morning and saddled his donkey, and took two of his young men with him, and Isaac his son; and he split the wood for the burnt offering, and arose and went to the place of which God had told him.

Then on the third day Abraham lifted his eyes and saw the place afar off.

And Abraham said to his young men, "Stay here with the donkey; the lad and I will go yonder and worship, and we will come back to you."

So Abraham took the wood of the burnt offering and laid it on Isaac his son; and he took the fire in his hand, and a knife, and the two of them went together.

But Isaac spoke to Abraham his father and said, "My father!" And he said, "Here I am, my son." Then he said, "Look, the fire and the wood, but where is the lamb for a burnt offering?"

And Abraham said, "My son, God will provide for Himself the lamb for a burnt offering." So the two of them went together.

Then they came to the place of which God had told him. And Abraham built an altar there and placed the wood in order; and he bound Isaac his son and laid him on the altar, upon the wood.

And Abraham stretched out his hand and took the knife to slay his son.

But the Angel of the Lord called to him from heaven and said, "Abraham, Abraham!" So he said, "Here I am."

And He said, "Do not lay your hand on the lad, or do anything to him; for now I know that you fear God, since you have not withheld your son, your only son, from Me."

Then Abraham lifted his eyes and looked, and there behind him was a ram caught in a thicket by its horns. So Abraham went and took the ram, and offered it up for a burnt offering instead of his son.

Genesis 22:1-13

There is possibly no more tender story in all the Bible short of the ultimate story this even prophesies: the sacrifice by Almighty God of His own, His only Son on the Cross. Abraham was not only experiencing the soul-jarring summons to sacrifice, he was struggling with a concept which went at cross purposes to everything He knew of God. You see, Abraham's God didn't demand human sacrifice as the surrounding pagan world practiced it. But God is leading Abraham, not merely to the top of Mount Moriah, He is bringing him to the pinnacle of understanding. It's the place God wants to bring every man eventually--every man who wants to walk with God.

GOD WANTS TO BRING YOU AND ME TO:

1. THE PLACE WHERE WE ARE WILLING TO TRUST *HIM*, EVEN WHEN EVERYTHING AROUND SEEMS TO SUGGEST HE HAS CHANGED HIS WAYS; AND TO

2. THE PLACE WHERE THERE IS NOTHING SO TREASURED BY US THAT WE ARE UNWILLING TO SURRENDER IT COMPLETELY TO HIS HANDS--EVEN TO EXTINCTION.

There are a thousand lessons in this incredibly wonderful passage of Scripture. Abraham's faith rose to action, believing that even if he *did* slay Isaac in obedience to God, the Almighty Faithful One would mightily, gloriously--and in line with His full promises for the future--raise Isaac from the dead!! (See Hebrews 11:18-19, which says exactly that!)

This is the ultimate *perfecting* in a man's walk with God--his arrival at a place of total trust, complete assurance: God will never fail His promises! God will never change His nature!

But the arrival at this peak in growth is not readily attained. It's the fruitage born from a growing, developing, progressing process of faith's lessons--at altars. For it is in the building of altars, in the encountering of God at distinct times in distinct ways, that a man's walk with God comes to increase and fruition.

And altar-building is never easy.

All Your Tomorrows

We're drawing to a conclusion, and I want to leave you with a vision of yourself as a lifelong builder of altars. I'm still building, and so is every man I know who has chosen to walk with God. But as you chart that course--like Abraham who walked this pathway of faith before us--I want to urge the remembrance of this practical counsel: There are basic keys to living as an altar-builder.

How do you build an altar? A number of things come to mind, but the thing that most impresses me about altars, as symbolized in the stone mounds arranged by the patriarchs like Abraham, is that *altars are built from hard things.*

Rocks.

The tough.

The unyielding situation.

A single difficulty, or a complete collection of hard things in life, can set up the possibility of an altar being formed.

This analogy of rocks being like life's "hard things" relates to the fact that rocks are the natural result of certain physical processes which formed them. I'm not an expert in geology, but I've read enough to know that stones or splinters of rock--granite and various other minerals--are the result of two primary forces:

(1) volcanic action or explosions, which

melt, cool, shape, and hurl rocks; and

(2) extreme temperatures, hot and cold, which crack and shatter larger masses of rock to smaller rocks.

For each of us, the building of an altar is often basically our choice to collect "hard things"--tough things that are a result of either explosions or extremities in our lives--and to bring them into arrangement before God.

Sometimes, things "blow up in our faces"--hard things that we need to learn how to take to the Lord.   Other times freezing cold (loneliness, rejection, depression) or emotional exception (anger, bitterness, harsh words) fill our lives with hard things. But this "altar lesson" calls us to learn what to do with those tough things. Our response will determine whether an altar will be erected, and the face of God sought, or if we'll try to handle the "roles" in other ways.

For one thing, we can just carry them--try to handle them as burdens of our own. Unsurrendered to "altar-building," they're an unwieldy burden, but many people have whole collections of hard things! "Hey, I've got problems you've never even seen before! In fact, I've polished up some of mine for display! Wanna see 'em?" Unarranged in prayer before God, our "hard things" can be paraded for their special designs and rare qualities, but they'll never be changed . . .

only collected.

Another thing one can do with life's "hard things" is to throw them at other people. Like a rock, a past pain or present difficulty can be hurled in anger: "If I've got a problem, it's gonna be yours, too!" And, Bammm!!

Or, life's hard things can simply be left lying there . . . neglected, as though to pretend they will go away on their own. But if not arranged before God in altar-building, hard things lying on the ground--undealt with--will soon cut someone's feet or trip another passerby. Passivity toward hard things doesn't work. Like rocks on a roadway, they'll remain a scattered mess in the path or split a tire of an unsuspecting driver.

God didn't intend any of us to be damaged by life's rocky hard things. They're simply a part of the world that we're living in. But it *is* God's intent to convert life's tough things to blessings; to fulfill His Word that "all things *do* work together for good for those who love God and are called according to His purpose." For this to happen, we need to take such "rocks" and turn them into altars--placing them before Him and arranging them in order.

And when you do, one thing remains.

As with ancient times, where the sacrifice was poured out on the altar, there's a contemporary counterpart for our action.

After the altar is built, we need: *to pour out our hearts!*

• Whatever the difficulty, open your heart completely.

• Whatever the frustration, declare your feelings without hesitation.

• Whatever the pain, let its fullness be laid in His presence.

• Whatever the anger, disappointment, or struggle--let your whole life be placed in His hands as you pour your heart's cry before Him.

And as you do, you'll find our Father's ability to deal with a heart that's opened itself--that's bared its fullest cry to Him.

So, the secret is to see life's hard things for what they are. They're the product of explosions and extremities--not to be carried, collected or thrown, but to be arranged before the Father. Then, to allow our heart to be poured out over the matter--

for His healing our hurt,

for His teaching our mind,

for His correcting our perspective,

for His soothing our soul,

for His removing our fears,

for His leading us beyond our rockiness into His revelation.

And as He reveals Himself, we'll find but another blessing that results when a person decides to walk with God. We'll find the power of altars to alter! To change our heart, charge us with wisdom, and call us with faith into His future for us.

That's why we all have this unalterable need of an altar.

It's the timeless pathway of all who would learn to walk with the Almighty--changed by His power to learn of His change-less grace and abounding purpose for us.

For you.

TALK ABOUT IT! Chapter questions to discuss with a friend.

1) Find a partner and pray together over the current "hard things"--burdens in your life--that need to be laid at Jesus' feet; name people before the Father in prayer and declare your forgiveness of them; ask the Lord to reveal ways for you to begin recon-ciliation with those with whom fellowship has been broken.

2) We have learned in our study that a better rendering of the biblical word "perfec-tion" is "maturity." God wants us to con-tinue to "grow up" in His way. List some life-patterns or areas you wish to grow in--mature in--during this season of your life.

DEVOTIONS

In CHAPTERS 12 through 22 of

GENESIS

Contributed by Bob Anderson

This devotional covers a critical section of Scripture. In Chapters 12 - 22 of the book of Genesis the Christian faith finds its deepest moorings: in the life of Abraham, the man referred to by the Apostle Paul as "the father of all those who believe"–those of us who walk by faith (cf. Romans 4:11).

Since Genesis is the "Book of Beginnings," our prayer is that this devotional in the life of Abraham will earmark the beginning of a whole new dimension in your walk with God.

(It is suggested that this devotional be used for stimulating discussion and prayer within a small group of men meeting regularly.)

☐ **Today's Text: Genesis 12:1- 3** *(key v. 1)*

1 **Today's Truth:** Abraham could have cleaved to physical "security and predictability" by remaining in his father's house and thus retaining control of his life. But laying all this down from a pure motive of obedience to God, he inherited wealth and eternal glory far beyond what his mind could envision.

Today's Thoughts: _____

_____

_____

☐ **Today's Text: Genesis 12:4-9** *(key v.4)*

2 **Today's Truth:** We can sometimes feel as though the season in life wherein God can use us has passed. But Abraham was already 75 years old when he began God's faith-walk adventure!

Today's Thoughts: _____

_____

_____

☐ **Today's Text: Genesis 12:10-20** *(key v. 17)*

3 **Today's Truth:** Abraham's sin of lying to Pharaoh's house adversely affected other lives. For this man, who would become *a blessing to nations*, this was a crucial lesson–one he would need to learn again–that of seeing how his moral decisions impacted others.

Today's Thoughts: _____

_____

_____

☐ **Today's Text: Genesis 13:1-4** *(key v. 4)*

4 **Today's Truth:** Abraham returned back to the beginning point of his journey but with new insight. His unhappy encounter with Pharaoh must have left him with a fresh reminder that doing things his own way instead of God's way will certainly lead to disaster.

Today's Thoughts: _____
_____
_____

☐ **Today's Text: Genesis 13:5-13** *(key vv. 8-9)*

5 **Today's Truth:** Abraham avoids his former pattern of seizing control to protect his own interests. This time he releases control and prefers his nephew over his own desires.

Today's Thoughts: _____
_____
_____

☐ **Today's Text: Genesis 13:14-18** *(key v. 14)*

6 **Today's Truth:** Abraham trusted God to take care of him and didn't seize the better grazing land from Lot–even though his culture would grant him such a right as the elder family member. Now God reminded him of the larger picture: we're not talking about grazing land, we're talking *destiny!*

Today's Thoughts: _____
_____
_____

☐ **Today's Text: Genesis 14:1-16** *(key v. 14)*

7 **Today's Truth:** This is a new side to Abraham we've never seen before: a man of military skill and courage. His experience in following God by faith ignited new strength and confidence which may have been a surprise even to him as it emerged.

Today's Thoughts: _____

_____

_____

☐ **Today's Text: Genesis 14:17-24** *(key v. 22)*

8 **Today's Truth:** As soon as Abraham returned from a victorious battle, it would seem Heaven and Hell both approached him seeking his allegiance. With danger now abated, it could be easy to compromise with the spirit of this world. But Abraham's commitment to God was firm.

Today's Thoughts: _____

_____

_____

☐ **Today's Text: Genesis 15:1-6** *(key v. 6)*

9 **Today's Truth:** Abraham wanted a logical explanation for his future–"Will Eliezer be my heir, God?"–that old control hang-up again. But as God reaffirmed His miracle method, Abraham believed. This lesson of releasing control to God had to be learned once again at a deeper dimension.

Today's Thoughts: _____

_____

_____

☐ **Today's Text: Genesis 15:7-16** *(key vv. 12-13)*

10 **Today's Truth:** Sometimes we receive the greatest revelations, wisdom, and comfort from the Lord during times of great horror and darkness. We may not understand all that God is doing in our lives at the present, but God encompasses all of time and sees well beyond our finite perspective.

Today's Thoughts: —————————————

—————————————————————————————

—————————————————————————————

☐ **Today's Text: Genesis 15:17-21** *(key v. 17)*

11 **Today's Truth:** When flesh is offered up in sacrifice to God, the Lord's revival fire will then burn in the midst of our lives. This typified Abraham's life: his fleshly ways were sacrificed so that God's redemptive plan could unfold through him.

Today's Thoughts: —————————————

—————————————————————————————

—————————————————————————————

☐ **Today's Text: Genesis 16:1-5** *(key v. 2)*

12 **Today's Truth:** Abraham was tempted to help God fulfill His promise. Maybe God, who tarried ''too long'' in bringing forth His promise, might be blessed by a helping hand! Hagar must be the answer! But again, the best human efforts to do God's work fall woefully short of His glory.

Today's Thoughts: —————————————

—————————————————————————————

—————————————————————————————

☐ **Today's Text: Genesis 16:6-10** *(key v. 10)*

13 Today's Truth: The Lord's tender lovingkindness was even shown to Hagar, who was unrelated to God's redemptive plan. Even though she was not to be the mother of the promised heir, still, God's words of comfort directed her to believe for *her own* destiny.

Today's Thoughts: _____

_____

_____

☐ **Today's Text: Genesis 16:11-16** *(key v. 13)*

14 Today's Truth: Although Hagar was an Egyptian, she called upon her master's God. Despite the present conflict, something of the glory of the Lord must have shown through Abraham's and Sarah's lives for her to forsake her ancestors' gods and trust in the God of Abraham.

Today's Thoughts: _____

_____

_____

☐ **Today's Text: Genesis 17:1-8** *(key v. 5)*

15 Today's Truth: God changed Abram's name ("Exalted Father") to Abraham ("Father of a Multitude"). It was the added breath mark, the Hebrew syllable "ha," that made all the difference in the world–because it was God's Breath on him begetting new character and destiny.

Today's Thoughts: _____

_____

_____

☐ **Today's Text: Genesis 17:9-14** *(key v. 10)*

16 **Today's Truth:** The rite of circumcision zeroed in on two critical issues: (1) God's people were to cut away their fleshly dependence; and (2) the fulfillment of God's promise would come through human flesh–but flesh deeply touched, even cut into, by God's intervention.

Today's Thoughts: _____

_____

_____

☐ **Today's Text: Genesis 17:15-27** *(key v. 17)*

17 **Today's Truth:** Abraham laughed not because of unbelief but because of how amazing the promise seemed to him. Yet even though he laughed, and pleaded again that Ishmael might be the son of promise (v. 18), God still called Abraham "a man of faith."

Today's Thoughts: _____

_____

_____

☐ **Today's Text: Genesis 18:1-15** *(key v. 12)*

18 **Today's Truth:** It's interesting to note the Lord's harsher reaction to Sarah's laughter compared to when Abraham laughed. It is evident that Sarah was still set in unbelief, not merely amazement.

Today's Thoughts: _____

_____

_____

☐ **Today's Text: Genesis 18:16-33** *(key v. 32)*

19 **Today's Truth:** Abraham interceded for the preservation of Sodom. But in this unique negotiating process, it was Abraham, not the Lord, who ended the negotiations.

Today's Thoughts: _____

_____

_____

☐ **Today's Text: Genesis 19:1-29** *(key v. 16)*

20 **Today's Truth:** Apparently, other than Lot and his family, no other righteous persons were found in Sodom. Could it be that other righteous people *had* lived in Sodom but had left in disgust instead of remaining to impact the wicked city for righteousness and thereby alter its future?

Today's Thoughts: _____

_____

_____

☐ **Today's Text: Genesis 19:30-38** *(key v. 31)*

21 **Today's Truth:** The girls incorrectly assumed that God could not provide husbands for them since their homeland had been destroyed. So they "took control" of the situation and their incestuous relationships produced two sons whose descendents became the enemies of the descendents of Abraham. The Moabites and Ammonites would become two of the greatest snares to the Nation of Israel.

Today's Thoughts: _____

_____

_____

☐ **Today's Text: Genesis 20:1-7** *(key v. 2)*

22 **Today's Truth:** One of the challenges of faith is to "connect all the dots"–meaning if we believe God can do a miracle in one area of life, we sometimes fail to believe He can be as proficient in another. Abraham believed God could provide Isaac as promised, but he failed to believe God would protect him in the midst of danger.

Today's Thoughts: _____

_____

_____

☐ **Today's Text: Genesis 20:8-18** *(key v. 17)*

23 **Today's Truth:** As imperfect as Abraham was, he was, nonetheless, a man of faith who interceded for others. His being a blessing was both at a personal level as well as at an international level.

Today's Thoughts: _____

_____

_____

☐ **Today's Text: Genesis 21:1-7** *(key v. 3)*

24 **Today's Truth:** Isaac means "laughter." Abraham and Sarah had laughed in struggling to imagine the impossible. Now the laughter is born from joy.

Today's Thoughts: _____

_____

_____

☐ **Today's Text: Genesis 21:8-14** *(key v. 12)*

25 **Today's Truth:** God Almighty told Abraham, the Father of Israel, to listen to his wife and comply with what she said. Yes, there were unique circumstances in this case, but spiritual headship embraces attentive listening to the words, heart, and vision of one's wife. Always.

Today's Thoughts: _____
_____
_____

☐ **Today's Text: Genesis 21:15-21** *(key v. 17)*

26 **Today's Truth:** It's touching that God "heard the voice of the lad." No voice is without significance. God takes seriously anyone who calls upon Him, no matter how weak or small that voice may be.

Today's Thoughts: _____
_____
_____

☐ **Today's Text: Genesis 21:22-34** *(key v. 33)*

27 **Today's Truth:** Our study in the book described an altar as being potentially anything. Here Abraham plants a tamarisk tree and calls on the Name of the Lord.

Today's Thoughts: _____
_____
_____

☐ **Today's Text: Genesis 22:1-8** *(key v. 8)*

28 **Today's Truth:** Abraham's mind must have been reeling! "My son–a human sacrifice!" Yet by now, Abraham's seasoned faith had learned that God's plans transcend human limitations and what our eyes alone can see.

Today's Thoughts: _____

_____

_____

☐ **Today's Text: Genesis 22:9-14** *(key v. 14)*

29 **Today's Truth:** The dramatic rescue of Isaac now passed, Abraham calls the place "The-Lord-Will-Provide." But was this man of faith amazed? He himself had predicted in verse 8 that "God will provide." One can imagine Abraham breathing a sigh of relief, "Well, it was a close one, but He came through, *again* . . . as He *always* does!"

Today's Thoughts: _____

_____

_____

☐ **Today's Text: Genesis 22:15-17** *(key v. 17)*

30 **Today's Truth:** Abraham began by trying to control events in his life. Now in the biggest test of all, he had totally relinquished control to God. And the reward was astronomical.

Today's Thoughts: _____

_____

_____

☐ **Today's Text: Genesis 22:18-24** *(key v. 18)*

31 **Today's Truth:** God says literally that the entire planet will be profoundly blessed through Abraham's descendants because of his obedience to God. What an incredible bargain! For obedience that took only minutes to fulfill, centuries of blessing would cover the earth!

Today's Thoughts: _____

_____

_____

Please note:

Our devotional covers Chapters 12 through 22 of the book of Genesis because it is within these chapters that Abraham's life-long pursuit of God's will is recorded, while Chapters 23 - 25 record the final key events in Abraham's life. Chapter 23 tells us of details surrounding Sarah's death and burial; Chapter 24 tells the story of Abraham's role in securing a bride for Isaac; and Chapter 25 is the account of Abraham's death.

For a comparative study, the following additional verses of New Testament Scripture may be referred to: John 8:39-58; Romans 4:1-25; Galatians 3:1-18; Hebrews 7:1-9; and Hebrews 11:8-19.

Additional Resources for
Biblical Manhood

Available from Jack Hayford and
Living Way Ministries

AUDIO CASSETTE MINI-ALBUMS (2 tapes)

Honest to God	SC122	$8
Redeeming Relationships for Men & Women	SC177	$8
Why Sex Sins Are Worse Than Others	SC179	$8
How God Uses Men	SC223	$8
A Father's Approval	SC225	$8
Resisting the Devil	SC231	$8
How to Recession-Proof Your Home	SC369	$8
Safe Sex!	SC448	$8
The Leader Jesus Trusts	SC461	$8

AUDIO CASSETTE ALBUMS (# of tapes)

Cleansed for the Master's Use (3)	SC377	$13
Becoming God's Man (4)	SC457	$17
Fixing Family Fractures (4)	SC217	$17
The Power of Blessing (4)	SC395	$17
Men's Seminars 1990-91 (10)	MSEM	$42
Premarital Series (12)	PM02	$50
A Family Encyclopedia (24)	SC233	$99

VHS VIDEO ALBUMS

Why Sex Sins Are Worse Than Others	WSSV	$19
Divorce and the People of God	DIVV	$19
Earthly Search for a Heavenly Father	ESFV	$19

Add 15% for shipping and handling.
California residents add 8.25% sales tax.
Request your free Resource Catalog.
Living Way Ministries Resources
14820 Sherman Way • Van Nuys, CA 91405-2233
(818) 779-8480 or (800) 776-8180

A MAN'S STARTING PLACE

A study of how
men become
mature in
Christ through
relationships

Jack Hayford

THOMAS NELSON PUBLISHERS
Nashville • Atlanta • London • Vancouver

Published in Nashville, Tennessee, by Thomas Nelson, Inc., Publishers, and distributed in Canada by Word Communications, Ltd., Richmond, British Columbia, and in the United Kingdom by Word (UK), Ltd., Milton Keynes, England.

ISBN 0-7852-7792-7

Printed in the United States of America

1 2 3 4 5 6 7 - 01 00 99 98 97 96 95

*This message was originally brought at
The Church On The Way.*

*It has since been edited and revised
for publication by Pastor Hayford,
in partnership with Pastor Bob Anderson,
Director of Pastoral Relations.*

TABLE OF CONTENTS

DEDICATION

I dedicate this opening book of this series to the thousands of men whom I've already watched set their sights on the high call of God in Christ our Lord--and follow it!

And I express thanks also to Bob Anderson, a man I've seen "truly 'become'" an effective agent of Christ in many circles of influence; and whose gifts and skills brought this book to completion. (He also is the writer of the sections on "All In The Doing" and the Devotional guide on 1 Samuel.)

I desire therefore that the men pray everywhere, lifting up holy hands, without wrath and doubting; in like manner also, that the women adorn themselves in modest apparel, with propriety and moderation, not with braided hair or gold or pearls or costly clothing, but, which is proper for women professing godliness, with good works. Let a woman learn in silence with all submission. And I do not permit a woman to teach or to have authority over a man, but to be in silence. For Adam was formed first, then Eve. And Adam was not deceived, but the woman being deceived, fell into transgression. Nevertheless she will be saved in childbearing if they continue in faith, love, and holiness, with self-control.

— 1 Timothy 2:8-15 (NKJV)

CHAPTER ONE:

GOD'S STARTING PLACE

It was Illinois-in-February, zero-biting *cold* as I walked down the small country path through snow a foot deep.

I was in the Midwest part of our nation to fulfill a speaking engagement, and have to admit the reason I was so enjoying that winter scene was very basic: I had *flown in* to speak, and could *fly right out* when I was done! It's called "Winter on demand"-- without pain!!

It was about 7:30 in the morning, and as I trudged along--earmuffs, scarf, heavy cap, and jacket and all--the sun was rising over the southeast, a purplish orange ball, cresting over snow-laden trees. As bitter as the cold was, it was a delightful, winter-wonderland moment. Even though frozen ice crystals fell as my breath touched the air, the morning was sheer magnificence. It was one of those precious, nonstressed moments, surrounded by God's awesome creation--the kind of moment I'd want to remember on a July day when I'm back driving L.A.'s freeways during rush hour.

As I continued walking--every step a crunch under my feet--I had no idea it was in this scene that God would meet me. I was entirely unprepared for what would become one of the most important assignments ever impressed upon my heart concerning how I was to lead as a pastor, and how I, myself, was to live in the ensuing years. This "prompting" I received from the Lord needs a context to clarify the significance of what He was about to say, so please allow a moment of background information.

Just a year before our small congregation had experienced a dramatic visitation of God's grace. In just one year from that point of visitation we'd quadrupled--grown from 100 people to just over 400. Of course, I hadn't the slightest dream that our church would take on the "mega" proportions it eventually has--serving 8,000 to 10,000 people in public services each week. The 400 was "plenty of miracle" for me!

But that morning, as my feet crunched the frozen country pathway, my heart was full. I'd seen a year of incredible blessing, and with that, here I was amid the beauty that surrounded me at that moment.

It was then that the words came:

"I want you to begin to gather men and to train them. As you do, I will raise up strong leadership for the future of this church."

10

Though I didn't understand all the implications at that moment, I did sense God's desire to build men--strong men, strong single guys, strong husbands, strong fathers who knew who they were. *"Gather the men and begin to teach them."*

Our "Men's Growth" Starting Place

It was about six weeks later I began the monthly men's meetings: Men's Growth Seminars. The first time we ever planned to meet, I made a direct invitation to thirty-five men; sending each a note, as well as putting a general announcement in the church bulletin. Of those I invited, eighteen came. So, we made a circle of chairs--a simple, up-close-and-together arrangement. We had a time of worship, and then I opened my heart to them about God's "word" to me. And that's how it started.

So, what happened that Illinois wintertime morning affected not only my life, but drastically--and very beautifully--the whole of the congregation I serve. For that event to which I'm referring, over 20 years ago, made an impact so great it still resonates through and orchestrates my thoughts, pastoral values, and ministry.

Over the years there have been multiplied thousands who have been influenced-- thousands of men who have been transformed. The direct result is that as our church has grown, there have been stable underpin-

11

nings, not only through vital Christ-exalting worship and Word-centered preaching, but by the roles filled with a cadre of committed, growing, sensible, submitted, godly men. Why should or why could such a strategy make so much difference?

The Issue of Creational and Redemptive "Sequence"

Let me make a head-on statement at the risk of generating sparks. In our sometimes militantly feminist society, it's more than likely that some people won't listen no matter how carefully I explain. But to begin, let me say: In most of His workings, God *starts* with men. Get that. *Men* are God's "starting place."

Fundamental to our whole study is this fact: *The shaping of a man is foundational to anything God seeks to do.*

I am in no way suggesting that men are superior to women. Neither am I hinting at any rejection or reduction of the value of women in God's Kingdom purposes. But this starts with a simple fact in Scripture--the *sequence in creation: "Adam was formed first"* (1 Tim. 2:13); and it's this sequence which God has chosen to preserve in His redemptive "order" of dealing with humankind.

There's a functional purpose to that order. It isn't that by making man first He prefers him. It *is* that *having* made man first

12

in the *initial* creation, He has chosen to deal with man first in His quest to recover what the Fall has brought about. Just as God in Creation's purpose started with man (in order to later form woman from his side, and thereby demonstrate the union and heart-commitment He intended the couple to have), so in redemption's purposes He begins with men to demonstrate something. That *"something"* is the objective of our whole study--the target of our men's ministries. Our objective is to recover something of understanding we men have lost about our responsibilities under God. But more about that later.

Right now, however, let it be made very clear--indeed it's obvious!--that God has not perpetuated this order or sequence because men are wiser, or more intelligent, or more gifted--or *anything else*--more than women.

For example, if we were to take a cross-sampling of the IQs of a mixed group of men and women, 50% of the women would be more intelligent than the men, more gifted, etc.--and vice versa. And I also want to assert that *some* feminist concerns are valid. It is unfortunate that it's taken our formerly male-dominated society so long to acknowledge the equality of women in many areas. In our Western culture--but even viciously worse in some others--there are still many places where women suffer from dehumanizing sexism and grievous injustice. *That is not part of God's design* and it *is*

13

offensive to His will. Such instances have nothing whatsoever to do with the principle of creational and redemptive *sequence* with which we're dealing.

So, God's dealing with men as His "starting place" has nothing to do with any system that demeans or restricts women. Nonetheless, God has appointed an "order" for processing His work in advancing His redeeming, recovering, releasing works among humanity. And things happen better and they happen faster when they are on God's terms. God starts with men, *not* because men learn better or faster—indeed, we in fact tend *not* to! But this still is God's order, and He has chosen to "initiate" what I'll call "releasing life" through men; i.e., things being released to divine order because men accept their responsibilities under that order. So, we deduce: *There are no second class citizens in God's Kingdom,* but there is a creational order which God has maintained in His redemptive purposes; an order that works best when men learn to accept their responsibility as the Creator intended.

But reactions do arise. Human arrogance still dares to say, "No, God! Don't do it that way. We have new insight. Look at it THIS way!"

The reactionary stance to God's sequential order may rise with accusations of male chauvinism. Others point to the obvious fact that men fail: "So why are they any better

14

than women for God's initiating His work?" And my answer is to emphasize: "Better isn't the issue; God's order or sequence *is.*" We refuse accusations of male chauvinism, stoutly opposing such practices. There is a radical difference between what I'm proposing and what male chauvinism does.

Male chauvinism is essentially the result of granting the *privileges of preference* to men without requiring of them the *responsibilities of leadership*. It's male chauvinism that toys with women and trumpets the hollow idea of men being "better." In contrast to this, we are NOT *persisting* in an argument for male preference or dominance, but *insisting* on a male's acceptance of his responsibilities in leadership. When *that* is realized, the man's "leader" role will never be used to limit or control the advancement or fulfillment of women, but to serve and assist the woman's highest possibilities--including *her* discoveries of leadership, influence, and biblical self-realization.

God's plan is for a man to take his leadership role--to learn of, to accept, and to exercise those *responsibilities* (not privileges) that thereby he might serve and assist God's means for the release of a woman's highest potential.

No! Chauvinists we're not!

In this vein, I believe stark honesty requires a dual admission. First, that Christianity has done more to recover and equalize the societal gap between men and women, and thereby to dignify womanhood, than any other social force or religious system on earth. Second, however, the same honesty requires an admission with regret. Some Christian traditions have in places and at times, whether intentionally or unwittingly, fostered some degree of male chauvinism they have based on a supposed "biblical" foundation. In seeking to distance ourselves from that injustice, we nonetheless still hold to true biblically based teaching. The Spirit of Truth in the eternal Scriptures shows God's intent. He points the way toward prioritizing the development of men--responsible men--without diminishing anything of a woman's potential. And when this way is honored, the end result will be the *maximizing* of each woman's greatest possibilities at every dimension, just as surely as it will the man's.

The history-changing invasion of Jesus Christ into the human scene was to make us all one and to bring salvation's victories to every individual, we all--regardless of gender--are made *winners*, now and forever! This is the spirit of our whole proposition in focusing Men's Ministries:

"There is neither Jew nor Greek, there is neither slave nor free, there is neither male nor female; for you are all one in Christ Jesus" (Galatians 3:28).

Christ has come not only to save us and to break hell's powers, but also to undo social injustice at every level. It's important to recognize that fact, because the above evidence (Gal. 3:28) of God's acknowledgment of equality between men and women tells us something. He not only is set on liberating people so that both men and women can become all that they were intended to be. He has also laid the foundation in His Word as to how this may come about on *His* terms; a plan which starts with His bringing men to learn their role.

Beginning With "A Man"

God is unapologetic about this plan He has of "starting things" with men. It's threaded throughout His Word.

- The human race began with a *man*--Adam.

- The vision of faith's promise--how to walk a pathway of faith with God--began with a *man*--Abraham.

- The Jewish peoples began with a *man*--Jacob; to whom God reached out and called saying: "I will make of you a great nation," and his twelve sons became the fathers of the twelve tribes of Israel.

- Israel's Deliverance from Egypt--which is a grand picture of God's whole deliverance program for all mankind through the blood of the Lamb--came under the leadership of a *man*--Moses.

• Israel's possession of Canaan came under the leadership of the *man*--Joshua; who led the people of God into their inheritance, and became the biblical "type" of Jesus, who as our Leader brings us into the possession of our God-promised destinies.

• The precursor of "Messiah," the royal prototype of the one who would become humanity's King, was a *man*--David; from whose line would come the Savior of mankind, Jesus, later called "the Son of David."

• And finally when God became flesh to rescue all mankind, He came as a *man*--in the form of His Son Jesus Christ; the ultimate *Man*, the Second Adam from Heaven, the Son of God!

In underscoring these facts, I would not, nor could I, dismiss the worth or the preciousness of womanhood. Nothing about God's order reduces the marvelous role of the woman nor suggests a heavenly rejection of her significance. And further and finally, let it be noted that the Bible specifically says, "God is not a man" (Num. 23:19). But neither is He a woman. God is neither male nor female. But *historically* and *redemptively*, God has most commonly led the way--releasing His purposes in the interest of ALL humanity--through the leadership of men.

"Maximum things" don't happen without seeing this "starting place."

TALK ABOUT IT! Chapter questions to explore with a friend.

1) What are four dramatic examples of God choosing men at pivotal moments in human history?

2) Think over how the world has viewed Christianity as chauvinistic. What are some factors you think might have given fuel to this misunderstanding? What key truths have been overlooked by the world mentality in their maintaining such a view?

3) What's a good argument for Christianity being the most dynamic liberating force for women ever? What contrast do you see in other cultures?

4) Do you see the difference between the issue of *sequence* and *preference*; that God's redemptive order is not based on "liking men more," but on "having made man first"?

CHAPTER TWO:
RELATING TO IT ALL!

Take a look. If a church is deficient in spiritual vitality, ask: "What place is being given to the development of men?" I think we'll find it generally true that when God breaks through in a church, it's because He's making a breakthrough with men. Women seem more ready in spiritual responsiveness, and that's a beautiful fact. And the good that happens when they do is no less wonderful for that. But there's a need to come full circle in a holy breakthrough in men. And I believe that's the reason the Lord dealt with me that day. When men are strong in the ways of the Lord, the expansion of the Kingdom of God not only advances, it accelerates. Spiritual manhood affects everything!

• Manhood on God's terms begets a new *single man's mind-set*, which creates a new cultural context with non-self-centered men who don't exploit women, and who understand their own life purpose and thereby serve God effectively.

• Manhood per God's design is foundational to fullest *husbandhood*. It's the beginning of a marriage that works because the man loves his wife as Christ loved the Church and gave Himself up for it.

• Real manhood is also foundational to fullest *fatherhood*. It is the prerequisite for well-adjusted children that they have a happy, "loved" mom, as well as a dad who is diligent to fill his role in the family unit.

• True manhood in Christ also touches the *business world* with unique impact. Men will become successful, knowing who they are as men, and not by reason of a falsely competitive machismo or by manipulative scheming, but instead through God's grace working His highest creative purposes *for* each one, they succeed. And,

• True manhood releases life in *the Church*, as the credibility of the relevance of Christ is manifest; as the notions of "spirituality equals unmanly" or "Christians are wimps" are buried--permanently!

So it is, if *manhood* is diminished, perverted, imbalanced, misunderstood, impotent or destructive--*anything* less than accurately reflective of the image of Christ--then the world takes a loss at every level.

Men in general will tend to be without direction and confidence.

Marriages will tend to become weak or be

dissolved.

Children tend to reproduce the rejection, loneliness or pain they grow up with.

Families tend to be unstable and deficient.

Businesses lose out.

The Church is stultified.

In short, men lead the way, whether for good or no good.

In contrast, understanding God's sequential order concerning men in leadership roles will bring God's release to everyone--men *and* women. True biblical teaching will elevate womanhood. *It will bring a holy freedom to both, men and women, and it will bring an ultimate equality between a husband and wife.*

Defining the Man as Head

The idea of being "head" has been sorely distorted and often exploited. To avert misunderstanding, let's take a quick look at a biblical definition of "the head"; a term which essentially points to the responsible role of the *married* man. But certain of these principles are spiritually true (if not always societally so) irrespective of a man's domestic status.

• "Head" means to provide leadership, not to suppress it; as with benevolent, serving leaders in a society.

• True "headship" serves the interests of those being led; as the physical body's head sees, speaks, hears, and thinks in the interest of the whole body (but without the body even the head is helpless).

• True "headship" is like a soldier "on the point"; as in the way he risks his own safety in the interest of the rest of his squad or platoon.

God never intended the man, as the "head," to be a domineering, dogmatic kind of overlord at work, to his wife, over his kids, or anywhere else. He intended the man to accept the responsibility of leadership. But, fellows, learning *how* that can happen is a difficult thing for every one of us. It's tough stuff for us to find out how we are to relate to each level of God's assigned responsibility and thus become what He intended us to be.

Often, the idea of a man filling his "leading" role is twisted or misconstructed to mean or be applied as some kind of "boss-ism," or "chief of the fiefdom." This mind-set was caricatured in the '50s TV series, "The Honeymooners," a classic which continues with wide acceptance in reruns, both for reasons of comedy as well as its reflection of our human foibles. Jackie Gleason's portrayal of Ralph Kramden was brilliantly hilarious, but also pathetically tinged with that distorted view still existent in some men: "I'm the king of the castle, Alice, and you?--You're nobody!" Remember how he would go on his strutting parade around the kitchen?

Everybody knew that *he* was the real nobody and Alice was who really "ran the store." It's the inevitable reversal resultant from a twisted view of authority. That scenario reflects the truly sad case of the man who doesn't see the failure and foolishness of the "king of the castle" mind-set; who doesn't understand that "to lead" means "to serve." Are there any of us who need to become clearer on this: that our "leading" role is *not* one of superiority, but to become a role of *service? As Jesus Christ our Lord, the Lord of Glory, became a Servant, we are called to be men--as He was.* Let's let Him bring us to the fullness of the discovered power that comes through discovered servanthood.

I sense that right now the whole Church is on the brink of something remarkable. Something new is stirring everywhere, and I sense it uniquely in things I perceive Him seeking to do among men. Jesus is determined to expand the borders of His Kingdom, Sir. And He's calling you and me--*today*--just as He did His disciples long ago! The hell-burnt ruins of Adam I--the fallen man--smolder around us. But Adam II has come to restore all things to the original created order. Let's all--each one of us--be among those men who hear what the Holy Spirit is saying to the Church, and who respond in step with His present redemptive works!

Maintenance, Servicing, and "A Clean Filter"

As men turning to God's redemptive plan, we need to let His wisdom *service us* so that *we* will be prepared to serve. God's "word" to men--to you, Sir, and to me--is "responsibility." He is calling us to accept responsibilities as He teaches us and calls us to responsibly live out what we're made to be. But we'll need His help, just as any equipment needs the helpful benefit of "servicing."

God put us together and He knows how we work. As the Designer and Engineer of our souls, He has prescribed a very specific program of maintenance. That maintenance program is clearly outlined in the Bible--the "Owner's Manual" for human life.

Have you seen the TV commercial of the auto mechanic talking about the need to regularly change your car's oil filter? He summarizes by saying if you don't regularly change the filter every so-many-1000-miles, a combination of things will happen--bad things. He notes that inevitably there will be deficiency in the operation of the engine and that eventually the likelihood of a breakdown is almost certain. So in persuading us to buy the oil filter "up front"--to get your engine serviced and preserve it from breakdown--he says, *"You can pay me now or you can pay me later!"*

I think God wants to get our attention the same way, wanting to service our systems of thought and life. He wants us to experience His "filtering" of our minds so the ways of thinking that characterize our world are filtered out. We men have a propensity to chest thump (at least privately); to suppose our own "do-it-my-way" philosophy is the best, even at the expense of God's ways. But until that "world-think" gets filtered out--until we let God regularly "service" how we think--we're going to pay an incredible debt as the "engine" sputters, or things "break down" in life. But how much better to "get serviced" *now* and get on with God's program. It isn't that God is threatening us with breakdown if we don't do it His way. But we *do* reap what we sow. It's far better to "pay up now" by having our understanding re-tooled and our minds purged of things that confuse and hinder the effective operation of God's system in our lives.

The choice to let God begin His work in you *now* will affect how you think about yourself; will affect how you relate to your friends and family; will affect everything to do with your business; and affect how you relate to matters in the Church--the Body of Christ. We can't afford *not* to be "serviced." No one in his right mind wants to "pay later."

So exactly how does a man choose to let God begin His work in him now?

Three Circles: Relating to It All!

Let's begin with the issue of a man's relationships: how he relates to life, to love, to leading--to it all! The starting place is with pivotal relationships and with relational understanding. Just as *God's* starting point is with men, a *man's* starting place is to find alignment with God's ways in his relationships. There are three primary areas of relationship which are critical in shaping us as men.

• Each of them has unique obstacles that can thwart us.

• Each of them has awesome potential to fulfill us.

• Each of them is so precious that both hell and heaven are intensely interested in possessing them.

These three circles of relationship are paramount to a man's development. The *first* is with God. The *second* is with his wife (or how an unmarried man thinks about eventually marriage). The *third* is with other men.

TALK ABOUT IT! Chapter questions to explore with a friend.

1) What are four areas of life in which men have been specifically ordained for leadership? Into which of these areas would you like to see the Lord move you?

2) Discuss the relationship between "authority," "responsibility," and "servanthood." Give one example of each attribute from Jesus' life.

3) Can you think of viewpoints or practices God may want to begin "filtering" from your thoughts or practice?

CHAPTER THREE:

POURING GOD A CUP OF COFFEE?

Read with me from Paul's first letter to Timothy, as the Apostle expresses his prayer for Christian men in a graphic picture:

"I desire therefore that men pray every-where lifting up holy hands without wrath and doubting" (1 Timothy 2:8).

That's a noble and manly picture! It clashes with the negative projections of spiritually committed men that the media has etched on our minds. An irresponsible use of stereotypes is so common in the secular media; so often portraying the spiritually inclined male as a pompously pious or heavy-handed religious bigot. With incredible regularity, (barring such rare wonders as *Chariots of Fire*, for example), a man of purposeful religious character is typically shown as devoid of genuineness, who generally turns out to be some "freako" living out the ultimate hypocrisy. A preacher is so often caricatured as frantic--foamingly threatening God's wrath in public, while everything he does in private is either hateful or corrupt, from beating his wife, to blistering his kids, to womanizing parishioners. How often it happens on the screen! The film or video plot ends with the "religious" man as the serial killer or the fake! The message which distills is always the same: (1) "Godly men" are phonies; and (2) God Himself is rendered as irrelevant for *real* men.

But the Bible has another kind of man in mind. The text calls for men with an open commitment to the living reality of His Person and Presence. The phrase, "lift up holy hands without wrath and doubting" calls to a *declarative* stance; it seeks a man who has *discovered a confidence* in his relationship with the Lord. This isn't some dandy dude who struts up to the throne of God, hands swinging upward with a casual or cutesy excitability. No! He's coming with *holy hands*--hands that have had something happen to them. They've been transformed! He comes before the Lord, with a countenance of openness and recognition, knowing that "I am received and accepted by my Father--the Mighty God!"

Paul is saying, "I would that men were like this": men of *faith* (that is, "without doubting") and men of *self-control* (not possessed by anger, "without wrath"). So much unbelief and anger dominates the modern male; unbelief because of ignorance of God's Word, and anger due to uncertainty. Much anger burns because of a low-grade irritation present from a nagging, yet often unidentified, sense of inadequacy--not having realized "something" in life. It's the cry of a man's inner being to seize his destiny, a destiny unfulfilled and seemingly light-years out of reach.

But here is a biblical call to a real relationship--to a friendship with God; to be able to freely come to Him for everything. It's a call to a friendship so intimate, it's as if God drank coffee, you'd pour Him a cup, and feel comfortable coming to Him...and then, to come and pour out your heart as well. Imagine it, just the two of you--God and son, "over coffee"--sitting there, as *friends*. Such a man will learn that his walk with God allows for such "pouring out," for *emptying* anger, pride, lust or anything else eating at him. God doesn't see this as though you're "flinging things" in His face; as though you were putting Him at fault, or as if your failures disallowed forthrightness with Him. Rather, this "pouring out" is a learning to "cast all our care on Him for He cares for us" (1 Peter 5:7).

Please make this distinction: there's a big difference between being "*saved*," as glorious as that is, and *learning* a *walk* with God in friendship. God becomes included in everything in your life. David, that fabulous earthen-vessel who showed us what a heart for God was all about even in the midst of his human frailty, often exhibited in psalm after psalm a great pattern for us to use in prayer.

• Phase I: He cried out, pouring forth his frustrations, fears, and anger at God's feet. But he didn't stop there.

• Phase II: He reaffirmed Who God is and all that God has done for him in the past.

• Phase III: Caught up with the glory of God's faithfulness and majesty, he praised and worshiped. The trash is taken out, the temple is cleansed, and worship is reinstated (check this pattern out in places like Psalms 57, 60, and 77).

This free-to-face-Him call is at the center of Christ's heart for men. Note how Jesus, having walked with His disciples for three years, one day said to them, "No longer do I call you servants...but I call you friends" (John 15:15). The Lord Jesus Himself wants you and me to walk in that intimate a relationship with Him! Praise God!

However, everything about our lives as men seems to work against it!

Not Without a Fight

Let's look at three things that seem to work against a man's possibilities of really having a confident relationship with God.

1. *The Painful Absence of Models.*

I wonder how many who read these words have had a complete absence of anybody to follow; never having someone you could watch in the formative years of your upbringing, about whom you could have said, "That's how a man is supposed to live!" Did you have anyone to watch who showed you a model of a man with peaceful, unfeigned confidence in his relationship with God, of whom you could say, "I want to be just like him!"?

I have heard so many sordid stories of authority figures--potential role models--who failed; fathers or teachers who violated or brutalized people, relatives who mocked or neglected family members, or pastors who seemed like such good guys but then turned out to be dishonest or immoral. Young minds get burned by corrupt images and their hope of just plain "good manhood" withers and dies.

Or maybe you had a good role model, but didn't have the opportunity to get close enough. Relationship with that man who seemed to be what you thought manhood was supposed to be about, never seemed to come within reach or schedule. There was only a kind of quiet distance between you and him, real but remote, like seeing but not being able to span the breadth of the Grand Canyon--nice view, but no touch, no warmth. Or maybe you grew up with a woman as the only leadership model in your life. There's no fault there; certainly no minimizing the worth of a woman's influence. But still you didn't have a *man* to show you the way to *man*hood.

Thus, in the absence of dynamic models to help form our lives according to the Lord's design, many men don't know how to respond as a godly man to life's situations, nor how, for that matter, to be a good role model themselves. Their fractured image of manhood tends to go on reproducing its painful deficiency--one generation after another. *Unless*...unless we break the chain and become God's man. Then, not only do *we* win, but we pass that wholeness on to others--whether to our sons or to other men.

Imagine a boy and his dad on the baseball field. Dad says:

"Now, son, when you go to the plate, you just put your feet about that distance apart...right. Now just take the bat...No, no, Son; just scoot the bat down a little bit. Give about two or three inches there--it's called 'choking the bat.' You'll be able to control your swing better--that's good. Now just take a couple of swings...that's it! Great!"

Think of that kid's advantage. There's somebody there to coach. And when he goes to the plate, whether he gets a hit or not, he'll feel a different degree of assurance--a confidence because *somebody* was there to "coach." And when the same boy goes home and drifts off to sleep at night, there's a faint glow inside. Because that somebody added to his self-worth. A confidence has been ignited that will spill over from baseball into life. Men in formative years need good models.

But there's a second thing that works against our having a confident friendship with God.

2. *The Abounding Presence of Corruption.*

Most men reading these words right now will go to a place of business tomorrow. There, whether it's sophisticated or crude in its tone or delivery, they'll be surrounded by the lewd, the corrupt and the foul. It may be in a pornographic desk calendar, obscene posters, crude speech, sexual innuendos, or coarse jokes. The air is blue with profanity or suggestiveness, and impurity is ever present.

Anyone who's worked as a janitor can tell you there's a world of difference between the women's and the men's restroom walls. The men's are scrawled with foul drawings, filthy words, and phone numbers to call for "action"--either sex available.

Or the corrupt may be business-oriented; the boss wanting you to sell a half-truth to a customer, or "fudge" on accuracy in reported figures.

So much about a man's life is surrounded by corruption, and it works against him. Even if in his heart he says, "I want to be a man that walks with God," he feels like Isaiah: "I am a man of unclean lips, and I live in the middle of a group of people of unclean

35

lips" (Isa. 6:5). The sense of unclean surroundings almost oozes into one's soul--osmosis from a corrupt environment. It brings a terrible disqualifying sense to the serious possibility of a man conceiving of himself as a friend of God.

With the absence of models and the presence of the corrupt, there's a third force that erodes masculine confidence in relating to God.

3. *The Consciousness of Our Own Failure.*

There are none of us who haven't sinned. The Bible says "All have sinned and fallen short of the glory of God" (Rom. 3:23). If we're honest, our souls *more* than agree. Our sins may have been very private and shielded or very public and known. We may even be widely respected and known for our social, occupational or even Christian success or service, yet a dark corner of our soul is still hooked by hell to a particular area of fiendish bondage.

Who among us, right now, may wish that this "hook from hell" could be yanked out; that the "puppet strings" compelling our sinning be cut? How many wish they could erase from mind the inescapable "replays" of pornographic videotapes you saw? Maybe it was only once; that day in a hotel room, far away from home and your family; when buttons were pushed for "late night adult entertainment" (what an insulting use of the word "adult"!) when your mind was invaded, and now your soul seems permanently stained.

You may well already have come to the Lord, have repented, and known He has forgiven you. But *still*, your mind has those scenes riveted in place. And the sad consequence is the awful absence of conviction you feel in your confidence toward God. In such a case, one's perception of his manliness can seem painfully shallow and the term "manhood" can sting with mockery in the presence of such a scarred self-image.

But the Bible doesn't say that friendship with God begins with an accomplished moral perfection. God doesn't mandate a track-record proof showing years of commitment to Him.

Friendship with God starts with coming to Him for forgiveness. In Christ, He banishes our record of failure and declares us "clean!" That's why we can walk into His presence with holy hands uplifted in praise-filled thanks.

"But," somebody says, "you don't know what my hands have done, or what they have touched, and what has rendered them unholy." And I agree, I *don't* know.

But God does.

And He who calls us to friendship with Himself knows something else, and He wants to remind you and me of it:

Whatever our hands have done in sinning, Jesus' hands have cleansed in salvation. And His hands were nailed through in order that your hands and mine might be cleansed by His blood!

Praise His Name--His *scarred* hands will *unscar* ours!!

In fact, let me urge you to take action right now. Would you just put your hands in front of you--there where you are--and say: "Lord Jesus, because of *Your* hands, mine can be holy right now. And I rebuke every spirit of condemnation that would seek to rack my mind or body with guilt!" Then, if you will--as Paul said in our text--lift your hands and praise the Lord "without wrath or doubting"; let *anger* over past failure be done with, and let *doubt* over your acceptance with God be resolved. *Lift up your opened, cleansed hands with praise!* Do it in the confidence that you have full forgiveness of sin, and in the assurance that you can walk in friendship with God in a holiness He'll grow into your character. Friendship with God is a viable possibility with real confidence for one grand, overtowering reason: *the blood of Jesus cleanses from all sin!* (1 John 1:9). That's the basis for our confidence.

TALK ABOUT IT! Chapter questions to discuss with a friend.

1) King David had a pattern of prayer found in a number of psalms. What three phrases characterized that pattern?

2) Name three forces of conflict that work against our having a confident relationship with God.

3) For which area of struggle do you need a brother to pray for you this week? Call and ask him to.

CHAPTER FOUR:

THE DYNAMIC DUO--
YOU AND YOUR WIFE!

Nothing's more pricelessly worth discovering on this earth! And few things are more derided, joked about or doubted-as-beautiful than a man's relationship with his wife.

Even if you're not married, you're going to like this chapter!

It's *so* important to us all--to our understanding our manhood--that I want to have you dig into the subject with a commitment to *think*...to think *deeply*.

In fact, brother, I'm inviting you to school for a chapter or two; because what follows is going to get "teachy." I say that, because I want to plow into a passage of scripture which holds the key to a foundational understanding of this very precious and vital relationship: a man with his wife. I'm asking you to gird up your mind to *think*--to look clearly into God's Word at life-impacting truth. So hang on, and let's go.

Let's start by tackling one of the most

misunderstood passages in the New Testament; verses 9-15 of our text in 1 Timothy, chapter 2. Please open your Bible and note especially the phrases in verses 11 and 12: *"Women adorn themselves in modest apparel...learn in silence with all submission...the woman being deceived..."* Then, also *"I do not permit a woman to teach or to have authority over a man, but to be in silence."*

These have historically been very problematic words, and this passage seems to have muddied relationships between men and women rather than clarified them.

Our objective in seeking to "solve" the tough questions this passage raises is found in the promise which occurs in verse 15:

"Nevertheless she will be saved in childbearing IF THEY continue in faith, love, and holiness, with self-control" (emphasis mine).

You see, in this verse there is a very desirable goal being realized: (1) a marital unity, (2) led by a man, which (3) brings special benefits to his wife and himself. The issue in this verse isn't just "having babies," but finding a fruitfulness in relationship which brings spiritual unity and its practical benefits. So it's worth "figuring out"--worth *studying through* this difficult portion of God's Word to find the fruitful potential of the promised dimensions of relationship shown. The goal is a distinct and blessed *partnership* and *friendship* with distinct benefits.

Looking at this text, I ask *every* man, irrespective of marital status, to consider the implications of the Scripture. As difficult as the passage appears initially, it delivers a wealth of ministry and enlightenment once we get over barriers of misunderstanding and distortion. (And I believe that any woman who would hear or read these words--*any* objective thinking person-- would say, "You know, that *does* make sense now that I see that. I didn't realize *that's* what the Bible meant here.")

Two Issues To Address

There are actually two issues in these verses. The second is more direct to our subject--i.e., a man's relationship with his wife. But the first, "modest apparel," recommends explanation lest anyone think either; (a) that this text is not relevant today, or (b) that the Bible is tinged with a sexist condescension toward women. We need to be convinced of the Bible's sensibility and integrity on this issue of a woman's appearance, because then we will more easily become settled in seeing and honoring God's sane, loving intent for *both* womanhood and manhood. Our grasp of the first issue ("modest apparel") will bring the second issue into easier perspective (how a man relates to his wife). And we'll see how "they continue" together in beautiful partnership and with practical blessings.

1. *Propriety, Not Prudery.*

The issue of appropriate apparel is found in verses 9 and 10, wherein Paul challenges "...that women adorn themselves in modest apparel with propriety." He says they should do so "in moderation, not with braided hair or gold or pearls or costly clothing."

Well, do we have a problem!

Somebody's shouting, "Hey, my wife, relative or daughter wears braids! What about it? Cut 'em off?" Somewhere someone's reading this and his wife is a lovely lady sporting a magnificent "corn row"--one of those stylized hairdos with multiple tiny braids all over her head! So, before we go any further--"Everyone, 'Attention!' I want you to know right now that God is *not* arbitrarily 'coming down on the case' of women with braids!"

The "braiding of hair" and the related injunctions in this Bible text were specific confrontations of a cultural context where these feminine styles were employed as a carnal "invitation"--a sort of sexual enticement. The text is not a divine order for a woman to dress like a pilgrim in order to be godly. But it does point to the need for discernment within one's culture; to recognize the difference between carnal dress and otherwise. The text in its time was opposing

43

"dressing to kill"; seeking to be publicly seductive, or to call attention to one's self in a sensual way. In contrast, the Bible says, a Christian woman will know the difference between what is a modest and appropriate dress that's truly beautiful, and what instead is dressing to arouse a man at a sensual level. Looked at within that light, the spirit of the verse is timeless.

2. When "Silence" May Be Golden.

Now we're ready for the "husband-wife relationship" part of this text. But strangely, it begins with a really tough nut to crack. Look at verses 11 and 12:

"Let a woman learn in silence with all submission. And I do not permit a woman to teach or to have authority over a man but to be in silence."

How could this demand build relationship!? Verses like this have been wielded with feminist fury and legalistic glee. It's the kind of stuff that infuriates the "liberation" woman and delights the male chauvinist! But for you and me, it brings honest questions. What's going on here?

Well, first, there's nothing in these verses to apologize for except: (1) the *misunderstanding* that has shrouded them; and (2) the *abusive applications* they've experienced. But what *God* says and how *people* apply it are often two very different things.

44

At first glance, "relationship with one's wife" hardly seems to be the topic of the text, for on the face it appears to say, "Ladies shut up, the man's in charge." But, of course, that's not what's being said at all.

Though "friendship" is not specifically spelled out here, a key in *relationship* is. Take a close look with me, because there's a principle found here on how a unique partnership may take place. *Let me say that again. You can find a key here to special relationship--a holy partnership--between a man and his wife!*

To begin, let's do some spade work with this text, studying two pivotal words. The first is, *"silence,"* occurring twice in verses 11 and 12; the other is *"man,"* at the end of verse 12; and when these are clarified in this text (just like the "braids" question), things become clear and practical.

a. Defining "Silence"

"Silence" (vv. 11, 12) is the Greek word *hesuchia,* which also is used in verse 2 of this chapter. Here prayer is encouraged that we may lead a "quiet" life. Obviously, the idea of "quiet" is not "speechlessness," but controlled speech.

Clearly, the intent of the appeal to women (wives) is not a demand for a corked-mouth or strapped-shut jaws. This is not a prohibition of speech, but rather this has to do with a quietness of demeanor; a call to not being "mouthy"--neither pushy, brash or haranguing.

b. Defining "Man"

Concerning the word "man," there are two Greek words; the most familiar being "anthropos" (from which we derive anthropology, the study of mankind). "Anthropos" occurs over 500 times in the New Testament. It's the most common word for "man," referring to man as (1) the male of the species, or (2) to mankind as a race. It's used both ways.

But far more specific in designating "man" is the word *aner*, which occurs here. *Aner* appears about 250 times in the Greek New Testament; and about 50 of those times it's translated "husband." Thus, when it's put together, this passage is clearly describing a husband-wife relationship (see vs. 15, "if they"). So it is, that verse 11 should read as a *marital* reference to couples, not as a *gender* reference to the total society. Please see this: the text is discussing something between husbands and wives in their relationship; God isn't telling every woman in the world she can't say anything if there's a man around.

So, we read, "Let a *wife* learn in silence with all submission and I do not permit a *wife* to teach or have authority over her husband but to control her speech."

This spade work isn't a construction of

my own. We're simply looking at what was obviously intended by the original text. However, someone may ask, "If that's true, why hasn't it been translated that way?"

In answering, I'm embarrassed to admit why I think it hasn't been, but I'll venture the following. I think it's because the Church is *still* going through a process of reformation--of recovering things lost during the Dark Ages. There's been an ongoing restoration taking place in the Church--ever since the 16th century. What was lost, polluted, corrupted or confused spanning well over a thousand years of Church history, is *still* undergoing rediscovery and recovery. So, with reference to this particular text, and the fact that some sectors in the Church persist with a low-grade chauvinism, the translation survives its near medieval form.

And please know this: In making this re-translation, correctly substituting "wife" for "woman," I'm not espousing or surrendering to some contemporary cause. I feel little obligation to sympathize with the feminist agenda. However, these words have a practical reason; one that's not oppressing but which can be releasing for the husband and the wife *both!* So, now let's decide *why* verses 11 and 12 are here, and *how* they can work out in practical experience.

3. Why the "Silence" Can Be Golden

The whole intent of these verses unfolds with simplicity and clarity when the issues we've just discussed are resolved. Paul is dealing with a very human set of facts about our distinctiveness as men and women.

Women, by nature, tend to be far more intuitive, sensitive, and responsive to spiritual things than men. In comparison, if there's a countering distinctive with men, it's almost solely in the advantage of their physical make-up--primarily muscular strength. In other words, men are usually stronger physically than women, and women are usually more spiritually responsive than men.

Now, I am not saying that women have more spiritual potential than men, but that they are generally far more responsive. Women have a far greater readiness to "hear" the things of God, to accept them and put them to application. It seems then that Paul, knowing this, is seeking to assist toward a climate in which a husband will more readily accept his spiritual responsibility. In that quest, he basically is saying, "Ladies, for there to come the maximizing of what God wants to do in the church, in your home, in your community, in your husband, you're going to have pull in the reins on your spiritual oratory. Because if you, however sincerely, get pushy with him or drill him about 'spiritual stuff,' he's going to withdraw even further."

Paul, still continuing with the wives, seems to be adding: "Dear lady, your husband probably already feels like something of a spiritual wimp, so don't compound it! He's never going to rise to the dynamic things of the spiritual realm and the Kingdom of God if he feels that somehow he's forever trapped far behind you. Your 'talking too much' may work against your and his best interest; only making him feel all the more a spiritual failure, and stifling his will to seek to grow."

I think the whole context of the New Testament shows that that's why Paul is saying this: "I don't want a woman to boss or cajole her husband, because I want him to learn to accept his leadership role. If she accepts it because he resigns it, he's never going to catch up." Sadly, since women are fully and equally *capable* of leadership, too many men are willing to forfeit their responsibility. By nature, they will tend to say, "Go ahead, honey--do all you want spiritually, but just keep it easy for me." But a woman controls the "gold"--the "silence" of a self-controlled bearing that can help her husband grow unto acceptance of spiritual responsibility!

Most men don't actually say, "Make it easy for me, I want to forfeit my role to my wife." And I'm not accusing any man of slothfulness, but it *is* clear that when it comes to responsible spiritual leadership, we men tend to avoid our leadership call. So the text encourages women to hold their natural tendencies in reserve, never to discourage her gifts being realized and surfacing; but rather, to point to the long-range benefit to them both if the wife will accept God's terms requiring this self-discipline.

So there *is* a call to "friendship" between husband and wife in this text. And once the relationship of husband and wife comes into alignment with God's order, amazing things happen. Where it's needed, a new joy and fruitfulness begin to be found in the marriage--something some never dreamed possible. And where they've been present, hell's flames will be extinguished in that home due to a new spiritual partnership. A new establishing of God's will--a virtual "heaven on earth"--can happen in the home, because the two are now learning a walk in spiritual and marital unity. It's a prerequisite to His Kingdom coming and dwelling in power in a home, a marriage, and a family.

So, our "difficult" passage (hopefully better understood now) points to something wonderful. And winding it up, verse 15 shows God's power and blessing working in the midst of such marital unity!

"Nevertheless she will be saved in childbearing if they continue in faith, love, holiness with self-control."

This verse refers to the Old Testament

story of sin's original impact on our race. The magnitude of that event transcends comprehension, for we have no idea what life must have been like before the Fall! But Genesis 3:16 shows that the bearing of children before the Fall might have been an easier thing for the woman. Today, of course, the majority of births come forth with great pain and travail, and the text is offering the prospect of some degree of "release" from this aspect of childbirth. So, at least at this point, a possible blessing awaits the couple who are learning the dimensions of spiritual unity we have been discussing. We are *not* told that *all* removal of birth's pain in travail is promised. So, if your wife has a difficult delivery, your or her godliness is not in question, nor is your marriage relationship necessarily being reflected upon by that fact.

But what *is* said is that there are scriptural conditions which can be met, "that they continue in faith, love and holiness with self-control." And the promise seems to indicate that when such growing mutuality occurs, *something beyond the curse* becomes released to them in their union.

Let's read it again, inserting what we've learned:

"*She*, (the wife) *will be saved* (released from the Fall's impact on childbearing) *if they* (the husband and wife) *continue together* (in growing partnership) *in faith, love, and holiness, with self-control* (basic disciplines of Christian growth)."

Looking at this promise, "something wonderful" seems to be being hinted at. If the power of Christ's redeeming work can impact the birthing process of a couple who are learning God's order together, might there be a more general blessing of "release" awaiting them? In Ephesians 5:20-33, where the flow of the husband's Christ-like "ministry" to his wife is shown for all its dynamic potential, another New Testament text points to brighter horizons. Between these two passages, I think God's Word reveals a progressing benediction of God's grace bringing couples beyond the impact of the curse in allowing for a "new beginning" of the husband-wife relationship. May I suggest that if a woman's bearing of children may be blessed, assisted, and advanced with greater ease because of the partnership she and her husband grow into, could the whole of the husband's/wife's "life-productivity" be affected? In other words, might all aspects of their life and destiny be "released" to broader dimensions of love, unity, and fulfillment *all because the husband (with her sensitive assistance) rises to fill his place in God's order?*

Here are some thoughts then, rooted in the *whole* of the Word, which convert a *problematic*, apparently legalistic text, to a *promise-filled*, life-giving one! Here are blessings of life-wide proportions; rich potentials when a husband and wife come into a growing "friendship." However, it's all contingent on the man taking his place.

My Personal Illustration:
Getting Checked About the Checks

Let me give a very simple example of "how" we men tend to resign responsibilities for "leading," and how this stresses marriages. The case may seem mundane, but maybe it can help you, Sir, to envision ways *you* need to accept responsibilities you might have neglected.

Years ago, during the first dozen years of our marriage, I would regularly bring my paycheck home and simply give it to Anna. *She* would deposit it, and *she* would pay the bills.

To my mind, this was right. It was her duty: "That's part of her job in keeping the house." And further, I felt that in giving her the money, I was displaying obvious trust in her. (How grand I thought I was! But I was later to discover it was not all that grandiose.)

Now, my wife is an intelligent woman. She was an honors graduate from college and is also experienced in bookkeeping, having done such work in a doctor's office before she and I were married. So when the problems arose in our "money matters"--and my, did they!-- it certainly wasn't due to an incapability on her part in managing the checkbook. But things degenerated. We both alternated feeling angry about it. The "money" task became an unexplainably difficult thing for her. She became very emotional, to a point that neither of us could explain it. There was no failure on her part--it wasn't that the checkbook didn't balance or that we got into trouble. But it did *weigh* on her, very heavily, and I was increasingly unsettled in my feelings about our finances (though it wasn't debt or neglect--just sensing "something's not right.")

Then one day, the Lord began dealing with me about what I was doing; or rather what I *wasn't* doing. He revealed to my understanding the REAL reason I was having her do the checkbook and taking care of paying the bills. It had been subconscious, but beneath it all I wasn't being trusting, generous or "grand." In actuality, the real reason I had assigned her the job was: *I didn't want the work or the responsibility!*

That's all there was to it.

Because I hadn't completely recognized it, I had never said, "Honey, you do this because I don't want to." I didn't even perceive my neglect--my forfeit of duty. But the Lord had begun to show me *very emphatically* that I was resigning a place of responsible leadership; that this was *something we were supposed to be doing together* instead of my casting the burden on her shoulders--a burden never intended for her to bear alone. (I must pause here, to touch on the opposite extreme. I ran into a guy one time who had the idea that taking the leadership in his household finances was to "control it all." He was the stingiest dude you ever ran across; doling money to his wife like each dime was an ingot of gold from Fort Knox. So here and now, let me emphasize, I am NOT talking about anything like that in my illustration. I'm talking about a partnership and understanding between couples, with a man learning to take his responsibilities.)

In Anna's and my case, when I took a place of responsible leadership and partnership, *everything* changed. It's something she remembers well. To say "new friendship happened" isn't off the mark. Struggling--in this case, over money matters--ceased dramatically. She grew happier all the time. And we had no explanation for this other than "something was released" when I owned up to a responsibility I had unwittingly forfeited.

The principle I'm illustrating is this: *When a man partners with his wife, a deeper union--yes, "new friendship"--can develop.* So ask the Holy Spirit to teach you practical ways to accept your leadership responsibilities. He will. And from that point, you can find new ways to grow with your wife "in faith, love, holiness and self-control" and *blessing will burst forth!* The effects of man's Fall through sin begin to be set into reverse.

That's called *"redemption!"* It's what this world, burned out from Adam I, is crying out for. People want to see it, and when they see that it's possible in you, Sir, they'll want to experience it themselves.

So, Paul's 1 Timothy 2 picture of a "holy-hands-man" is anything but the picture of the religious prude or a pious bigot. A stance of openness--of friendship and intimacy with God, turns a man into a person whose warmth of relationship with God overflows into a warmth of relationship with those in closest proximity with him--especially his wife. His growth into a husband's God-given role of leadership in the home brings comfort and peaceableness to the woman he loves.

TALK ABOUT IT! Chapter questions to discuss with a friend.

1) Because of the unique nature of this more demanding study portion of our book, consider rereading this chapter noting the following:

a) What the Bible *really* says about a woman's appearance and dress; i.e., that He doesn't prohibit loveliness--only carnal appearance.

b) What the Bible *really* says about a woman being "silent."

c) What the Bible *really* means in urging a woman's reserve in speech, so as not to discourage her husband's spiritual responsiveness.

2) Take time to discuss your own thoughts as to how the "release" potential of a husband and wife "continuing together" according to 1 Timothy 2:15 could affect your relationship.

CHAPTER FIVE:

IRON SHARPENING IRON

Please believe this: The Bible shows that *a man who would become the maximum person God can cause him to become is a man who discovers the power and blessing of partnership with other men!*

That's the principle moving us as we look at the third type of relationship key to our "becoming." To our relationships with God and our spouse, we add our relationships with men.

Now there's nothing explicit in our 1 Timothy, chapter 2 passage about relationship or friendship with other men. But what *is* in this text, is what I believe explains the reason why men usually avoid relating to other men; why men tend to "go it alone." If we can see *what* that may be--see *what* obstructs our willingness to open up to moving into partnership with other men--then maybe we can get over one of our greatest hurdles and begin to develop as fully growing men.

Jesus established this need for partnering,

man-to-man relationships on New Testament terms. He, Himself, gathered a dozen men together--shaping them to become shapers of the whole world, and their impact has continued right to this present day. Thus, "gathering men, for the sake of shaping them through interaction with one another under God, was initiated by Jesus. And that's your and my call!! Whether we are pastors of a church, new believers in Christ, men of long-term knowing God, guys wanting to influence our friends for the better--the *breakthrough* happens when we *break out* of isolation!

Contrary to popular belief, men aren't born. *Children* are born--men are *formed.* And the Bible says men help "form" each other: "As iron sharpens iron, so a man sharpens his friend" (Proverbs 27:17).

Carved, designed, and shaped--males are processed into true manhood. At the core of that process is one crucial component: man-to-man relationship. Prioritizing the cultivation of such relationships according to God's created order is in line with His blueprint for full manhood.

Ah, but we've hit a snag right there; snagged on the word "manhood." For many of us, the very term "manhood" may cause us to squirm, because it carries emotional baggage for some, and possibly conveys unachievable responsibility to others. Say the word "manhood" and some men may

immediately recall the times in his childhood when he was picked last for the baseball team. Or it may bring back the fresh
emotions of last month when he was laid off
at work--"How can I face my peers as a
failure?!" Say "manhood" and some women
may instantly feel complex emotional recol-
lections of all the times their "manly" husbands forced their desires and preferences
on them to the annihilation of their own
sensitivities or feelings.

"Manhood," for many simply lacks a
definition with substance and value. Everybody knows what Indiana Jones is made of:
guts and glory--we've seen it big and loud on
the screen. But for something as basic as
street-level, life-in-the-real-world "manhood," the kind that successfully functions
on a daily basis within every venue of life,
definitions are obscure. So in seeking to be
God's man in a confused, sometimes oppressive world, some men simply choose to
"give it my best, and wish for better." And
there *is* a way to the "better." A living way.

The Process Of Becoming

True manhood is resourced in Jesus Christ.
Don't let the simplicity of that statement
blow by you. Since it *sounds* "religious" it
might only conjure a mental dullness toward
its earth-moving potential. But religious
rhetoric doesn't change lives, God's
reality--living truth does, and Jesus Himself
is Truth Incarnate. *His indwelling your*

manhood is what this book is about. He is the only salvation for a battered or ambiguous male identity, and He's the provider of substance to bring definition to your manhood and mine.

It's God's intent to reproduce Jesus in us: "For it was fitting for Him, for whom are all things and by whom are all things, in bringing many sons to glory, to make the captain of their salvation perfect through sufferings" (Heb. 2:10).

That's God's design--getting the glorious image of Jesus Christ to be reproduced in any person who will ask Him to do so. It works for *both* genders! In Christ, women can be *truly* liberated and celebrated, and in Him men can finally escape the world of "self-help" programs and *machismo* power tactics. However, being conformed into the image of Jesus can't be done Lone Ranger style. One of the chief scalpels that God has chosen for shaping us into His image is the dynamic of personal friendships--man-to-man relationships. This is an essential, practical biblical principle, and one of a man's key starting places.

More Than A Greeting Card

Friendships not only reflect the man, but they can make him what he is. They form him. They decide his depth, his qualities, his skills and his destiny, for we're told, "He who walks with wise men will be wise, but

61

the companion of fools will be destroyed" (Prov. 13:20).

The topic of "friendship" could smack of something perceived only at the Hallmark card level--a nice word with nice sentiments. But the irresistible force and life-destiny-impact of "friendships" is more than a greeting card concept. We dare not overlook it, especially as men committed to Christ's man-to-man methods. How many of us--do you?--tend to find escape routes seeking to insulate us from encounters or relation-ships calling us to man-to-man commit-ment. That course forward toward relation-ships may make us feel our real identities are threatened, tempting us, instead, to buy into those things which only feed our fanta-sies. But what we need for starters is to move toward personal honesty with ourselves and others into friendships/relationships which foster transparency and identity-renovating selflessness.

Can faking the appearance of "having it all together" be more important to me than the actuality of my being available to being "sharpened" into Christ's image? I hope not! Because for me to be available for growth means for me to be willing to admit need.

That's not very macho, is it?

Yet admission of our needs seems to be at the core of God's dealing with humanity--from coming to an altar and admitting my need for the Savior, to learning to "confess your faults to one another, and pray for one another, that you may be healed" (James 5:16). So, for starts, I simply need to admit my need for partnership with other people--other men--in order to advance with Christ and grow in Jesus victoriously.

There's a profound shaping of men that happens when we *come together* and learn to *grow together* in Christ. John wrote these words, "If we walk in the light as He (Christ) is in the light, then we will have fellowship one with another."

Notice: if we'll get together (true "fellowship" in Christ) there's something that will happen to us all--"The blood of Jesus Christ *keeps on cleansing us from all sin!*" That's the way the tense in the original Greek text puts it!

Progressing in fellowship brings progression in victory over sin's clutchings at a man's body, soul, and spirit!! In other words, as we--you and I--walk in the light with other brothers, there is a *progressive sense* of what has already been *positionally secured* in Christ. Your and my *past* sin was totally covered, atoned for in Christ, and forgiven completely when we came to Him. But *present* sin still finds occasions to tempt and try us. Our humanness is not overthrown because we received Christ. That doesn't diminish the reality of our salvation, but present sin must be faced and dealt with. That's why, in walking with Jesus, I need to also walk with my brothers in Him--to "walk in the light" of a growing relationship of friendship, partnership, and accountability.

As a result, through a loving and brotherly confronting of one another--not with ridicule but with honest-to-God, face-to-face realism--our trusting transparency ("in the light") *advances* the work of righteousness in each of us. Through our "fellowship with one another" we can discover a special operation of the sanctifying blood of Christ. The promise here declares it, and it's progressive in its ongoing work: "The blood of Jesus, His Son, *keeps on cleansing me* from all sin!" (Paraphrase, 1 John 1:8). We'll study this pathway to such transparency and accountability in another of our *Power To Become* books for men, but first we each need to decide to *accept the terms* of such a need for "friendship with other men."

We need one another.

That's the reason for men's gatherings--large and small--among Christ's own! Nothing is a greater passion with me. In my own pastorate, I would even sacrifice Sunday morning preaching if I needed to, in order to meet with the men of my church. Thankfully I don't have to make that choice, but my priorities are clear. I want to touch the point from which everything springs: *Men.*

As pivotally important and essentially necessary as this "man-to-man relationship" need is, and as clear-in-the-Bible it is shown to be Jesus' method, hosts of men never allow themselves to become subject to that kind of possibility for fellowship. So often, a men's fellowship in the Church of Jesus Christ becomes only a kind of "hail fellow well-met" get-together--paint a building, mow a lawn, play on a team, even have a Bible study.

Those, of course, are all good things for men to do. But men's activities are not a substitute for men coming together and interfacing at a personal, spiritual dimension. There's a reason why this doesn't happen more commonly. And as we move toward conclusion of this study, let me tell you why I think we men back away from openness toward each other.

TALK ABOUT IT! Chapter questions to discuss with a friend.

1) Describe the relationship between the power of "the blood of Jesus" and "walking in the light" with your brothers. What is "walking in the light"?

2) Have you identified your own reactions, if any, to the mention of the word "manhood"?

3) In what ways, no matter how small, have you felt tempted to "go it alone" when you really should have relied on brothers in Christ? Identify "excuses" which preempt your involvements.

CHAPTER SIX:

BECOMING INSTRUMENTS OF HIS REDEMPTIVE POWER

We're finding our starting place in partnership with God's. Since He's determined to make men His catalysts in the broad extension in His Kingdom purposes--from personal levels, to family, to the church, to the world--how can we cooperate? The answer to that question is in discovering keys to relationships. And now, we've come to the place of seeing how you and I can overcome our greatest hindrance to becoming "relational" men.

We have asked, "Why don't we men more readily open to relationships?" I think our text contains an insightful fact about us men; one which points to the heart of our problem in "getting together" and thereby in our "getting *IT* together." Look at our text:

"But Adam was not deceived but the woman being deceived fell into transgression" (1 Timothy 2:14).

There is something far more poignant about these words than meets the eye of the casual reader. Ask yourself, why is this reference to the original sin made here? And, why is the role of each--a man and woman--noted separately from one another in their transgression? In answering this, look first at how Adam and his wife are each described as participating in the Fall of the human race into sin.

• *The man*--Was not deceived, he consciously disobeyed (verse 14; also see Rom. 5:19);

• *The woman*--Being deceived, she fell into sin (verse 14; also see Gen. 3:1-6).

These are radically different descriptions, which I am persuaded the Holy Spirit has given for important reasons. This distinction unlocks a perspective to which I invite you; one which can help us not only see what the original man might have become, but what we as redeemed men *can* become.

If I recall *any* observations on this tender passage in verse 14, it's usually been tied to the earlier "prohibition" regarding women speaking. The intimation has always seemed to be that, somehow, "The woman was deceived" because women are gullible, if not stupid. "Look how the serpent deceived her," I've heard preachers intone. To hear them one would think there has never been such a thing as a *man* being deceived! But

68

every one of us knows the opposite is true--we've all been deceived! And there is no way that "the woman being deceived" can be construed to suggest women, generically, are any less intelligent or sensible than men, then or now. So what *is* the point? The point is that the Bible is pressing a significant issue into view.

Look at the awesome issue which distills from distinguishing the role of each of the first couple in the Fall. In this passage:

(a) *which is describing God's desire to see men stand forth in bold relationship with Him;* and

(b) *which is urging women to relate to their husbands in a way that will increase the likelihood of their responsiveness toward God.*

Here, the Holy Spirit notes an important difference between men and women. It's this: When the Fall of the first couple occurred, the most guilty party was the man, who consciously disobeyed. This is not to imply the woman was less sinful, but the text clearly states she was motivated differently on that occasion than the man. She was a victim of deception, not *conscious* disobedience: in stark, biblical contrast "Adam was not deceived," but *consciously rebelled.*

Again, let me stress that this distinction is not to imply that either Adam or his wife were more or less guilty than the other in the final analysis. But I believe in this text the Holy

Spirit has provided an important insight which seems intended to open our understanding. It is here we are given understanding as to why men are so slow to open themselves to God, to their wives, to each other; and why women seem not to share this reluctance.

I think God's Word discloses right here an answer to our peculiarities within our genders. I don't think it's a factor consciously responded to, but a study of our humanity--male and female--certainly confirms the likelihood that a *spiritual imprint* is carried in our souls which differs at the point of our God-responsiveness. Women, almost uniformly, respond more readily to spiritual matters, to God's Word, and to one another in general than men tend to do. Men, almost uniformly, withdraw or retire from spiritual matters, openness to God, and from one another.

I want to suggest that deep within the psyche of every man, though undiscerned and unlearned, there is a residue of subconscious remembrance that he--the man--is *more responsible* for the Fall of the race than the woman. It appears that men bear a *spiritual imprint* which is almost haunting in nature, as though to say, "Sir, in the person of your 'megagreat' grandfather Adam, you failed *in the light* of 'knowing better.' It's too late! You fouled your chance, so *never* embarrass yourself again by opening to that 'light'; you'll only fail again!"

70

"But wait," someone cries, "the woman partook of the fruit first!" And that, of course, is true. But come with me back to the Garden scene. It's there that I want to take a fresh look at the event of the Fall of man; to see what *did* happen and what *might* have happened.

What Did Happen?

According to Genesis chapter 3, the woman, when confronted by a satanic incarnation in the form of a serpent was completely deceived by the devil. As we have noted, this is no argument against her being fully responsible for her sin. But we have also noted, the *climate* of her consciousness was one of passive delusion rather than one of aggressive disobedience, and she ate the fruit. Imagine the setting:

"My," she sighs. "I...I..." she speaks, bewildered by the change coming over her; attempting to interpret the moment, exclaims, "It certainly *tastes* good!" Her thoughts begin to frame the patterns of fallenness: "My goodness, what sudden insight. I don't know why we ever hesitated!" Here's the victim of deception, musing over the moment. Deceived, and now sin-bound.

The brevity of the biblical text does not provide a timing sequence for us, but it was apparently soon thereafter when she brought the fruit to her husband. And Adam ate it.

It is at this point we join the revelation of the Genesis record to the words of our text in 1 Timothy. According to the Scripture we are told that Adam sinned, *not* as deceived, but as consciously disobedient. The man *knew full well what he was doing.* Probably not present at all at the time of the woman's temptation, and thereby not beguiled by the serpent, here he is--looking face to face with the woman's offer: "To sin or not to sin."

Eve's approach isn't to be blamed. It isn't as though she said, "Come on, *sin!*" But, far more likely, she came to Adam with something more on the order of an approach born of her bewilderment and newly-fallen state of mind: "My husband, this is not the evil we thought it was. Come and take some of this for wisdom's sake."

But Adam knew better, and in his sinning he disobeyed as one undeceived--with his eyes wide open.

A Different Garden Scenario

But what *might* have happened in the Garden? What if Adam had responded another way--a redemptive way--when Eve had fallen? When he saw her coming, when he heard her speak, what might he have said instead? Instead, imagine him--broken and with tears--crying, "Oh, my beloved! Why, oh why? You ate it! Death has already begun in you, and you are blind to it. Oh, my dear one, you are going to die! No, my wife! As dearly as I love you, I cannot--I will not violate the Creator's will. I *will* not eat of this fruit!"

And there, suddenly, she would have stood nakedly aware of what she had done. Now the charm of the serpent's device has been blown away, and she leaves the scene, overcome with a deep sense of shame. Then...

Coming now in the cool of the day, the Father of all Creation approaches Adam. And as Adam prepares to meet Him at their usual time of fellowship, the Father sees a pained expression on Adam's face. He asks, "Adam, where is the woman?" And even before Adam responds, the Father says, "She has eaten the forbidden fruit, hasn't she?"

"Yes, Father."

Silence. Then...Heaven's Lover speaks: "Then she must die." And there is nothing but broken-hearted love in the Father's voice as he says it.

"But Father," the man implores, "I love her." A pause, and again, "I love her...and *I don't want her to die!*" Tears fill human eyes for the first time, as the man weeps with an impending sense of loss.

The Father replies: "I understand. And I would wish her to live as well. But the eternal decree requires it. She must die." There is another moment of pained silence, then the Creator speaks again: "Yes, I weep too, but she must die: that is, O Adam, *unless another dies for her--in her place.*"

And the man, at first surprised--but then with understanding of the divine economy, looks up. With a firm resolve and a readiness of response; not with haste but with a measured cadence, now having dried his eyes, he speaks: "Then, Father, let *me* be the one. I will take her place in death, for I love her and long that she not be stolen unto death by the evil one."

"But wait!" someone shouts. "How can you create this story! On what authority do you propose such a possibility might have been present?" And my answer is:

Because that's the way The Story actually goes. Not, of course, that the *First* Adam fulfilled his leadership role as the one who "was created first"; *not* that through obedience and sacrifice he became an instrument of redemption.

No. The *First* Adam forfeited that role through *disobedience.* But the *Second* Adam came, and He *did* die! And He died on behalf of one whom He calls *His* Bride, His Church, *so that she may live and not die.* Jesus Christ fulfilled the redemptive role which today is made the model for the redeemed man's relationship with his wife: "...Husbands, love your wives as Christ loved the Church and gave Himself for her" (Eph. 5:25). But

74

not only do men rarely fulfill this role, we also shrink from man-to-man commitments which would help us grow in our potential as leaders who minister redemption's grace and power to others. It seems that somehow all sons of the first Adam sense that our earthly forefather has bequeathed a failure to us. It seems that as men we somehow have had a scar burned into our collective masculine psyche; a sense of disability fulfilling our spiritual role; a subtle inner voice which shouts, "Your father failed as a man and so will you! He missed becoming an instrument of redemption, and neither will you ever be able to become an instrument in God's hands!"

Even when we each receive the salvation brought to us by Adam II--the Lord Jesus Christ, Son of God (1 Cor. 15:22), the lingering, inherent sense of our violated role as "man" haunts us. Farcical renditions of the original sin story--shallow joking of, "Well, the woman ate first"--still disallow our escape from the fact that even though she was deceived, it was the *man* who consciously disobeyed; who forfeited obedience, embraced his own way, and learned nothing of a role he might have in redemptive possibilities. (And in passing, may we witness the incredible grace of God toward womankind, hearing the Lord say of the deceived woman "Of *her* seed the serpent's head will be crushed"--Gen. 3:15; granting her a role in redemption's processes.)

Yes, *both* sinned.

Yes, *both* will need salvation. And *both* will taste of grace as surely as they tasted of sin's fruit.

But the stamp has cut deep in the souls of the male of the species. The die of death has been cut, and remade us over and over again: men who fail their role. You see, my brothers, everything around us tends to argue toward our repeated fallibility. It timelessly tends to discourage our readiness to respond: "I don't want to open up to other brothers, because then it calls me all over again--(1) to *obedience* and (2) to *become an instrument of redemption.*"

But instead--now, please--listen to me; and *come!*

Let us each be shaken free of the coward-ice that lurks in every one of our souls because of the failure of our distant father, Adam. *Through Jesus our Savior, we have been born of a new Father; and He is able to restore, renew, rebuild, and release us!*

There is *another* Adam; Christ our Living Lord. His name is Jesus, and He's come to *live in you and me.* By His power He can enable my obedience and my openness to become an instrument of His redemptive grace. With resurrection mightiness He will work in and through us, *reproducing* the fullness of His life; not only in *cleansing* of our soul with saving blood to assure us of

76

heaven, but in *overflowing* our being with His personal presence--*dwelling* within us to nurture our growth and to impact our world through us!

I call you, dear brother, my friend, to learn the way of relationship; of friendship with the Father, of friendship with your wife, and of friendship with other brothers, so that you can become the maximum man God wants you to be. And as that begins, you will find a new release start in things around you. Results are not always immediate, but the impact will begin to become manifest: in your home, your relationships, your business, your church...and your world. God grant that it be so. Pray with me:

"Lord, I yearn to be free from the failure-scarred image of Adam. Not that sinless perfection can be mine this side of heaven, but in order that sin's crippling impact upon my male psyche would be reversed and so that I can be transformed into the likeness of Christ, I now invite You to move in my heart. I give Your Holy Spirit permission to work in me as it pleases You. I ask that You would *create within me* a new understanding of my role as a man according to Your original design in creation. And I ask that You would *release through me* Your leadership dynamic to be expressed in love, power, sensitivity, and wisdom to everyone I contact. In short, Father, please come and dwell in the midst of

77

every relationship I have. Let me become an effective instrument of Your redemption; certainly in my family, but also among my friends, with other men, within the business community, and everywhere I go. Lord, Your Kingdom come, Your will be done on earth--here where I live and move every day--just as it is in heaven. Amen."

TALK ABOUT IT! Chapter questions to discuss with a friend.

1) On what grounds is the possibility proposed that Adam might have become a "savior" of his fallen spouse?

2) In what ways can a man still "die" for his wife--selflessly laying down his life for hers?

3) Describe where you would like the Lord to free you from bondage patterns of your family.

IT'S ALL IN THE "DOING"

Receiving biblical teaching with an open heart is vital. But *"doing it"*--putting legs on the truth you've learned--is Christianity.

A national ad campaign for a line of sports shoes recently used a direct command for its sales pitch: "Just Do It!" It aptly reflected the spirit of the competitive edge. For no race is won by mere philosophy or good thoughts--you have to DO it--which in our spiritual race means: get off the proverbial couch, move from the prescribed Starting Place and press toward the mark of our high calling down the King's Highway!

Application: get with men. On a regular basis, meet with several men with whom you can (a) generate mutual, consistent support in prayer, (b) teach one another things the Lord is showing you in your life, and (c) learn a new level of transparency in the process.

We strongly encourage each of you reading these words to prayerfully select several brothers with whom you can meet at breakfast on a regular basis. We say "breakfast" as a suggestion because an early meeting can often clear most busy schedules; and we say "regular" because that's how trust can be developed within your group.

Jesus exampled for us *breakfast time* transformed into *discipling time*. John chapter 21 is a precious passage about the Risen Lord and his relationship with His disciples. The trauma of the cross behind Him, and the glory of the resurrection accomplished, Jesus didn't meet His disciples that morning amid some awe-inspiring Transfiguration-like glory, or on a mountain top with lightning and thunder rumbling about. Instead, He fixed breakfast for them...a very "family" thing to do. He "dined" with them and it was intimate and relational. Springing out from this fellowship setting, Jesus discussed with Peter a top priority on His mind: *the importance of feeding the sheep*.

Breakfast. Feeding the sheep. There's a message there.

The *occasion* is discipling fellowship at breakfast, the *agenda* is nourishing the sheep at our table--us included.

And it can change your life. Because Jesus is there.

In setting up such a meeting time with some brothers, here's a few considerations to keep in mind:

1) Find some brothers with whom you feel

free to be open and candid about your own areas of need and struggle. But don't let the group get too large. The bigger it is the tougher it is to really "open up." Target size: 3-4 men.

2) Set a regular meeting time once or twice a week.

3) Agree together that you are committing to meet weekly for a season of time, say, for four months.

4) Pray for each other. Share your struggles and victories together.

5) You may want to consider using the devotional on the following pages as a spring board for discussion. And, in essence, fulfill the Lord's command to "feed my sheep." God has ordained that we men be leaders. But we're also His sheep.

So, "let's do lunch" . . . (or breakfast). . . and then link arms, join hearts, and put our shoe leather into the race of "becoming" men who look unto Jesus, the Author and Finisher of our faith as we grow together!

DEVOTIONS
IN THE BOOK OF 1 SAMUEL

Contributed by Bob Anderson

The following devotional is designed for stimulating discussion and prayer within a small group of men.

1 Samuel was chosen because it provides a rich reference for studying relationships. In fact, it reads somewhat like a good screenplay: rich characters, relational conflict, struggles for power. Yet through it all, we see God's persistant faithfulness moving in the midst of imperfect humanity. And there are dynamic lessons to be learned by witnessing how God worked in the key relationships of Samuel, David, and Saul.

☐ **Today's Text: 1 Samuel 1:1-28** *(key: v. 28)*

1

Today's Truth: Hannah was "lending" her son, Samuel, to the Lord in dedication. But the Hebrew term for "lent" does not mean to give temporarily, but to give *unconditionally.*

Today's Thoughts:_____

_____

_____

☐ **Today's Text: 1 Samuel 2:1-36** *(key v.18)*

2

Today's Truth: Samuel's childlike openness to the Lord was a condition of heart he never outgrew.

Today's Thoughts:_____

_____

_____

☐ **Today's Text: 1 Samuel 3:1-21** *(key v. 20)*

3

Today's Truth: Samuel's pattern of waiting tenderheartedly upon the Lord in private, eager to hear His voice, eventually resulted in a national promotion from the Hand of Omnipotence.

Today's Thoughts:_____

_____

_____

☐ **Today's Text: 1 Samuel 4:1-22** *(key v. 22)*

4

Today's Truth: Christ in us is our hope of glory. Though the devil can't separate us from the love of God in Christ, he *does* try to diminish God's glory in us by stealing our confidence in our foundational identity in Christ.

Today's Thoughts: _____

_____

_____

☐ **Today's Text: 1 Samuel 5:1-12** *(key v. 4)*

5

Today's Truth: The "mere" presence of God in a place topples the powers of hell. And the presence of God is most forcefully fostered when God's people worship Him.

Today's Thoughts: _____

_____

_____

☐ **Today's Text: 1 Samuel 6:1-21** *(key v. 19a)*

6

Today's Truth: These men looked for or sought out the power of the ark instead of God's presence. God's call to us is always for relationship, not for seeking spiritual power.

Today's Thoughts: _____

_____

_____

84

☐ **Today's Text: 1 Samuel 7:1-17** *(key v. 12)*

7

Today's Truth: Samuel set up a stone of testimony saying, "Thus far the Lord has helped us." Following his example is wise: keeping a personal record of God's faithfulness to be remembered at future times of discouragement can bring renewal of strength.

Today's Thoughts: _____
_____
_____

☐ **Today's Text: 1 Samuel 8:1-22** *(key vv. 19-20)*

8

Today's Truth: Israel cried out, "We want to be just like other nations!" and it became a horrendous snare to them. Embracing conformity to this corrupt world brings defeat.

Today's Thoughts: _____
_____
_____

☐ **Today's Text: 1 Samuel 9:1-27** *(key v. 20b)*

9

Today's Truth: Israel's desire was for Saul, a leader who "looked good" (see 1 Sam. 10:23-24). We would later see God's idea of a king: David, a man after His own heart.

Today's Thoughts: _____
_____
_____

☐ **Today's Text: 1 Samuel 10:1-27** *(key v. 6)*

10 **Today's Truth:** Saul was filled with the Spirit of God and changed into a new man. The sobering reality is: he didn't *stay* changed by walking closely with his Lord.

Today's Thoughts: _____

_____

_____

☐ **Today's Text: 1 Samuel 11:1-15** *(key v.14)*

11 **Today's Truth:** Samuel said it was time to "renew" the kingdom, which meant the people were to unify together to rededicate themselves to the purpose of their kingdom. Gathering with brothers at breakfast to pray is a great way to "renew God's Kingdom" in force.

Today's Thoughts: _____

_____

_____

☐ **Today's Text: 1 Samuel 12:1-25** *(key v. 20)*

12 **Today's Truth:** Samuel puts his finger on the human tendency to shy back from the Lord after we're convicted of serious sin. But God's call is for us to immediately repent, be forgiven, then resume serving Him with all our hearts.

Today's Thoughts: _____

_____

_____

□ **Today's Text: 1 Samuel 13:1-23** *(key vv. 9-12)*

13

Today's Truth: Anyone in authority must also be under authority himself. Even when confronted about his wrongdoing, Saul quickly blamed everyone but himself.

Today's Thoughts: _____

_____

_____

□ **Today's Text: 1 Samuel 14:1-52** *(key v.45)*

14

Today's Truth: The Lord's relationship with Jonathan took priority over Saul's rash oath even though Jonathan was technically in violation of the king's edict. God's mercy flows even when men are ready to judge and cast stones.

Today's Thoughts: _____

_____

_____

□ **Today's Text: 1 Samuel 15:1-35** *(key v. 22)*

15

Today's Truth: To obey is better than sacrifice. Of course, there'll be sacrifice along the way of obeying God. But He's not looking for ways to deprive His people of good things. Ultimately, the fruit of obedience will be godliness with contentment and blessing with no sorrow added.

Today's Thoughts: _____

_____

_____

☐ **Today's Text: 1 Samuel 16:1-23** *(key v. 7)*

16 **Today's Truth:** Thank goodness--the Lord looks on the heart and not the outward appearance! It's wise to "do a heart-check" and regularly monitor our attitudes and motivations. The Psalms reveal that David did--a lot!

Today's Thoughts: _____

_____

_____

☐ **Today's Text: 1 Samuel 17:1-58** *(key v.45)*

17 **Today's Truth:** One of the greatest confrontations of all time: David & Goliath. Whether your Goliath is a financial crisis, a broken marriage, or an uncertain destiny, the battle is the Lord's. David's small stone guarantees it.

Today's Thoughts: _____

_____

_____

☐ **Today's Text: 1 Samuel 18:1-30** *(key v. 11)*

18 **Today's Truth:** Like the Kingdom of God, jealousy can start as a small mustard seed. Given place and left unchecked, it can yield murder in the heart and even become a spear in the hand. Not only confessing and forsaking sin, but praying for the further blessing of the envied person brings freedom.

Today's Thoughts: _____

_____

_____

☐ **Today's Text: 1 Samuel 19:1-24** *(key v. 9)*

19

Today's Truth: God isn't hurling demons at Saul, but we see that in the absence of the Spirit of God, men are vulnerable to hell's forces--sin being the "welcome mat" for bondage.

Today's Thoughts: _____

_____

_____

☐ **Today's Text: 1 Samuel 20:1-42** *(key v. 41)*

20

Today's Truth: Jonathan and David typify the amazing love God can work between men. It is a rare kind of relationship, but it's nothing beyond God's ability to work in your own experience if you simply ask Him for that caliber of friendship.

Today's Thoughts: _____

_____

_____

☐ **Today's Text: 1 Samuel 21:1-15** *(key v. 9)*

21

Today's Truth: God not only gave David victory over Goliath; now the very weapon of his enemy was in his hand. We, too, are more than conquerers through Him who loves us!

Today's Thoughts: _____

_____

_____

☐ **Today's Text: 1 Samuel 22:1-23** *(key v. 22)*

22 **Today's Truth:** Amazing as it is, David claimed he was responsible for the death of the priests slain by Saul. Whereas Saul typically rolled his guilt onto others, David did the opposite. He was keenly sensitive to the impact his actions had on others. *That's* responsibility!

Today's Thoughts: _____

_____

_____

☐ **Today's Text: 1 Samuel 23:1-29** *(key v. 12)*

23 **Today's Truth:** David's acceptance of spiritual responsibility and discipline saved his life and the lives of the men with him. As priests of our home, our everyday decisions can be either life-giving or life-diminishing.

Today's Thoughts: _____

_____

_____

☐ **Today's Text: 1 Samuel 24:1-22** *(key v. 26)*

24 **Today's Truth:** David was grieved for so little as cutting Saul's robe. If we, like David, want to be a "man after God's heart," we should follow his example by not returning evil for evil.

Today's Thoughts: _____

_____

_____

☐ **Today's Text: 1 Samuel 25:1-44** *(key v. 39)*

25 **Today's Truth:** David gave room for the wrath of God. Instead of taking matters into his own hands, he let God avenge his enemies.

Today's Thoughts: _____

_____

_____

☐ **Today's Text: 1 Samuel 26:1-25** *(key v. 21)*

26 **Today's Truth:** Saul repents--the right thing to do, but far too late--after destruction has run its course and reached maturity in his life. Jesus is quick to forgive us of all sin--but why wait to repent until after seasons of sin have burned a hole in the tapestry of our lives?

Today's Thoughts: _____

_____

_____

☐ **Today's Text: 1 Samuel 27:1-12** *(key v. 9)*

27 **Today's Truth:** David's raids served as corrective surgery for future generations, slaying the evil of false demon gods along with the societies that served them. As believers we are assigned to demolish spiritual strongholds with at least as much diligence.

Today's Thoughts: _____

_____

_____

☐ **Today's Text: 1 Samuel 28:1-25** *(key v. 17)*

28 **Today's Truth:** Saul served as Israel's king for 40 years. David would also reign for 40 years. What made the two kings so dramatically different was their heart-responsiveness--or lack of it--towards the Lord. The final hours of each king's life reflected the decisions of a lifetime.

Today's Thoughts: _____

_____

_____

☐ **Today's Text: 1 Samuel 29:1-11** *(key v. 6)*

29 **Today's Truth:** When a man walks closely with the Lord, even his enemies will admire his character and integrity.

Today's Thoughts: _____

_____

_____

☐ **Today's Text: 1 Samuel 30:1-31** *(key v. 6)*

30 **Today's Truth:** David strengthened himself in the Lord and sought His council, even when impaled by grief over a kidnapped wife and surrounded by bitter people ready to stone him to death. Accusing God or others was the furthest thing from David's lips.

Today's Thoughts: _____

_____

_____

□ **Today's Text: 1 Samuel 31:1-13** *(key v. 6)*

31 **Today's Truth:** To analyze the different substances comprising Saul's heart--which led to his tragic end--and the heart of David, as imperfect as he was, may be one of the most valuable studies a man of God can make. Same occupation, same God, same nation, same historical period, same opportunities for good and evil . . . yet the two men ended up in dramatically divergent destinies. Truly, all the decisions each man made in response to the Lord throughout their lives respectively, added up to one conclusive, final bottom-line result for each.

Today's Thoughts: _____

_____

_____

_____

_____

_____

_____

A MAN'S CONFIDENCE

*A study of how
men become
confident in
life through
mastering guilt*

Jack Hayford

THOMAS NELSON PUBLISHERS
Nashville • Atlanta • London • Vancouver

Published in Nashville, Tennessee, by Thomas Nelson, Inc., Publishers, and distributed in Canada by Word Communications, Ltd., Richmond, British Columbia, and in the United Kingdom by Word (UK), Ltd., Milton Keynes, England.

Unless otherwise noted, Scripture quotations are from the NEW KING JAMES VERSION of the Bible. Copyright ©1979, 1980, 1982, Thomas Nelson, Inc., Publishers.

ISBN 0-7852-7791-9

Printed in the United States of America

1 2 3 4 5 6 7 - 01 00 99 98 97 96 95

TABLE OF CONTENTS

Beloved, if our heart does not condemn us, we have confidence toward God.

And whatever we ask we receive from Him, because we keep His commandments and do those things that are pleasing in His sight.   1 John 3:21-22

The Lord is merciful and gracious, slow to anger, and abounding in mercy. He will not always strive with us, nor will He keep His anger forever.

He has not dealt with us according to our sins, nor punished us according to our iniquities.   For as the heavens are high above the earth, so great is His mercy toward those who fear Him;

As far as the east is from the west, so far has He removed our transgressions from us. As a father pities his children, so the Lord pities those who fear Him. For He knows our frame; He remembers that we are dust.   Psalm 103:8-14

CHAPTER ONE:

RECOVERING CONFIDENCE

The moon was just rising over the college campus, casting long shadows which slanted across the brick staircase where I stood, dejectedly looking down the curved pathway to the courtyard below. I was in my first year of studies for the ministry–dedicated to everything I believed God wanted me to be. But I was defeated!

The immediate reason for my depression was a very recent instance of failure–of yielding to besetting sin which dogged my path and recurrently struck condemnation to my soul.

As I sat down on the casement beside the stairs, I brooded over my failure. I wasn't feeling self-pitying, I was simply beaten by my own humanness, and trying to figure out how to square things with God. I had mixed feelings. I'd failed often enough in this same way that I felt dishonest coming to God again with my sorry tale of stumbling.

It was a Sunday evening, and the campus was empty. My fellow students were either out ministering someplace, or worshiping at the campus church not more than a hundred yards from where I sat. But I was on the outside–and felt it deeply; not being outside of church or my circle of friends, so much as *well* outside a circle of *confidence*. I *did* know I was saved, at least I supposed that hadn't changed, since I knew that God is long on grace. But what I didn't know was how to shake the weight of guilt on my soul; a heaviness that hung like metal weights all over me, for I felt unworthy even to *ask* for forgiveness. When you've asked to be forgiven for the same thing over and over, you begin to wonder if God will even take you seriously if you ask again.

I was yet to enter into a fuller grasp of God's truth which would eventually insulate me against this kind of attack. It's that wilting assault on the soul which seems to beset hosts of Christians who are just as sincere as I was that evening, but who haven't found the key of confidence in their relationship with God. But something was about to happen. In His mercy, God was about to whisper to me by His Holy Spirit; to whisper a set of words from His Word which would become the *real* beginning of an abiding spiritual confidence I would eventually come to learn to live in.

8

It's still an unforgotten moment.

Though decades have passed since I sat there in that campus setting, my soul wearied to near despair, I still recall the sound of the Voice which spoke to my heart–timeless words you can find engraved in His Eternal Word:

> *"If we confess our sin, He is faithful and just to forgive us our sin, and to cleanse us from all unrighteousness." 1 John 1:9*

It wasn't as though I had not heard those words before; indeed, I had memorized them as a child. But there is a world of difference between reading, hearing, or remembering a set of words, and having them *revealed* to your spirit! And that's what happened.

Suddenly, it was as though the moonlight swelled to sunlight, as though chains snapped and a helmet of lead was removed from my mind. I KNEW God had heard my request for forgiveness. I KNEW He did not view me as a minced-minded compromiser. I KNEW He was both forgiving me and freeing me. I KNEW I was being–*that moment*–cleansed and released.

I KNEW IT!!

And my heart rose with a joy which seemed to leap inside me, as despair, defeat, and depression melted before the power of

God's Word which had just been made gloriously alive by the Holy Spirit's voice to my soul. It was a release and rejoicing which I earnestly pray might be yours; might be the portion of any and every believer who has ever been badgered by the crushing weight of condemnation's force.

As I stood from where I had been sitting on the brick casement, I virtually felt I could fly. And the most gratifying thing about that whole encounter with God's redeeming, releasing truth was the overwhelming sense of *confidence* which possessed my heart.

> *"Beloved, if our heart does not condemn us, we have confidence toward God."* 1 John 3:21

Confidence.
    The settled peace of certainty
    in the soul.
Confidence.
    The knowledge that you can
    achieve a goal.
Confidence.
    The inner sense that all is
    right and well.
Confidence.
    The breath of heav'n that snuffs
    the fires of hell.

The Right "Stuff"

This book has to do with a man's confidence *toward God*. It's based on the proven fact that until *that* arena of confidence is secured, all other efforts at *self*-secured confidence will inevitably prove inadequate. We're all creatures who have been brought into being with a dual capacity for life–both physical and spiritual. Any effort at treating life on half its terms is doomed. You and I must deal with our *spiritual* base of confidence first, or our other realms of supposed strength are without the "stuff" that makes life work–and *last*. A mound can be built of sand and stones, mixed with water, and a sandcastle erected with temporary splendor. But without the ingredient of concrete mixed in, the sand and stone will only last until they meet the rain, wind, or waves. And in the same way, the *spiritual* facet of a man's nature must be mixed *in* (not mixed up!). Only the integration of spiritual understanding–proportionately fit into the whole of all the other components which constitute a person's life–his duties, family, vocational goals, interests, and education–can bring a solid substance to life.

In our book-to-book studies for men, our target is to find the way to "mix in" the solidifying "stuff" of spiritual reality, so that every man, any man–YOU!–can cultivate that balance in life which gives the proper place to the spiritual aspect of your personality. Confidence in the spiritual realm is not readily achieved. This is because everything about attaining spiritual confidence is the reverse of the way most of us have gained confidence in other areas of our lives.

Usually, we men gain confidence through what we *achieve*.

Recognition.

Athletics.

Education.

Ownership.

Clothes.

Competition.

Conquest.

And on and on.

Earth-level confidence rises when successes are achieved and usually diminishes when failure impacts or the unexpected overthrows our best-laid plans.

An anticipated sale collapses.

An athlete's musculature is damaged.

A planned marriage is called off.

A promising investment turns to nothing.

It's a mere truism, but it deserves repeating: "Success" is only as long as success lasts. And when success comes to its end–even if it's been lifelong–*every* man ultimately has to come to terms with the spiritual aspect of his being: his relationship with God.*

Defining "Confidence"

There's where confidence finds its base–its foundation–and that provides a beginning. But how do we *build* on that foundation when our own humanness seems to fail and our confidence for growth seems shaken? To answer, let's first establish the definition of what we mean by "confidence." Let's open the dictionary a minute.

---

* In the back of this book, I've included a few words of guidance for anyone who may not have established a beginning point–a "newborn" point of life in knowing the Lord, God Almighty. Take time here–right now–if you haven't found THE KEY TO LIFE yet; for coming to know Jesus Christ, the Son of God, is the beginning place for attending to the spiritual part of your nature. Going back to the early sand-stone-cement analogy, the place you go to "bring it all together" and to "make it stick," is to the Cross of Christ, in faith and to your knees in prayer with humility before your Creator. But let me proceed now, on the assumption that you, Sir, have begun your life in Christ.

13

The word "confidence" has four essential uses or applications:

1. Confidence refers to "firm belief, trust, reliance."

2. Confidence refers to "the fact of being or feeling certain."

3. Confidence refers to "the belief in one's own abilities."

4. Confidence refers to "a relationship of trust in secrecy."

Impressive by any standard of analysis is that the *first* definition which asserts "belief, trust, reliance" is not only primary and foundational. It's exactly the real and the only path to a *lasting* confidence–the eternal kind. And look at those other three parts, and see how all secondary meanings of the word depend upon WHERE and IN WHOM you place your *first* point of confidence. *All* "feeling certain," *all* "belief in your ability," and *all* "trusting relationships" stem from the fountainhead of well-placed confidence. For a man to have abiding, transcending confidence, his relationship with God must become one of solid assurance and unshakable stability.

But how many forces war against that kind of relationship?

TALK ABOUT IT! Chapter questions to explore with a friend.

1.   What are several false foundations upon which we men sometimes build our confidence?

2.   What are four essential definitions or applications of confidence in a man's life?

3.   Tell how you, in recent years, have transferred your confidence from a false foundation to one that is valid and biblically based.

CHAPTER TWO:

THE CRIPPLING EFFECTS OF CONDEMNATION

Condemnation is exactly that: it's *"crippling!"* It reduces a person to a stumbling, uncertain pathway in his walk with God. Under condemnation:

- There is no joy;

- Spiritual vision is clouded;

- Holy motivation is sucked empty; and

- Living for God can become a fearful pilgrimage of uncertainty, pain, and exhaustion.

The New Testament Greek word for "condemnation" is *katakrinō,* meaning "judgment coming down on." It strongly conveys the idea of a person being *brought down by that which is against them.* How perfectly that describes the feelings experienced by a person as the result of feeling condemnation. And it's a tragic non-necessity: nobody needs to feel condemnation if he knows the truth.

I want to pass on the secret to triumph

over condemnation. Because of what I have witnessed condemnation do in my own life, and what I know it can do in yours as well, I want to partner with you to assure mastery over this monster.

It's of more than passing or merely personal importance that condemnation be whipped. There are three specific negative effects that condemnation has on a person. The first is:

1. Condemnation shakes our assurance toward God.

Shaken assurance. It's a kind of spiritual/emotional drain-off. It deadens the soul's sensitivities. Instead of singing:

> *"Blessed Assurance, Jesus is Mine,*
> *Oh what a foretaste of glory divine";*

Have you ever felt like grinding out:

> *"Shaken assurance, Jesus ain't mine,*
> *Oh what a sick taste of hell's lies and mine."*

Assurance can be shaken so unpredictably. I dare say that *everyone* reading my words has had the experience. You wake up one morning, and there it is–for no apparent reason. Unpredictably, suddenly, without explanation, you climb out of bed feeling a heaviness in your soul.

Your thoughts begin to percolate: "Hey,

man! What did I do wrong? I feel like God's left me. He must be really ticked off!" It might be overcast outside, but whether it is or not, it is in your soul–and you *know* that something *must* be wrong: "Heaven's dark. Situation's bleak. I'm dead meat, spiritually."

And I've found when gloom-clouds gather and confidence flees, very soon you'll also hear a sly voice whispering to your soul; listing at least a half dozen reasons why you deserve to be feeling this way.

It's not the voice of God.

No, Sir. It's a self-appointed representative from hell who has swaggered into the room and begun to reel off "helpful suggestions"; arriving to "clear up" any mystery as to *why* you feel unholy, unwelcomed by God; why you feel unfit to serve Him.

"Aha! There's no doubt about it!" hisses the vindictive intruder. "That prideful attitude you allowed when driving home yesterday–it angered God! And don't forget, you didn't put money in that homeless person's basket at the supermarket! You know the Word: 'Whatever you've done to the least of the brethren, you've done to Jesus'! You heartless pig!"

But the Bible unmasks this intruder: he is our Adversary, the devil! (1 Peter 5:8). The Scriptures call him "the accuser of the

18

brethren" (Rev. 12:10), and he takes detailed notes on every point of our human vulnerability, waiting for the most opportune moment to make his recitations. And brother, whether it's the devil or our own minds harking back to our failures, have you found what I have? *The most frustrating thing about it is, his accusations seem so disgustingly accurate!* Every pinprick of hell, every argument of my mind–they both tell me things that are *true*! "You did that! You failed here! You know what you thought! And *God doesn't like that*. It's small wonder you *feel* so crummy, man. You *are* crummy!"

Satan will even use Scripture against you. He'll proof-text his accusations with mastery. He did while tempting Jesus in the wilderness, so don't be surprised if he attempts the same with you!

Or if the whole truth won't work, he'll try half-truths. Or gross exaggeration. And if you've gained strength to resist in one area and remain confident in the face of condemnation, the hosts of hell assigned to your case will go to 'plan B.' Or 'plan C.' Hell's minions are tireless in trying every possible avenue of assault, hoping you'll "buy" into their condemnation council. The enemy will be satisfied to establish *any* degree of condemnation into which he can escort you. And of course, the worse, the better. It may be anywhere from feeling: "Oh God, I feel I'm a damned soul–lost forever; I've committed the Unpardonable Sin"; to your simply feeling, "Well, today's 'shot!' I'm so 'out-of-sync' with God's best plans for me, I'm as useless to Him as a brass door knocker! Maybe some other day I'll 'count' for Him. Some other time, but not today." Wherever you may find yourself on the scale of condemnation it makes little difference, because at any point it shakes confidence of our acceptability to God.

2. Condemnation cripples our confidence in daily living.

The Bible reveals God's desire to give us confidence in many ways. For one, when he begins His work in us, He promises that He'll continue it until Jesus Christ comes.

> ". . . Being confident of this very thing, that He who has begun a good work in you will complete it until the day of Jesus Christ." Philippians 1:6

He also says He is committed to completing everything involving me and my development.

> "The Lord will perfect that which concerns me; Your mercy, O Lord, endures forever; do not forsake the works of Your hands." Psalm 138:8.

But all such precious, dynamic words

from heaven tend to fall on a numb soul when condemnation has begun its work. That's because condemnation tends to "anesthetize" us–to blur or blind our sight, dull our sense of the truth that would otherwise liberate us. When condemnation clouds hang low, you can't seem to perceive God's truth as you normally would. You become spiritually hazy–can't see straight. As a result, though you launch into a new day, you feel defective even before you start; feeling anything except certainty that today is the Lord's, and it's going to be a good day.

The soul freshness wilts. The machinery of your spirit feels "gunked up." "Now that I think about it," your mind argues, "this is all probably something I deserve." And the case seems closed, even though it's argued on the basis of something that happened: "When was it, now? About five weeks ago? Five days? Five hours?" Although, "I think I asked God to forgive that," I still conclude, "Well, I *deserve* to feel crummy anyway. I *deserve* the guilt I feel."

And brother, as certain as the "just deserts" may be if you measure them on the scale of *human* justice–God has intended something for us that's arranged on a different basis. It's called "our redemption in Christ!" and in that circle of grace there are facts and promises the precise *opposite* of what we judge ourselves to deserve. But before we look at God's "better idea," let me

21

agree with one thing. If you or I are only judging what we deserve on the terms of any program of legal justice *outside* Christ, then I'll agree: we *do* deserve a bad day; we *do* deserve the absence of God's presence; we *do* deserve the removal of confidence. Yessir! In fact, to put it as a blunt bottom line: we both *deserve* to go to hell!

-IF the ground we stand on is devoid of the blood stains of Jesus;

-IF we stand on the grounds of God's law and that alone. And,

-IF the scope of our self-assessment is based strictly on the sweat and merit of our performance, outside of divine grace–

If *these* are the parameters which govern our feeling right toward God and good about ourselves, then *yes*, we *deserve* to feel condemned. When we surrender to our feelings on the terms of such human reasoning, rather than submit in faith to the truth of God's Word, we're destined for futility.

The fastest we will ever ascend in spiritual confidence will be a slow crawl. The highest we'll rise will only be a slight incline gained, from the pit of our own unworthiness and condemnation to an earth-level limitation of self-generated, self-achieved "confidence."

This level of confidence, based on efforts at reinstatement through a desperate groping for self-merit–for *anything* to justify ourselves before God–is totally fruitless. Yet, how many succumb to inner thinking somewhat like the following?

> *"I'd ask God to help me, but I feel like I fumbled so many times that I'll just, sort of, work my way through <u>this</u> day, and then see how I do. By the end of the day, maybe I'll have racked up some merit points and I'll feel better about asking God to accept me."*

And suppose you *do* do better that day. What then?

Will you come to God and say, "Lord, now that You've seen how really hard I've tried, could I negotiate with You on the basis of my merit points I think I've earned?" Will you recite your accomplishments, and conclude, "So, Lord, I think because I did so much better today, it seems now–at least I feel better thinking so–that maybe *I* deserve *You* to do something for *me* now. (Pause) I DID do better today, didn't I, God?"

But brother, that system doesn't hold an ounce of weight or contain a grain of truth. In the terms of Scripture, it's blind, barren, and worst of all, hopeless. Yet it *is* the way our minds work, isn't it? Sure it is! And it's cockeyed!!

If either of us is determined to live in the realm of self-gained-merit to find spiritual confidence, it's going to be a very long, wearing trip, because to do so means we'll be functioning in the "deficit economy" of human effort. But if we choose to move into the dimension of what God Himself has provided for us in Jesus Christ, then an entirely new arena of possibility opens to us, because *there*–in Christ–is an economy of infinite resource. Our Lord Jesus has *provided* and Father God has *secured* something for us which we could never afford to acquire on our own. *It's the very righteousness of God Himself,* and we'll look at more on that later.

But first look at the third and last of the things we're seeing that condemnation does to torment people. Along with shaken assurance and crippled confidence,

3. Condemnation evaporates our certainty for ministry.

This third crippling effect of condemnation pinches off God's life flow through us to others. Have you experienced that condition I described–waking up, feeling crummy, facing the day with a defeated disposition: "Just gonna have to stumble through this one"? And what happens?

The day begins, and you've no sooner walked into the office, onto the campus, or got onto the job, when a brother in Christ comes up to you and says, "Boy, am I glad to see you. Listen, man. I'm really having a problem, and I sure need you to pray with me. Could we do that now, or later today?" What do you feel like saying?

"Forget it!"

Naturally, we'd never *say that*, but it's exactly the way we feel. At least *I* have, haven't you? The impression instantly flashes inside your soul, which, if put into words, goes something like: "Me, pray? Ha! Listen, buddy–rather than *me* pray for you, let me tell you the best thing you could do for yourself: get as far away from me as you can, because you'll be better off the further you go! If you want to get something from God, put space between me and you. I'm a dead stump: a walking spiritual vacuum."

Sound familiar? Such thoughts come because you feel disqualified.

"Ministry? Me?"

You feel even if you *were* to pray for the person, the words would bounce back in your face; hollow words from the lips of a spiritual non-entity, empty prayers with nothing of substance or worth, composed of words which are a mockery, void of true spiritual confidence–a dynamic confidence you so deeply sense is missing. "Nothing's gonna happen through me! I'm a jinx!"

This syndrome is so common, this tendency of succumbing to feeling totally disqualified, yet it's so seldom admitted. And when this terrible sense of evaporated certainty for ministry occurs, look what happens. My confidence toward *God*, my confidence in His work in my *life*, my confidence for what *I'm* to be that day, and my confidence for touching other *people* with spiritual power–it's *all* just had the Rototiller of condemnation chew gutters of mud through what should have been a garden of fruitfulness. At the very least, we feel demoted–notched well below the "Society-of-Saints-Qualified-to-Minister-Effectively." And this syndrome hangs on. That dark cloud can rise in ugliness anytime. It happens to all of us. And it happens often and will recur until we learn to deal with condemnation effectively. But there is an answer for a man's confidence toward God.

The solution is the truth of God's mighty Word: "In Your light we see *light* (for) . . . the entrance of Your Word gives *light*" (Psalm 36:9; 119:30). Hear it! The fountain of life-giving, truth-shedding-light is *only* in the Word of God, and in Its light we can be permanently led out and kept free of condemnation's clutches. So having identified this darksome monster, and the way it undercuts our assurance, confidence, and ministry, let's open the portals of *Light*. Darkness, shadows, and gloom of soul can be set running–scattered like night before dawn–when we know how to turn that light on.

TALK ABOUT IT! Chapter questions to explore with a friend.

1. What are three specific negative effects that condemnation has on a person?

2. What are several ways by which we try to justify ourselves before God?

3. Can you share any experience in which you felt hindered–due to condemnation–while trying to minister to another person? How did you overcome it?

CHAPTER THREE:

DISCERNING BETWEEEN CONDEMNATION AND CONVICTION

There is no greater basis for a man's confidence than *eternal life*. For one glorious reason, the very term thunders truth of everlasting destiny–security in the heavenlies without end. But eternal life is more than just non-ending life, as blessed a reality as that is! Eternal life is a *quality* of life as well as a *quantity!* That is, there is more than an eternal *sum total* to it, but there's a *surpassing substance* to it. And one of the great confidence-building qualities it provides is the authority that is available to everyone who receives eternal life. The *founding* authority we receive is an authoritative right to affirm, to assert, and proclaim that you *are* a child of God–a son *in* His Son, Jesus Christ! Read it:

> *"But as many as received Him, to them He gave the right to become children of God, to those who believe in His name." John 1:12*

This is an authority conferred upon us by God's will; a position *in Christ* and a pronouncement, "We *are* God's sons!" It's to be walked in and to be lived in *with confidence and certainty* at all times by every believer in Jesus.

But unfortunately, we don't always feel that way. Real sin and personal failure have a way of dimming the brightness. So we need an answer for dealing with the darkness that gathers when we actually *have* sinned and need forgiveness.

Dealing with Sin

1 John 1:7 is an incredibly lovely verse. It makes a moving promise of *ongoing power* through the blood of Jesus Christ when we walk in His light and abide in the fellowship of God's people.

> *"But if we walk in the light as He is in the light, we have fellowship with one another, and the blood of Jesus Christ His Son cleanses us from all sin."* 1 John 1:7

In this verse the Greek text literally emphasizes how the blood of Jesus *keeps on cleansing us* from all sin; how an ongoing, continuous purging process is sustained. That's the environment I invite you to begin and live in, as we walk in the light of Christ's love, His Word, and in the circle of loving, supportive fellowship. But the essential role we have in making this promise work is being wise to deal with sin when it touches, taints, or tarnishes our life with Christ. When the Lord *convicts* us–that is, *points out failure*–we need to respond. But in order to respond *rightly* we need to differentiate between conviction (God's dealing with us about sin) and condemnation (our laboring under guilt without resolving it).

The Difference Between Condemnation and Conviction

Dear brother, it's important that we understand that for us to gain continuous triumph over condemnation, you and I need to recognize this one fact: *condemnation does have grounds to assault us*. Because we do in fact sin, we have sinned, and we are sinners–because of this, we are ever and always vulnerable to being defeated by condemnation. With this fact, because the Holy Spirit faithfully deals with the heart of each humble, honest believer in Jesus, we will regularly sense His conviction when we sin. When He is grieved, we'll know it (Eph. 4:30). However, since our human inclination to condemnation often *feels nearly the same* as conviction does in our soul, we need to gain discernment. So let me make an important distinction between these two biblical terms: conviction and condemnation.

God *does* convict us of sin, but *conviction* is different from *condemnation*. We never need mistake one for the other again–ever.

You ask, "How, Jack? How can I know the difference?"

The answer is clear and unmistakable, for a lifetime of walking with Jesus and in the Word of God has taught me this simple, distinguishing fact: Condemnation *defeats,* but conviction *draws.* Let me elaborate.

Condemnation will always seek to separate you from God. You'll feel driven away by hopelessness and shame. You'll feel unworthy; feel you can't approach Him, and that there's no way in. You'll feel unaccepted–a helpless reject. But there's a holy contrast with conviction.

Conviction will always summon you to God. Conviction beckons you to come to Him, and to say, "I've sinned, but my Savior is waiting to wash me from it all." You'll hear the heart of God's love beating with mercy and promised forgiveness.

No, Sir, the Lord doesn't convict us to punish us, but to get us to repent so His forgiveness can be lavished on us! And the same Holy Spirit that convicts us of sin also convinces us of the adequacy of the righteousness given us in Jesus; He also loves to remind us of the fact that Satan is a beaten adversary, and that we are free to come to the Savior!

This past week, even while working on this message, I had a disappointing experience of failing–of stumbling into an instance of sin. I'm sorry it's not my only sin of recent date, but let me illustrate how we all seem to stumble as I humbly acknowledge my own failure. Just as *you* are determined not to sin, yet sin still subtly finds ways and means to gain a place in your imperfect soul at times, *I too* am committed to living right before God. However, this past week was one of those occasions when I let something slip. It happened like this.

I was involved in a time of recreation with a friend, and during the course of the afternoon at one point I made a remark that was essentially true in content–that is, *technically* true, but it wasn't *completely* so.

I had no sooner said it than I realized I had "hedged," and that there was actually more factual information related to the statement; facts which would qualify the "truth" I had framed in a way so as to be more advantageous to me by leaving the rest of the truth unspoken.

I hadn't really set out to deceive my friend; I really *wasn't* calculating to lie or tell a half-truth. But I did honestly "slip"–slipped into my dilemma, and suddenly saw how I'd been caught in a self-engineered verbal trap. After I said what I did, I began to ponder my dilemma: "I think I should have mentioned the further fact that . . . ." But, well, it was minutes behind us now. We were involved in an athletic activity plus an ongoing conversation, and it really wasn't convenient–it would seem "stuffy"–to jump back to my earlier "slip," I thought. So I decided to skip it. I laid aside the idea of returning to clarify my words and simply forgot about it.

But that evening, at home after I had finished dinner and had gone up to my study, as I sat down to write, the whole incident flashed across my mind. It wasn't because I engaged in some sort of introspective search, raking my soul to find out if I'd failed God that day. In fact, by then, I wasn't even conscious of having done anything that displeased the Lord. Until . . . until suddenly the impression came clearly to my mind: "Your statement today to (my friend's name) wasn't entirely right."

Now *if* I had plotted or planned to tell a half-truth, I would have been feeling guilty the whole rest of the afternoon. But I hadn't. So when this thought came to me, rather than bypass it neglectfully *or* endure condemnation's slow grind, I did two things–immediately.

First I said, "Lord, You've shown me the

33

squeak-point in my personality that gave room for the sloppy statement I made. You've helped me see the way I emphasized only *part* of the truth so as to enhance my own appearance. In doing so, I see how the truth not only became unbalanced and clouded, but I see how I was relying on my 'management' of the truth to enhance my appearance and advance myself."

I continued in prayer: "Lord, I ask You to forgive me for both: the slip of truthfulness, and the slowness to acknowledge it. And also Lord, please strengthen me at that point of weakness which You've just shown me in my own character."

I haven't related the actual content of my verbal compromise, because I fear that in fact too many would think it too small to deem worthy of my concern. If I were to tell you what my statement had been, you'd possibly–indeed, likely–say, "But Pastor Jack, that wasn't that big a deal!" But you see, brother, the Holy Spirit *did* deal with me about it, and that makes anything a *big* deal! And I've learned that if I keep sensitive to His convicting me about seemingly "small deals," I'll become protected all the more against falling carelessly or "slipping" into *big* failures. The Lord doesn't want to badger us, but He does want to keep our conscience sensitive. And confession of sin when the Spirit points out what *He* thinks is important is always a wise course. Don't rationalize conviction of sin. Confess it.

I did.

And then, after prayer, I did a second thing. I called my friend.

When he answered the phone, I said, "You know, I really feel dumb calling, but this will only take a minute." I hurried ahead.

"You remember this afternoon when I said (and I described the instance)?" He said he did.

"Well," I went on, "there is another added fact that casts what I said in a different light, and I need to fill out all the pieces."

I continued, explaining, "I didn't mean to intentionally mislead you, but after I'd slipped into a half-truth, the Lord profoundly dealt with me about it–this evening, after I got home." I proceeded to tell him the added information, and when he heard the whole story, he chuckled. "Jack, that's really okay. I understand and accept your feeling the need to tell me. But really, like I said–It's OK."

The truth of the matter is, it would have made no difference at all to my friend. But hear me, brother. *It made a difference to the Lord.* And that made it make a difference to me!

Now, the most obvious point in my telling this is to illustrate how the Spirit's voice *convicts;* to help urge dealing with "sin-when-I-see-it-as-sin," rather than sloughing off conviction, rationalizing, or being indifferent about it. But here's a deeper point.

If I were to have only said, "Lord, I confess my sin," and then claimed, "Praise God, I'm under His grace and all my sins are forgiven!" I'd have left something else half done. I would have failed to move on to the decisive actions required for "walking in the light"; that is, exposing what was hidden, and taking steps to ensure unbroken integrity in my fellowship with a brother as well as with God. To fail to follow through at the second point would be to end by backing out on the key issue spiritual maturity requires: keeping my relationships uncluttered–with both God *and* man!

To "walk in light" means to confront sin. Because sin *is* a factor in all our lives, confronting it is important. But we need to learn to do that in an atmosphere that's *without* condemnation! Conviction is *not* something God wields like a sword over our necks, lovelessly slicing His critiques at us. He's not in the business of dealing in a heavy-handed, condemning manner. Rather, to the contrary, in His infinite mercy, gentleness and graciousness, God is constantly reaching out to assist us in the process of being freed from sin in all its most sinister or most subtle ways. That's His business as our Redeemer, Incredible Lover, and Savior from sin, marvelous in patience and lovingkindness, with a mercy beyond our ability to find out.

But He does bring us to confrontation with sin.

> *"If we say that we have fellowship with Him, and walk in darkness, we lie and do not practice the truth. If we say that we have no sin, we deceive ourselves, and the truth is not in us. If we say that we have not sinned, we make Him a liar, and His word is not in us."*
> *1 John 1:6, 8, 10.*

Those three verses focus a demanding point. They say that if I'm having fellowship with God, and yet I insistently, intentionally, and by my own will walk in the darkness of self-justification or indifference to sin, then I'm not walking in the truth. And there's no way in the world I'm going to escape feeling condemned if I'm in willful pursuit of that which is contrary to the way of the Lord!

Hey, listen! I'm not talking about accidental failures, fumblings, or evidences of your human weakness. That's another issue, even though those matters–like my own slip I described–are in a different league from what these verses of scripture are addressing. They point up the danger of not coming to terms with any willful pursuit of sin–my own will, my own way, my own sin. If these are unrepented of when you're *convicted*, you *will* bring inevitable feelings of condemnation upon yourself, and that condemnation is inescapable apart from repentance. This book's message and the promised hope it holds do not apply unless a no-slack-for-sin mindset governs our commitment. I may sin, but I won't excuse it, I'll confess it.

The above verses remind us that sin needs to be confronted–to be dealt with *regularly*. They aren't to drum sin's guilt into our system, but to trumpet truthfulness into our ears. Their point isn't to negate the beautiful things God says about our forgiveness in Christ. No! The point is to show me that I'm living a dumb-fool, ostrich-kind- of-life if I stick my head in the sand of supposed "grace" and say, "Hey, man, know what? I just don't have a sin problem. Not me, brother! Nada."

But we *do*. We all do. I do, you do, etc. And that's not a matter of issuing a license for more sin, by excusing myself with a glib, "Don't expect me to be perfect" as a pious excuse for lolling in self-indulgence.

So the bottom line is: There's no way to be freed from condemnation without first confronting the reality of sin. Whether I'm a person who has walked in the sanctifying grace of Jesus Christ for most of my lifetime or a newborn babe who just received Jesus this week, the same need is present. We need to recognize that you and I are people with whom the sin problem is very real, both around us and in us. Indeed, there are fragments of it in our flesh. They're fragments that we'll never be wormed free of until Jesus gives us another body at His coming, and so, we need to face the reality of sin, but we need to face it both wisely and honestly. Wisdom will keep us in the light of the Word, and in the fullness of that light of truth, two things will happen: (1) We'll be kept free from condemnation, and (2) we'll keep honest in dealing with sin.

Conviction will always point out sin, but only to drive us to deal with it, not drill us with guilt. Condemnation doesn't stand a chance when conviction is responded to with confession. Because confession, in the light of the power-cluster of confidence-building verses we're about to study, will neutralize the crippling effects of condemnation:

• Your assurance before God will be secured;

• Your confidence in life will rise with joy; and

• Your fruitfulness in ministry will be

certain, continual, and abundant.

It's all possible through the power of God's words of truth from His Word of Truth!

TALK ABOUT IT! Chapter questions to explore with a friend.

1.   What is the chief difference between conviction and condemnation?

2.   What are two things of which the Holy Spirit convicts us ongoingly?

3.   There is no way of being free from condemnation without *first* confronting the reality of _____.

CHAPTER FOUR:

THE POWER-CLUSTER VERSES

The stories of believers who succumb to a less-than confident experience are painfully too common. For example, I recall the story of a person I'll refer to as Glen. He wrote to me about how he had carried a sense of guilt and condemnation for 20 years of his life. Almost all of those years, he had known Jesus Christ as his Savior, having a genuine confidence he was born-again. But still, he never could completely shake the gnawing sense of guilt that related to past episodes in his life. His letter referred to a transforming Sunday–one day when I related a message centered on a power-cluster of verses; a set of scriptures which had a tremendous life-changing impact on him. By his own testimony, that power-cluster "broke the bondage" to condemnation! The truth of God's Word set him free and changed his life as the condemning spirit which had so tormented him for two decades was crushed!

Those same verses, which brought such a resounding victory in this one person's life, have done the same for many who have testified of the same release. This power-cluster constitutes the verses I want to study with you now. But here are a half dozen verses which can provide effective weaponry for keeping the taunts of condemnation at bay when they attack you, and assuring your being equipped against this vicious, lying enemy of our souls.

First, let me list the six verses from God's Word which I have been referring to as "the power-cluster" verses. I've called them that because they remind me of the air-warfare tactic of "cluster-bombing." This has been a means employed for decades of battle, insuring that a target is totally obliterated–that the enemy has no remaining point of retaliation. In the same way, my objective is to see your heart and mind grip the reality in these texts of scripture in a way that will make them your weapons against the Enemy. Thus, *every* time he seeks to deceive you with condemnation, you can obliterate him with these tactical weapons of God's eternal, unchanging truth.

The six verses which have found "cluster-power" in my own experience are: 1 John 1:9; Romans 8:1; Isaiah 1:18, 44:22; Micah 7:18, 19; Psalm 103:11, 12; and Hebrews 10:17. They are equally divided into two sets of three: the *root* of reality, and the *fruit* of rejoicing. Let me outline them briefly, then elaborate.

I. THE ROOT OF REALITY

A. 1 John 1:9 - The reality of God's readiness to forgive.

B. Romans 8:1 - The reality of God's justice in forgiving.

C. Isaiah 1:18; 44:22 - The reality of God's totality in forgiveness.

II. THE FRUIT OF REJOICING

A. Micah 7:18, 19 - Rejoicing in overwhelming mercy.

B. Psalm 103:11, 12 - Rejoicing in an undiscoverable record.

C. Hebrews 10:17 - Rejoicing in an unreclaimable past.

God's Readiness To Forgive

"If we confess our sins, He is faithful and just to forgive us our sins and to cleanse us from all unrighteousness." 1 John 1:9

This was the verse that the Holy Spirit breathed into my soul that night as I sat in despair on the brick casement in the center of my college campus that moonlit night. Here's a dual concept about God's nature that we need to see.

First, see God's readiness and reliability to forgive: "He is *faithful* to forgive us, and

43

to cleanse us from ALL (get it, *ALL!!*) unrigh-teousness." Perhaps nothing moved me more than the sudden revelation that God wanted to show me *His* faithfulness not-withstanding my *un*-faithfulness. I was amazed at the immediate sense I felt of this grand fact: God is incapable of unforgiveness! If the simple condition of confession is met, He cannot, He will not, He is unable to deny His commitment to be a Forgiver!!

Further, this forgiveness is not delayed to see how you or I will do another day. It is present-tense, on-the-spot, here-and-now forgiveness! And that sets up the second feature of the matter: He performs His forgiveness as totally as He does quickly: ". . . to cleanse us from ALL!"

Oh, how my heart leaps at that word! And may yours as well, dear brother. God is not operating an installment plan in forgiving us, as though increments of guilt were "washed away" on the basis of our performance over a season of days, weeks, or months. Get it! ALL is forgiven–And right NOW!

God's Justice In Forgiveness

"There is therefore now no con-demnation to them who are in Christ Jesus." Romans 8:1

Our first verse included a significant

phrase: "He is . . . just" as well as forgiving. This verse in Romans brings us face to face with that gigantic truth.

When the Bible says that IN CHRIST there is NO CONDEMNATION, we are being told that, literally, " There is no more judgment of the court being brought down upon or against us any more." Such words remind us of a fact we must never forget: Heaven's laws cannot be broken without a price being paid. In other words, God *must* remain just at the same time He is loving.

The fact of your sin and mine is that it cannot simply be forgiven "out of hand," so to speak. Forgiveness must have *grounds*; that is, the problem of sin's penalty cannot be dispensed with as though a clerk tore up the price tag on a suit and gave it to you free. Even if you receive it without cost, somebody has to pay for it.

So it is with the clothing of God's righteousness–the highest-priced suit ever worn by a man. That garment of perfectly tailored salvation and forgiveness which the Father gives us when we put our faith in Jesus Christ is only available because Jesus paid for it with His life-blood. And the reason that payment was so worthy was because of His perfect sinlessness.

Thus it is that the *grounds* of our forgiveness have been established in that God's justice–His inviolable laws which require payment for sin–was completely satisfied. The life of His sinless Son was exchanged to balance the scales of justice which required payment for *my* sin, for *your* sin–for *all* sin.

There was a popular song years ago, and you'll still hear it sung occasionally: " Though it makes Him sad to see the way we live, He'll always say, 'I forgive.' " That song is true, but in a distorted way; a half-truth worse than an entire *un*truth. By featuring His forgiveness *alone*, God's love is paraded, without accountability for God's justice; God's forgiveness apart from the price of Jesus' Cross. He does say, *and always will*–"I forgive." But He also says that forgiveness comes solely through His Son.

Further, because God says Jesus satisfied the demands of heaven's justice, in effect God says, "In forgiving you, I will attribute to you my Son's record of sinlessness and at the same time abolish your own personal record of sin and sinning!" The impact of such a concept is staggering to *anyone* who truly wraps his mind and heart around it. No analogy can come close to being a faithful representation of this amazing reality, but here's a simple picture to help us.

Say, you have a Gold MasterCard, Visa, American Express, or some such credit tool. And you have this Gold Card because you've run up $66 trillion of indebtedness. Now, the obvious stares at you: there's simply no way you can ever pay it. However, there is a fellow cardholder, named Jesus, who offers to put your debt on His card. His account is debt free, and His resource is capable of "handling" any amount transferred. But as though that weren't enough, He *now* takes on your card's obligations. In essence, you switch account numbers; switch identities. So the Bank will now come *after Him* instead of you, as they seek payment on the debt.

And brother, that's what happened! The price was death, and death *did* come after Jesus as He went to the Cross to make the full and final payment for our indebtedness-our sin. And at that point, as He died on the Cross, for judgment's and condemnation's purposes–for satisfying justice's demands–He was *you* and He was *me*. In a way transcending imagination He bore all of us and our sin on the Cross, becoming the ultimate payment for the penalty of our sin.

So the debt was paid. Our account balance before God is zero. We owe no penalties to God's justice for our sins. Payment's been made.

We are justified, and now no judgment can be "brought down against"–no condemnation. The Judge–the Living God–has made a statement in the courtroom of heaven as the Judge of the universe. The gavel has sounded and He has said, "I declare all of those who have received My Son as Savior as having the same degree of guiltlessness that He has." And He is *just* in doing that, as well as loving and forgiving, by reason of the fact that Jesus Himself bore all sin, paid sin's price, and rose again to prove it was all true. It was impossible that death hold Him, because our sin which He bore could find no control over Him. And in rising from the dead, He now comes as Heaven's attorney, declaring: "The Judge's case is dismissed. You've been pronounced 'Not guilty,' and totally accepted in the sight of the Judge of the heavens–Almighty God." You're justified–acquitted of any record of sin against you! *There is* therefore no condemnation'–no case whatsoever against you in the chambers of divine justice!" Hallelujah! Shout it again–HALLELUJAH!

Now that's true, and our praise is proper. There *is* no "case held against me," that is, no judgment "coming down on my head." But that doesn't mean there isn't an occasional battle over this decision heaven's court has declared.

Dealing with the Enemy's Torment

Someone says, "Right! If there is 'Now no condemnation,' why do I feel it sometimes?" The answer involves two related reasons.

First, as human beings, our memories

often haunt us, conjuring the past like a recurring nightmare or an endless video-tape rehearsing one failure after another. Second, we are still vulnerable to the Adversary's ploys. A relentless Adversary, the devil tirelessly comes as a prosecutor, accusing us as a lying Lawyer from hell. He *does* have a case, in *half*-truth. He is taunting us for real sins, but he wants to press his charges without reference to what Jesus has done for us and what we have received in Him.

Picture a courtroom.

Bill, a believer in Christ, has just failed. Anxiously, gleefully, the Lawyer-from-hell runs into the Courtroom of the Universe and slams down a report of the crime: "Bill sinned!" This hellish attorney is seething; driven by a perverted mixture of loathing and delight: "Bill's dead this time!" And claiming Bill's failure justifies his argument, the devil presents his case against Bill before God, our Father and Judge.

But Bill has earlier conferred with his Heavenly Attorney, Jesus, whom he met earlier before the adversary's present court date. Bill had already put the case of his whole life *totally* into the hands of Jesus, via his confession of sin. So when the Judge asks the Defense to come forward, our Heavenly Attorney presents the blood of His Cross and His sinless life as grounds for the

49

Judge to refuse to accept the Liar's true charges. Jesus says, "Yes, Bill sinned. But I hold up the evidence of what has been accomplished on My Cross." And brother, when He does that, that blood is still as crimson and fresh in power as the day it poured forth from our Heavenly Attorney's own veins! So it is that our Father, the just Judge, looks at the two cases—one *against* Bill and one *for* him, and He says, "I've studied the evidence, and I find the defendant 'not guilty!' The evidence of the Blood is greater than the evidence of Bill's failure!"

The Lawyer-from-hell shoots out of his chair screaming, "On what grounds, Your Eminence? This man broke YOUR law!!"

And the Father narrows His gaze, His eyes burning with righteousness, and addressing Satan, the prosecuting attorney, He points His finger at His Son, whose scars and blood still speak in heaven, and says, *"On the grounds of the payment you see standing before you.* Case dismissed!" And the thunder of His gavel drives the prosecuting lawyer from the room.

Racing down the halls in fury, the Lawyer-from-hell vows to himself to find another child of God who perhaps does not have the same degree of understanding that Bill had; someone who will not so immediately and thoroughly confer with the Heavenly Attorney, so that the case may be decided so quickly and so completely. The Lawyer-from-hell knows he can't easily separate such a child of God from His inheritance of eternal life, but he'll still seek to plague him through distortions of the written Word; he'll attempt to wreak an agony of mental and emotional litigation for weeks–maybe years, if he finds a child of God who is ignorant of the great truth: "NO CONDEMNATION!"

God's Totality of Forgiveness

" 'Come now, and let us reason together,' says the Lord, 'Though your sins are like scarlet, they shall be as white as snow; though they are red like crimson, they shall be as wool.' " Isaiah 1:18

There's nearly a holy touch of humor in this verse.

I don't know why it is that I picture this at the table on the patio of Anna's and my house, but I do. It is as though I see God saying, "Come here, Jack. I want to talk with you–We're going to 'reason together.' "

That's where the humor begins; I mean, who is capable of "reasoning" with Ultimate Intelligence, with the Mastermind of the Universe? But God still says, "I want you to think this through–let us reason together."

Then, having said that, He adds words that from our human point of view are absolutely *un*-reasonable. He adds:

"Everything that has indelibly stained your record is going to be expunged. There is no failure so severe, no sin so destructive, no guilt so deep, no action so depraved, corrupt, or damaging, that it can survive the penetrating power of the cleansing agent I am using."

Listen to His reasoning. He is basing His "reason" *on His terms*–Christ's Cross–not on ours. Our "reasoning" will end up arguing that it's all too gracious and all so undeserved. Our minds will plead guilty upon remembrance of our failures, and the residue of our past will stare us in the face and scream that we're fakes who are pretending a piety we don't possess. But God keeps saying, *"Come on now! Reason with Me,"* which is His way of saying, "I want you to think like I do." That dimension of "thought" is described elsewhere in this same prophecy of Isaiah's. God is speaking, and says:

> *"For as the heavens are higher than the earth, so are My ways higher than your ways, and My thoughts than your thoughts."*
> *Isaiah 55:9*

God's appeal to us is that we *not* appeal to our *own* reasoning, but to HIS! He isn't unreasonable in declaring such forgiveness, because the reason for it all is JESUS! And it is from the roots of these truths that we are called to taste, eat, and delight in the fruit of rejoicing!

TALK ABOUT IT! Chapter questions to explore with a friend.

1. There's a dual concept about God's nature reflected in 1 John 1:9, "He is faithful and just to forgive us our sins. . ." How do these two facets of God's nature relate to you personally?

2. How would you describe the doctrinal concept of "justification"?

3. In what ways is Satan like a "Lawyer-from-hell"? On what grounds is a child of God able to withstand the accusations of the Lawyer-from-hell?

CHAPTER FIVE:

MASTERING GUILT
AND CONDEMNATION

Isaiah was a man like you. He was conscious of his limitations at a time that God was calling him to become an instrument in His hands. Listen to him:

"Oh, God–It's awful. I don't have anything together! My mouth betrays me, I don't talk like a man whom You'd call Yours; in fact, my lips seem fouled by the things I've said. And worse, Lord, everything around me is like that. How can I become a whole man, much less a holy one, when everything around me smacks of human sin and hellish trash?"

You say, "Did a prophet say that?" And Isaiah did. You can read it in Isaiah 6:5, and the setting is significant. It was right at the time the Lord was seeking to show this one man that He had higher purposes for him than he had ever imagined. Could it be that's exactly where God is in dealing with you?

My paraphrase above is not exaggerated in the least. What Isaiah experienced of a *sense of disqualification* is so common to us men, maybe we'd be wise to all make one of our middle names "Isaiah" as a reminder.

But in making that reminder, we would end with a positive power, for Isaiah's sense of condemnation was smashed by God's cleansing power: "Look ... Your iniquity is taken away and your sin is purged!" (Isaiah 6:6).

And that, Sir, is the purpose of this book, to bring you to a place of *ministry readiness*; not as a religious professional, but as God's-man-on-*your*-job! It begins with knowing the *root* system in the power-cluster, but it climaxes with knowing the song of rejoicing which flows from the *fruit* of the power-cluster.

It's a holy wine. And it makes you sing, like Isaiah was ignited to sing: "Sing ... for the Lord has done it!"

Done what? Listen, here's what!

> *"I have blotted out, like a thick cloud, your transgressions, and like a cloud, your sins. Return to Me, for I have redeemed you!"*
> *Isaiah 44:22*

Isaiah's discovery is one that invites your and my sharing. Hear the truth that *shouts* the dimensions of our forgiveness. To measure the scope of this salvation is to find its measurelessness, but in hearing the thunder of heaven's announcement about my sin's banishment and my total acceptance, I can't help but sing.

Sir, I ask you to prepare to lift your voice in song. But only after you've taken a drink from the wine born of the power-cluster of the grapes of God's graciousness. Read, then sing:

Rejoicing in Overwhelming Mercy

"Who is a God like You, pardoning iniquity and passing over the transgression of the remnant of His heritage? He does not retain His anger forever, because He delights in mercy. He will again have compassion on us, and will subdue our iniquities. You will cast all our sins into the depths of the sea."
Micah 7:18-19

Hear that!? Sins *buried* in the depths of the sea! Are you aware that the deepest point in the oceans of this world are further down than the highest point of the mountains on earth? The message: There's nothing I've "run up" as a debt of sin, that the sea of God's forgiveness can't cover–and bury! Sing!

"O the deep, deep love of Jesus,
Vast unmeasured boundless, free!
Rolling as a mighty ocean

In its fullness over me."

Samuel Francis

"Buried in the deepest sea,
Yes, that's good enough for me.
I shall live eternally,
Praise God, my sins are gone!"

Helen Griggs

Rejoicing In Your Undiscoverable Record

> *"For as the heavens are high above*
> *the earth, so great is His mercy*
> *toward those who fear Him; as far*
> *as the east is from the west, so far*
> *has He removed our transgressions*
> *from us."*   Psalm 103:11, 12

There is a studied effort on God's part to make a picture so clear in our earth-bound minds that we can't forget it. "As far as the east is from the west" is a tangible figure any thoughtful mind can grasp. If God had said, "as far as the north from south," the distance would be impressive, but not immeasurable. It is approximately 12,500 miles from the North Pole to the South Pole. Once that trip is traversed, the very next instant–from any point south–a new direction is established: *back to the north.* And unfortunately, that's what many people do with their sin. They take it to one end of God's promise of forgiveness, then carry the

57

load "back north" again, making wearying cycles of repeated conjurings up of memories of failure. But God's Word won't allow that, not with the clear image He's engraved on its pages: *"As far as east from west."* Get it straight once and for all: that's *eternally apart, permanently removed, gone forever.*

One never comes to the end of that distance. It's as though God put a rocket into orbit, with the payload made up of our sins. Then, having orbited the earth–whirling to the east from the west–it gained escape velocity and now has been launched into the infinite, black void of space, plummeting into the depths of the universe. Brother, it will never return; our forgiven sins will never find re-entry. Sing!

> *"Amazing grace, how sweet the sound,*
> *That saved a wretch like me.*
> *I once was lost but now am found,*
> *Was blind but now I see!"*

> John Newton

> *"Cleansing power, in this hour*
> *Wash my heart and all sin erase.*
> *Blood of Jesus, flow and free us,*
> *Lead us Lord to Your resting place."*

> JWH

Perhaps the master stroke of all texts in the power-cluster is found in these mighty words which occur three times in the Bible, as though God wanted to establish a "three-fold witness" to this rich reality: *Heaven FORGETS the record of our past!*

> *"Their sins and their lawless deeds*
> *I will remember no more."*
> *Hebrews 10:17 **

How can this be? How can the greatest mind in the universe "forget"? Isn't forgetfulness a sign of mental weakness? Well, consider this.

If you or I could take the most unpleasant memory of our lives–the one thing that most comes back in a nightmare; the remembrance of the worst moment we've ever experienced; if we could selectively slice such ugliness from our memories forever, wouldn't we consider that capability a great *power?*

Of course we would!

So, listen: God is saying He has that power! He isn't saying He *can't* remember our sins anymore. We're not dealing with a senile parent who's losing a grip on His memory. Rather, this text teaches us of an

---

*(see also Jer. 31:34; Isa.43:25; Heb. 8:12)

active, committed Redeemer who says, "I *will* to forget those sins." And He's telling us that the very thing you and I feel would be a *power* if *we* were capable of it, is a power He possesses. And He not only says *that He does have the power to forget our sin, but that* He has and *will* do it. He has selectively removed from our record all the sinful facts of our lives!

Some time ago I was touched by what a brother shared with me. After having failed at a point of sin often besetting him, he had prayed, saying, "Lord, I don't even feel I deserve to come to You today about this... I've failed this way so many times. I'm here today because I did it again." Then, he said, "The Holy Spirit whispered the words of the Father to me, and said, *'Did what again?'*"

"Did what again?" Can you hear it? It was only in *that* moment that my friend said he truly understood how fully Father God means, "Their sins I will remember no more." After we have confessed our sins, not only have they been removed completely from the books of heaven, but by His power God has chosen to remove them *forever* from His mind!

Why? Only because of the Cross of our Lord Jesus Christ.

I was also profoundly impressed by a story someone shared with me after a message I brought from this text: "I will *remem-*

ber their sins *no more!*" They said: "Pastor Hayford, as you spoke of God forgetting our sins, though I believed what you were saying, I had difficulty understanding how it could be. Then the Lord brought to mind something that happened where I work.

"I work about 30-35 miles north of here," the person continued, "and just last week a thunder storm struck, and a lightning bolt hit the transformer on the power line behind our office where I work. Because it didn't actually destroy anything visible, at first we took little notice. But later we discovered that when that bolt struck the transformer, a power surge coursed through our computer systems and everything that had been input for that day had been totally and irrevocably erased!

"When I stepped to the office door and looked out where the lightning struck, the telephone pole appeared to me as though it were a giant cross, with the burned out transformer just hanging there on the pole. And as you spoke tonight, it struck me: Jesus was the one who, hanging on the Cross, transformed us from death unto life by totally absorbing the lightning bolt of divine judgment for our sin. Just as He bore the payment of death for my sin, He also occasioned a power surge of God's might which went shooting into heaven's records of our sins and totally erased all the memory banks!"

My eyes misted. But my heart sang as I heard this analogy. And I bid you, brother–go forth as a *Man Alive* in Christ! Go forward singing!

> *"And can it be that I should gain*
> *an int'rest in the Savior's blood?*
> *. . . Long my imprisoned spirit lay*
> *Fast bound in sin and nature's night*
> *Thine eye diffused a quick'ning ray,*
> *I woke, the dungeon flamed with light!*
> *My chains fell off, my heart was free,*
> *I rose, went forth and followed Thee."*

Charles Wesley

The Grapes of Grace

The fruit of rejoicing which comprises the power-cluster of anti-condemnation verses are the Grapes of Grace–not wrath; and they blend together to make a holy wine, not a heady one. Think about it, Sir.

Have you ever noticed how bold some people become when they drink? How happy (even if only temporarily)? How open and tender?

All those traits distill from the wine of earthly vineyards, but in this cluster of fruit-filled verses we're looking at, there is genuine *confidence* for any man.

- Confidence that brings a boldness in your stance before God.

"Let us therefore come boldly to the throne of grace; that we may obtain mercy and find grace to help in time of need." Hebrews 4:16

- Confidence which brings happiness (and <u>not</u> temporarily!)

". . . Believing (in Christ), you rejoice with joy inexpressible and full of glory, receiving the end (that is, 'the objective') of your faith–the salvation of your souls."
1 Peter 1:8, 9

- Confidence which brings openness and tenderness to others.

"In this is love, not that we loved God, but that He loved us and sent His Son to be the propitiation (covering) for our sins. Beloved, if God so loved us, we also ought to love one another." 1 John 4:10, 11

A man's confidence is not simply for his own blessing, but to breed and beget a way of life that moves–

- from boldness born of an assurance in God's presence;

- to joyfulness in positive, encouraging behavior toward and around others;

- to transparency and sensitivity in relationships with people, showing the love and gentle strength of God Himself.

Like *all* truth, the secret of mastering condemnation and learning to live in confidence is to *"set free." First,* to set you free from the crippling impact of guilt's memories and condemnation's lies. *Second,* to set you free from carnal presumption which would be indifferent to sin or would rationalize self-indulgence. *Third,* to set you free in the light of instant forgiveness, knowing it flows when instant confession is made by a fully repentant heart which refuses to live in a way that grieves the Holy Spirit. *Fourth,* to set you free to know, glow, and show the radiant realities of the power-cluster verses which keep your own soul free from condemnation and which equip you to minister anti-condemnation truth to others. And *finally,* to set you free to let the genuineness of this God-designed order of confidence make you a man of humble boldness, holy happiness, and open tenderness.

It's the life-style of the man whose confidence is in Christ.

> *"No condemnation now I dread;*
> *Jesus, and all in Him, is mine!*
> *Alive in Him, my living Head*
> *And clothed in righteousness divine*
> *Bold I approach th'eternal throne*

And claim the crown
  through Christ my own.
Amazing love!
How can it be
That Thou, my God,
  shouldst die for me!"

Charles Wesley

TALK ABOUT IT! Chapter questions to explore with a friend.

1. Five specific ways of mastering guilt and condemnation were mentioned in this chapter. Can you cite three of them and discuss how you've experienced success in any one of them recently?

2. Discuss one of the three dramatic illustrations given in this chapter which demonstrate how God has dealt with our sins.

3. Why hasn't God removed our sins from us as far as the north is from the south?

Scriptural Ammunition Against Guilt and Condemnation

The following pages are four sets of the "power-cluster" verses. They are intended to be removed from this book and to be used for memorization, to keep in your wallet or Bible, and extra sets are included for you to give to other men.

The Power-Cluster Verses

1 John 1:9
**The reality of God's readiness
to forgive.**

"If we confess our sins, He is faithful and just to forgive us our sins and to cleanse us from all unrighteousness."

Romans 8:1
**The reality of God's justice
in forgiving.**

"There is therefore now no condemnation to those who are in Christ Jesus, who do not walk according to the flesh, but according to the Spirit."

Isaiah 1:18; 44:22
**The reality of God's totality
in forgiveness.**

" 'Come now, and let us reason together,' Says the Lord, ' Though your sins are like scarlet, they shall be as white as snow; though they are red like crimson, they shall be as wool.' "

"I have blotted out, like a thick cloud, your transgressions, and like a cloud, your sins. Return to Me, for I have redeemed you."

Micah 7:18, 19
Rejoicing in overwhelming mercy.

"Who is a God like You, pardoning iniquity and passing over the transgression of the remnant of His heritage? He does not retain His anger forever, because He delights in mercy. He will again have compassion on us, and will subdue our iniquities. You will cast all our sins into the depths of the sea."

Psalm 103: 11, 12
Rejoicing in an undiscoverable record.

"For as the heavens are high above the earth, so great is His mercy toward those who fear Him; as far as the east is from the west, so far has He removed our transgressions from us."

Hebrews 10:17
Rejoicing in an unreclaimable past.

"Their sins and their lawless deeds I will remember no more."

The Power-Cluster Verses

1 John 1:9
The reality of God's readiness
to forgive.

"If we confess our sins, He is faithful and just to forgive us our sins and to cleanse us from all unrighteousness."

Romans 8:1
The reality of God's justice
in forgiving.

"There is therefore now no condemnation to those who are in Christ Jesus, who do not walk according to the flesh, but according to the Spirit."

Isaiah 1:18; 44:22
The reality of God's totality
in forgiveness.

" 'Come now, and let us reason together,' Says the Lord, 'Though your sins are like scarlet, they shall be as white as snow; though they are red like crimson, they shall be as wool.' "

"I have blotted out, like a thick cloud, your transgressions, and like a cloud, your sins. Return to Me, for I have redeemed you."

Micah 7:18, 19
Rejoicing in overwhelming mercy.

"Who is a God like You, pardoning iniquity and passing over the transgression of the remnant of His heritage? He does not retain His anger forever, because He delights in mercy. He will again have compassion on us, and will subdue our iniquities. You will cast all our sins into the depths of the sea."

Psalm 103: 11, 12
Rejoicing in an undiscoverable record.

"For as the heavens are high above the earth, so great is His mercy toward those who fear Him; as far as the east is from the west, so far has He removed our transgressions from us."

Hebrews 10:17
Rejoicing in an unreclaimable past.

"Their sins and their lawless deeds I will remember no more."

The Power-Cluster Verses

1 John 1:9
**The reality of God's readiness
to forgive.**

"If we confess our sins, He is faithful and
just to forgive us our sins and to cleanse us
from all unrighteousness."

Romans 8:1
**The reality of God's justice
in forgiving.**

"There is therefore now no condemnation
to those who are in Christ Jesus, who do not
walk according to the flesh, but according to
the Spirit."

Isaiah 1:18; 44:22
**The reality of God's totality
in forgiveness.**

" 'Come now, and let us reason together,'
Says the Lord, ' Though your sins are like
scarlet, they shall be as white as snow;
though they are red like crimson, they shall
be as wool.' "

"I have blotted out, like a thick cloud,
your transgressions, and like a cloud, your
sins. Return to Me, for I have redeemed
you."

Micah 7:18, 19
Rejoicing in overwhelming mercy.

"Who is a God like You, pardoning iniquity and passing over the transgression of the remnant of His heritage? He does not retain His anger forever, because He delights in mercy. He will again have compassion on us, and will subdue our iniquities. You will cast all our sins into the depths of the sea."

Psalm 103: 11, 12
Rejoicing in an undiscoverable record.

"For as the heavens are high above the earth, so great is His mercy toward those who fear Him; as far as the east is from the west, so far has He removed our transgressions from us."

Hebrews 10:17
Rejoicing in an unreclaimable past.

"Their sins and their lawless deeds I will remember no more."

The Power-Cluster Verses

1 John 1:9
The reality of God's readiness to forgive.

"If we confess our sins, He is faithful and just to forgive us our sins and to cleanse us from all unrighteousness."

Romans 8:1
The reality of God's justice in forgiving.

"There is therefore now no condemnation to those who are in Christ Jesus, who do not walk according to the flesh, but according to the Spirit."

Isaiah 1:18; 44:22
The reality of God's totality in forgiveness.

" 'Come now, and let us reason together,' Says the Lord, 'Though your sins are like scarlet, they shall be as white as snow; though they are red like crimson, they shall be as wool.' "

"I have blotted out, like a thick cloud, your transgressions, and like a cloud, your sins. Return to Me, for I have redeemed you."

Micah 7:18, 19
Rejoicing in overwhelming mercy.

"Who is a God like You, pardoning iniquity and passing over the transgression of the remnant of His heritage? He does not retain His anger forever, because He delights in mercy. He will again have compassion on us, and will subdue our iniquities. You will cast all our sins into the depths of the sea."

Psalm 103: 11, 12
Rejoicing in an undiscoverable record.

"For as the heavens are high above the earth, so great is His mercy toward those who fear Him; as far as the east is from the west, so far has He removed our transgressions from us."

Hebrews 10:17
Rejoicing in an unreclaimable past.

"Their sins and their lawless deeds I will remember no more."

Receiving Christ As Lord and Savior

It seems possible that some earnest in-
quirer may have read this book and somehow still never have received Jesus Christ as
his personal Savior. If that's true of you,
that you have never personally welcomed
the Lord Jesus into your heart, to be your
Savior and to lead you in the matters of your
life, I would like to encourage and help you
to do that.

There is no need to delay, for an honest
heart can approach the loving Father God at
any time. So I'd like to invite you to come
with me and let's pray to Him right now.

If it's possible there where you are, bow
your head–or even kneel, if you can. But in
either case, let me pray a simple prayer
first–then, I've added words for you to pray
yourself:

My Prayer:

*"Father God, I have the privilege of joining
with this child of Yours who is reading this
book right now. I want to thank You for the
openness of heart being shown toward You,
and I want to praise You for Your promise,
that when we call to You, You will answer.*

*"I know that genuine sincerity is present
in this heart, which is ready to speak this
prayer, and so we come to You in the Name
and through the Cross of Your Son, the Lord*

Jesus. Thank You for hearing." (And now, you speak your prayer.)

Your Prayer:

"Dear God, I am doing this because I believe in Your love for me, and I want to ask You to come to me as I come to You. Please help me now.

"First, I thank You for sending Your Son Jesus to earth to live and to die for me on the Cross. I thank You for the gift of forgiveness of sin that You offer me now, and I pray for that forgiveness.

"Do, I pray, forgive me and cleanse my life in Your sight, through the blood of Jesus Christ. I am sorry for anything and every-thing I have ever done that is unworthy in Your sight. Please take away all guilt and condemnation, as I accept the fact that Jesus died to pay for all my sins, and through Him I am now given forgiveness on this earth and eternal life in heaven.

"I ask You, Lord Jesus, please come into my life now. Because You rose from the dead, I know You're alive and I want You to live with me—now and forever.

"I am turning my life over to You, and turning from my way to Yours. I invite Your Holy Spirit to fill me and lead me forward in a life that will please the Heavenly Father.

"Thank You for hearing me. From this

day forward, I commit myself to Jesus Christ the Son of God. In His Name, Amen."

DEVOTIONS

IN THE FIRST EIGHT CHAPTERS OF

ROMANS

Contributed by Bob Anderson

The Book of Romans is widely regarded as the greatest exposition of Christian doctrine in the entire Bible. The plan of redemption is developed throughout the whole epistle, building with clear logic, graced with holy passion.

The song writer's words, "Our hope is built on nothing less than Jesus' blood and righteousness," reminds us of Romans set to music. The grounds for our confidence truly is on Christ the Solid Rock–and no exposition has ever presented a stronger, more exhaustive legal case for that confidence than Romans.

(It is suggested that this devotional be used for stimulating discussion and prayer within a small group of men meeting regularly.)

☐ **Today's Text: Romans 1:1-7** *(key v. 4)*

1 **Today's Truth:** Jesus' Sonship was actually "declared" or reaffirmed by His Resurrection. Because we, as believers, are ''in Him'' as sons, therefore our sonship is assured beyond any doubt because *His resurrection guarantees it.*

Today's Thoughts: _____

_____

_____

☐ **Today's Text: Romans 1:8-15** *(key v.12)*

2 **Today's Truth:** Even the Apostle Paul, being the "powerhouse" leader he was, still needed to have his faith strengthened by fellowship with others.

Today's Thoughts: _____

_____

_____

☐ **Today's Text: Romans 1:16-19** *(key v. 16)*

3 **Today's Truth:** The Gospel is the *power of God.* We rarely question that–until it comes to God's power to totally forgive us. Condemnation makes us feel like God might *try* to forgive us, but "His batteries could be too weak for such a large job."

Today's Thoughts: _____

_____

_____

☐ **Today's Text: Romans 1:20-32** *(key v. 20)*

4   **Today's Truth:** Though God is invisible to our physical eyes, He has emblazoned upon every horizon throughout the earth His signature of glory which proclaims: "I AM HERE!" He wants all to be saved if only they will seek Him.

Today's Thoughts: _____

_____

_____

☐ **Today's Text: Romans 2:1-4** *(key v. 1)*

5   **Today's Truth:** A recipe for condemnation: judging others for doing things you yourself do! However, if we ongoingly forgive others, confess our sin, and repent earnestly, infinite grace is ours.

Today's Thoughts: _____

_____

_____

☐ **Today's Text: Romans 2:5-11** *(key v. 11)*

6   **Today's Truth:** There is no favoritism with God. So the chief issue is: if our lives are hidden with Christ (the *only* Favored One) in God, then we are *all favored* via Christ's righteousness–for He loves us all equally!

Today's Thoughts:_____

_____

_____

☐ **Today's Text: Romans 2:12-16** *(key v. 16)*

7 **Today's Truth:** Terrifying words: "when God will judge the secrets of men." But if our "secret sins" have all been exposed through confession and repentence, and they have been sent away as far as the east is from the west, then we can have confidence in the day of His appearing! Hallelujah!

Today's Thoughts: _____

_____

_____

☐ **Today's Text: Romans 2:17-29** *(key v. 29)*

8 **Today's Truth:** God's plea is for internal righteousness of heart, not outward religiousness. In the parable of the Pharisee and the tax collector in Lk. 18:10-14, the sinner who humbled himself and asked for mercy was justified before God.

Today's Thoughts: _____

_____

_____

☐ **Today's Text: Romans 3:1-8** *(key v. 4)*

9 **Today's Truth:** God is *true*. The Greek word, *alethes*, means: genuine, real, ideal. He is incapable of falsehood and is therefore absolutely faithful to keep all of His promises.

Today's Thoughts: _____

_____

_____

☐ **Today's Text: Romans 3:9-18** *(key v. 10)*

10 **Today's Truth:** The sooner we realize the full extent of the depravity of man–that is, our own hopeless state as sinners, the sooner we'll learn to seek God's righteousness and not our own. "Blessed are the poor in spirit " refers to those who recognize their spiritual poverty, and who trust in the Lord's resources instead of their own.

Today's Thoughts: _____

_____

_____

☐ **Today's Text: Romans 3:19-26** *(key v. 24)*

11 **Today's Truth:** "Redemption" is a power-packed word. The Greek term, *apolutrosis*, describes a master ransoming a slave, and freeing him from a yoke of bondage.

Today's Thoughts: _____

_____

_____

☐ **Today's Text: 3:27-31** *(key v. 27)*

12 **Today's Truth:** Although few of us may be tempted to approach God on the basis of our own righteousness, we often fall prey to an inverted form of that logic: based on our *un*righteousness, we feel unworthy to come to Him and be forgiven (cf. Heb. 4:16: "Let us come boldly . . .").

Today's Thoughts: _____

_____

_____

☐ **Today's Text: Romans 4:1-4** *(key v. 3)*

13 Today's Truth: Abraham's faith was *accounted* to him for righteousness. The Greek term, *logidzomai*, from which we get the English word *logic*, means God "computed, calculated, summed up, and reasoned" that Abraham was righteous because of his faith (and even *that* was a gift.) After all, based on God's eternal principles of redemption, it was only *logical*.

Today's Thoughts: _____

_____

_____

☐ **Today's Text: Romans 4:5-10** *(key vv. 6-8)*

14 Today's Truth: In respect to categorizing sins, we often think of murder and adultery as the all-time "biggies." Nevertheless, David's sin in both of these areas was forgiven and blotted out.

Today's Thoughts: _____

_____

_____

☐ **Today's Text: Romans 4:11-19** *(key vv. 17-18)*

15 Today's Truth: God's creative power is released in "hopeless" situations when we simply believe His Word rather than circumstances. Abraham's body was dead to procreation, but today the nation of Israel proves his "hopeless" circumstance was a lie.

Today's Thoughts: _____

_____

_____

☐ **Today's Text: Romans 4:20-25** *(key v. 25)*

16 **Today's Truth:** We *know* our sins are paid for because Jesus died on the Cross. We *know* we are justified before God because Jesus rose from the dead. So the next time you feel *un*justified, escort your doubts to the empty tomb. And celebrate.

Today's Thoughts: _____

_____

_____

☐ **Today's Text: Romans 5:1-5** *(key v. 5)*

17 **Today's Truth:** God's love: *agape*, conveys God's undefeatable benevolence and unconquerable goodwill wherein He always seeks His children's highest benefit no matter what weaknesses or failures they are struggling with.

Today's Thoughts: _____

_____

_____

☐ **Today's Text: Romans 5:6-11** *(key vv. 8-9)*

18 **Today's Truth:** It's a mind-boggler: when we were in our *worst* state–"still sinners"–Christ did the *most* for us. Now as His kids, how "much more then" shall we be saved to the utmost.

Today's Thoughts: _____

_____

_____

84

☐ **Today's Text: Romans 5:12-16** *(key vv. 14-15)*

19 **Today's Truth:** Even without our sinning in the likeness of Adam's transgression, just being *in Adam* results in the sentence of death through the universally inherited sin nature. Conversely, being *in Christ* is the "lock and seal" of life.

Today's Thoughts: ⸻⸻⸻⸻

⸻⸻⸻⸻⸻⸻⸻⸻⸻⸻⸻⸻
⸻⸻⸻⸻⸻⸻⸻⸻⸻⸻⸻⸻

☐ **Today's Text: Romans 5:17-21** *(key v. 20-21)*

20 **Today's Truth:** Two actions of God's grace in our lives: *abounding* and *reigning*. One speaks of ample quantity–more than enough; the other speaks of ruling power through righteousness.

Today's Thoughts: ⸻⸻⸻⸻

⸻⸻⸻⸻⸻⸻⸻⸻⸻⸻⸻⸻
⸻⸻⸻⸻⸻⸻⸻⸻⸻⸻⸻⸻

☐ **Today's Text: Romans 6:1-6** *(key v. 4)*

21 **Today's Truth:** Total identification with Christ! We can look at our heinous past sins and say, "Oh my–I'm dead meat!" And in Christ, that's exactly right. We're dead! That sinful man is dead. Now we can walk in confidence knowing that the "dead weight" of our past sins is gone; the new man created in Christ is alive!

Today's Thoughts: ⸻⸻⸻⸻

⸻⸻⸻⸻⸻⸻⸻⸻⸻⸻⸻⸻
⸻⸻⸻⸻⸻⸻⸻⸻⸻⸻⸻⸻

□ **Today's Text: Romans 6:7-11** *(key v. 11)*

22 **Today's Truth:** To reckon yourself dead to sin and alive unto God takes practice. *Reckon* means "consider it a fact." Even when you feel alive to sin and dead to God, God has a different judgment on the issue!

Today's Thoughts: _____

_____

_____

□ **Today's Text: Romans 6:12-16** *(key v. 16)*

23 **Today's Truth:** Since we are all "wired for sin," sin stands by ready to dominate us if we simply *present* ourselves to it. Give sin an inch, and it seeks to consume our lives. Instead, let's "tap in" to obedience, which leads to righteousness.

Today's Thoughts: _____

_____

_____

□ **Today's Text: Romans 6:17-23** *(key v. 19)*

24 **Today's Truth:** The more we yield ourselves to sin, the easier it is to keep sinning. But the same goes for righteousness. It, too, seeks to be our master.

Today's Thoughts: _____

_____

_____

☐ **Today's Text: Romans 7:1-6** *(key v. 6)*

25 **Today's Truth:** Now, with our deliverance from the law established, God can deal with us as sons rather than as debtors. That certainly does not eliminate the issue of obedience, but now there's a loving family relationship in which obedience takes place.

Today's Thoughts: ―――――――――

―――――――――――――――――――

☐ **Today's Text: Romans 7:7-12** *(key v. 12)*

26 **Today's Truth:** The Psalmist cries out, "I love Your law!" (Ps. 119) for it is a light to our feet. Yet though the law is perfect, it is totally powerless to help us obey it. We need a Savior.

Today's Thoughts: ―――――――――

―――――――――――――――――――

☐ **Today's Text: Romans 7:13-19** *(key v. 19)*

27 **Today's Truth:** Thank you, Paul, for identifying with our struggles! His admission of personal struggle is not to give us license to sin (cf. 6:15-23!), but rather to encourage us that we're not alone in our battle for holiness.

Today's Thoughts:――――――――――

―――――――――――――――――――

□ **Today's Text: Romans 7:20-25** *(key v. 25)*

28 **Today's Truth:** Paul's cry of victory is not because the struggle ceases, but because of recognition that human strength is surpassed by the power of the Resurrected Christ!

Today's Thoughts: _____

_____

_____

□ **Today's Text: Romans 8:1-11** *(key v. 2)*

29 **Today's Truth:** The law of the Spirit of life in Christ provides the assistance of Omnipotence for our victory. Our pilgrimage, however, requires that we ongoingly learn HOW to yield to, trust in, obey, and rest in God's Spirit–a discipline which may require a little more than one month for us to perfect!

Today's Thoughts: _____

_____

_____

□ **Today's Text: Romans 8:12-23** *(key v. 18)*

30 **Today's Truth:** Such blessed assurance: whatever sufferings we know in life, the glory that shall come later *can't even be compared to them*–it's so far off the scale of measure!

Today's Thoughts: _____

_____

_____

☐ **Today's Text: Romans 8:24-39** *(key v. 37)*

31 **Today's Truth:** We are *more* than conquerors through Christ (as if being *mere* conquerors wasn't enough!) because of the content of all eight chapters preceding this verse. In the courtroom of heaven, picture the Father as the Judge, the Son as our Attorney, and the Holy Spirit as the Jury–not to mention the fact that we were acquitted long before this court came into session! Now here's a test:

What do the proclamations of Romans 8 work in your heart:
> *"confidence"* or
> *"CONFIDENCE!!!"* ?

Today's Thoughts: _____
_____
_____
_____
_____
_____

Additional Resources for Biblical Manhood

Available from Jack Hayford and
Living Way Ministries

AUDIO CASSETTE MINI-ALBUMS (2 tapes)

Honest to God	SC122	$8
Redeeming Relationships for Men & Women	SC177	$8
Why Sex Sins Are Worse Than Others	SC179	$8
How God Uses Men	SC223	$8
A Father's Approval	SC225	$8
Resisting the Devil	SC231	$8
How to Recession-Proof Your Home	SC369	$8
Safe Sex!	SC448	$8
The Leader Jesus Trusts	SC461	$8

AUDIO CASSETTE ALBUMS (# of tapes)

Cleansed for the Master's Use (3)	SC377	$13
Becoming God's Man (4)	SC457	$17
Fixing Family Fractures (4)	SC217	$17
The Power of Blessing (4)	SC395	$17
Men's Seminars 1990-91 (10)	MSEM	$42
Premarital Series (12)	PM02	$50
A Family Encyclopedia (24)	SC233	$99

VHS VIDEO ALBUMS

Why Sex Sins Are Worse Than Others	WSSV	$19
Divorce and the People of God	DIVV	$19
Earthly Search for a Heavenly Father	ESFV	$19

Add 15% for shipping and handling.
California residents add 8.25% sales tax.

Request your free Resource Catalog.
Living Way Ministries Resources
14820 Sherman Way • Van Nuys, CA 91405-2233
(818) 779-8480 or (800) 776-8180

A MAN'S INTEGRITY

*A study of
how men can
develop in Godly
character*

Jack Hayford

THOMAS NELSON PUBLISHERS
Nashville • Atlanta • London • Vancouver

Published in Nashville, Tennessee, by Thomas Nelson, Inc., Publishers, and distributed in Canada by Word Communications, Ltd., Richmond, British Columbia, and in the United Kingdom by Word (UK), Ltd., Milton Keynes, England.

ISBN 0-7852-7795-1

Printed in the United States of America

1 2 3 4 5 6 7 - 01 00 99 98 97 96 95

This message was originally brought at
The Church On The Way.

It has since been edited and revised
for publication by Pastor Hayford,
in partnership with Pastor Bob Anderson,
Director of Pastoral Relations.

TABLE OF CONTENTS

Chapter One:
Integrity of Heart—
Preventative
Against Confusion

As the shimmering waves of desert heat seemed to part momentarily, the mirage of a lake turned to a vision—no, the *actuality*—of a city. And there, in the distance, he saw the massive city gate of Gerar—one of the five power centers of the Philistine people.

Abraham estimated they would enter these gates in perhaps an hour, at which time his large camel caravan, populated with family and servants, would finally enjoy rest after the wearying 75-mile journey from Mamre through the Wilderness of Zin.

With his destination now in view, the man's mind became active. Political strategy was foremost in his thoughts. Though knowledge of this city was common— Gerar controlled an important caravan route between Egypt and Palestine— Abraham did not know its king well at all. It was this uncertainty about King Abimelech that most troubled him. He wasn't sure exactly how this king of Gerar would deal with him and his estate.

"I ought to be safe," Abraham calculated,

"but should remain on guard."

Having entered the city gates, Abraham soon halted his caravan before what appeared to be the main entrance of the palace. He considered for a moment how to best approach this unfamiliar and unpredictable ruler.   Then his attention was seized by the swift approach of a small but official-looking man—Gath, the royal messenger.

Running towards Abraham and Sarah with frequent bowings to the ground, the sight of Gath caused Abraham to fear the worst; then, leaning over to Sarah's ear, he whispered something to which she nodded in agreement.

Smiling so broadly that it incited suspicion, Gath was finally close enough to speak, "My lord, your humble servant welcomes you to the glorious city of Gerar! King Abimelech wishes to find peace and favor in your sight!"

Abraham dismounted and bowed in response. "Your servant Abraham comes to you in peace and goodwill."

Gath bowed again, then turned his attention to the beautiful woman. "And may the wife of my servant dwell in peace."

"Ah," he hesitated but for a moment, "*this* woman? She is my sister." Abraham exchanged glances with Sarah. The reason for the earlier whispered remarks was now occasion for their agreed deception—"Say you're my sister, for the king might kill me to have you." It was a common understanding in this ancient world that an alien man with a beautiful wife was a "temporary citizen." Abraham, an outsider to this king's realm, was in need of great caution. Politically, this was a very touchy situation.

"Ah! Indeed!" Gath bowed again— smiling at Sarah in a new way. Then, quickly ordering his servants to bring water for the travelers, he abruptly excused himself and sprinted to the Palace entrance. Abraham's heart beat faster as he considered the possible meaning of the messenger's sudden exit.

Inside the palace, Gath burst through the doors with a rush—racing into the king's private chamber. Reflexively, King Abimelech whirled around with his sword in combat position ready to strike, causing Gath to throw up his arms in a moment of short-lived terror, "No, my lord! It is I, Gath!" The king relaxed his sword, but not his scowl.

"What is it!" Abimelech demanded— obviously irritated by the brash entry.

Gath cowered momentarily, then beckoned his king to the balcony with great excitement, "Come, my king, I pray thee—come, O my lord; look and behold. I have found my king the most beautiful woman ever to set foot in Gerar! If it pleases the king, I will bring her to you. Behold! Is she not the sister of Abraham our valiant guest?"

Abimelech looked down at the caravan lined up in the streets below. He squinted into the daylight and fixed his eyes on the woman seated at the head of the entourage. Even at this distance, her beauty spoke eloquently. It was the kind of beauty built from the bone.

Gath couldn't stop chuckling or nodding his head up and down. He would certainly be rewarded for this, he thought to himself as he glanced back and forth between the king's softening countenance and the prize discovery.

"Summon the woman," Abimelech said.

Gath vanished like a gazelle.

Rising up from a deep bow, Gath lifted his eyes up to Sarah while speaking to Abraham, tittering giddily between phrases, "Your handmaiden has found favor in the sight of my lord, the king. If it pleases my lord, King Abimelech offers many gifts in exchange for this fair handmaiden!"

Abraham briefly buried his eyes in his hands. "Egypt! This is Egypt all over again!" he silently murmured to himself. His thoughts flashed to that day twenty years ago, the last time he, through fear, had bartered this way, claiming his wife as his sister and laying at risk her chastity. It was an agreed ploy he had convinced her to use long ago.

On that occasion, Sarah had been summoned by Pharaoh to be his new possession, and Abraham's first embarrassment at such deception had been turned to deliverance by the grace of God. How could he be doing this again!?

Now, seeking to submerge his inner shame, he lifted his eyes from his hands to find Sarah staring right at him. There was a pause. Then Abraham tapped the camel's legs to kneel.

Sarah gave her husband her hand and dismounted. ("It is a natural and mature agreement," the man reasoned—forcing his mind to adapt some point to his defense. "And in reality, we are step-brother and sister." It was true—but Sarah's eyes and his own sense of shame could not be denied. There was no compensation by any line of reason for this peculiar behavior.) But all this flashed in a moment's glance between them. It was done, and now with a quick, "O God, help me," the plan was in motion.

Gath's greedy eyes stared at the dismounting woman excitedly, and almost babbling and chuckling intermittently and ceaselessly, he moved to take her hand.

Before leaving with the royal messenger, Sarah looked at Abraham one more time—a deep, penetrating look that, within its flash, held a lifetime of acquired meaning. As she did, Abraham was the first to look away, and with that, she had been surrendered to the king's messenger.

It was evening, and now King Abimelech was awaiting the arrival of this beautiful new woman. For hours, she had been being prepared with bath oils and spices by other members of Abimelech's harem. Soon she would be ready for entrance into the king's private chamber.

Finally, the doors opened, "My lord, the king!"

A valet escorted a magnificently beautiful woman through the doors into the royal bedroom quarters.

"She is called Sarah," he announced, then promptly left, closing the inner curtains and outer doors, leaving the two alone.

Sarah was hesitant as she looked around the room uncomfortably. The royal decoration of the bedroom was stunning, but certainly of little interest to the woman. Then her eyes turned to Abimelech.

The king tried to smile but found it awkward. He had never felt self-conscious in the presence of a woman before. Until now.

"Why?" he wondered to himself as he finished filling two cups with wine. The king motioned for Sarah to come closer, as he seated himself upon a mound of colorful silk pillows. And, as the woman drew nearer, he could smell the intoxicatingly sweet frankincense and myrrh perfumes wafting about her.

Sarah stood silent for several moments as the king held his gaze on the oil lamp he was igniting. Finally, Sarah sat down across from him on the soft pillows.

The moment was growing increasingly tense, and Abimelech began feeling somewhat impatient with himself. He was having difficulty even looking up from the lamp into her face at such close range. With an uneasiness that surprised him, the king finally forced his gaze upon the woman's large, dark eyes. Lit by the soft, warm lamplight, Sarah's beauty all the more hid her age.

The king searched for words. "So tell me of your people."

Sarah took a slow, deep breath and began to unfold the story of how God, Possessor of Heaven and Earth, called her people to a promised land. As she spoke, Abimelech wrestled with distraction. It wasn't just her unusual countenance, it was her presence—or A PRESENCE. "Who IS this woman? Rather, Who—*what is this Presence I feel prohibiting my advances?*" Abimelech wondered silently. "Perhaps my recent loss of sleep has fogged my mind. Yes, that's it. Loss of sleep."

But as Sarah concluded her story, the king could only nod with a pretense of understanding, groping with her words about a God worshiped by her and her brother—the God called, "Possessor of Heaven and Earth."

Finding few words and feeling feebly out of control, his eyes slunk back to the lamp's now-dimming flame, the wick running dry of oil. He reflected silently, then sighed, and rising to his feet, he called to his servant. He strode to the window, his back turned to Sarah, who remained seated, wonderingly awaiting the outcome of the moment.

The servant entered, "Yes, my lord!"

The king continued looking out into the night. And without explanation simply commanded, "Escort the woman to her room."

"Yes, my lord."

*   *   *   *

It was several minutes later—Abimelech

14

was crawling into his bed, shaking his head. He had expected to have great pleasure this evening with his newest acquisition. But for a reason he didn't comprehend, he had sent the woman away.

His thoughts drifted to the mysterious sheik who had freely given up the prize maiden in goodwill. "Abraham," he whispered to himself, lazily searching his memory as he drifted off into a sleepy haze.

Then it happened.

The Voice.

It was a roar, but ever so quiet. Cutting like a sword, but not hateful. Terrifying, but soothing. The Voice was more than words, it was the Voice of THAT Presence!

"Indeed you are a dead man," the Voice intoned. "The woman whom you have taken—she is a man's wife!"

Abimelech's nerves would have catapulted him out of his bed, but his muscles did nothing to respond—he lay frozen. He could hardly hear the words of his own reply to the Presence. With his heart pounding in his ears, he raised himself, leaning on his arms, and shouted in dismay: "Did he not say to me, 'She is my sister?' And she, even she herself said, 'He is my brother.' In the integrity of my heart and innocence of my hands I have done this!"

Silence. Then the answer:

"Yes, I know that you did this in the integrity of your heart. Therefore I also withheld you from sinning against Me; for I did not let you touch her.

"Now therefore, restore the man's wife; for he is a prophet, and he will pray for you and you shall live. But if you do not restore her, know that you shall surely die, you and all who are yours."

*   *   *   *

It's a spell-binding story. And it's in this event, elaborated from the twentieth chapter of Genesis, that we have our first biblical use of the phrase *"integrity of heart."* Our imagination's rendering of the text is consistent with the historical events in Genesis 20:1-7, and as we conclude with the actual conversation between God and Abimelech, we touch the nerve endings of a mighty truth.

When Abimelech pleaded his case, insisting that "In the integrity of my heart and innocence of my hands I have done this," *God agreed with him!* "Yes, I know that you did this in the integrity of your own heart."

As confrontive as God was in addressing King Abimelech, the Lord *was NOT without abundant mercy toward him!* God knew that the pagan king was ignorant of the facts. He knew that Abimelech didn't know Sarah was really the wife of Abraham. And even though this pagan ruler did not have the same degree of revelation as God had given Abraham, he nonetheless displayed a fundamental reverence for God as Creator, which manifested in a consequent sense of duty. Integrity had been preserved in his heart. He was a man who acted upon that degree of integrity he *did* possess, and God honored his heart's intent. As a result of Abimelech's pursuing the wrong thing *ignorantly*, the fact he did so in *innocent* ignorance prompted God's mercy, who prevented him from stumbling into sin and its confusing aftermath.

But above all, standing as the towering, transferable truth which we today may learn, is the fascinating point in God's response, essentially saying: "I withheld you from sinning against Me because your heart was honest in your error; therefore, I did not let you touch her."

God didn't let him touch her!

We don't know exactly how He worked His first expression of mercy, but God sovereignly kept the king's hands off of Sarah! (Regardless of how God may actually have orchestrated such a prevention, Abimelech must have wondered why he just "couldn't get around" to enjoying this new addition to his harem!)

Further, in a second expression of mercy, the Lord warned him of his sin and of impending judgment. God gave him full revelation about the dangerous situation he was in and the punitive consequences that were about to unfold. Why did God go to such an effort in keeping Abimelech from the sin he was about to commit? What is different about this case than any other sinner's sinning? The difference is that here, *God saw the integrity of Abimelech's heart, even though he was misinformed.* And hereby, the first lesson the Bible teaches about "integrity of heart" is: *if a man's heart is honest with God, that integrity will help prevent him from stumbling into error and becoming trapped by sin.* In other words, God can find a "handle" in an honest heart, to turn it and keep it from its own confusion. It's a summons to learn to maintain such a heart of integrity.

But the inverse of this lesson is equally true. If my heart, sir—or yours—wills to have its own way, with an inner knowledge that our actions or words are in opposition to or in violation of a God-given inner sense of "right," God will abandon us to our own devices.

So, in introducing us to the power potential of maintaining our hearts' integrity, remember: fidelity to live in integrity begets a kind of "mechanism" built into the life; a preventative promise of God's readiness to intervene when we fall into situations of inexperience, unawareness, or unpreparedness. God will protect us—as long as our hearts are committed to a stance of integrity.

The steps of a good man are ordered by the Lord, and He delights in his way. Though he fall, he shall not be utterly cast down; for the Lord upholds him with His hand.
Psalm 37:23-24

As long as I walk in "the steps of a good man"—that is, as a man committed to heart-integrity, no matter how imperfect or weak I may be—the Lord will uphold me with His hand. He will be my Protector, Defender, Director, and Teacher.

It's time to start now, brother. What the past may record of failure can be forgiven through repentance and faith in the cleansing power of the Blood of Jesus Christ. Then, *beginning now*, irrespective of how little proven integrity or "honesty with God in your own heart" you may currently possess in your character, if you act on it, speak from it, and live by it from now on—God will give you abundantly more!

19

For if there is first a willing mind, it is accepted according to what one has, and not according to what he does not have.

2 Corinthians 8:12

Chapter Two:
The Integral Parts
of "Integrity"

I was awakened that morning with a directive to speak on the subject "integrity." My one problem was that I didn't have a message on that theme prepared—in fact, I'd never brought a whole study on the idea. And so it was I was seated in the back seat of the car carrying me to my speaking assignment (just two hours away) frantically researching my biblical text and language resources for all the background on "integrity" which I could find. I'm happy to say, with praise to God for His grace, that I arrived with a sermon—in fact, one which the Spirit of God blessed wonderfully. But I also arrived with a bevy of brand new discoveries (at least for my part!) on the concepts undergirding this frequently used word.

Integrity is a powerful term! It is loaded with implications of honesty, trustworthiness, dependability, reliability and faithfulness, but what *exactly* does *integrity* mean—especially, "integrity of heart"?

Perhaps the best starting place is to look at cognate words (associated words) in our own English language, because the concepts there are remarkably illustrative of the precise meaning of the Hebrew word for "integrity," *thom*. In English, at least three key words virtually jump onto the chalkboard for analysis, all being clear relatives of "integrity": *integer*, *integral*, and *integration*.

Most of us were introduced to the word "integer" sometime early in our junior high math class. *Integer* is the word for a "whole number"; i.e., in contrast to fractions, integers are complete numbers—one, two, three, four—as opposed to one-third, three-tenths, or sixteen thirty-sevenths. This focuses the fact that when we are discussing integrity of heart and life, we are looking at *unfragmented—commitment, undivided attention, undiminished priority*. David was praying for this kind of heart when he called upon the Lord saying:

"Teach me Your way, O Lord; I will walk in Your truth; *unite my heart* to fear Your name" (Psalm 86:11, emphasis author's).

All of us know moments at which a quiet "ping," deep within the soul, has signaled a warning—an appeal that we *not* sacrifice a value, neglect an issue, surrender a moment, or violate an inner awareness of righteousness. But with uncanny ease, either you or I can silence that "ping" (which sometimes sounds like a giant "GONG!" trying to stop us) and plunge

22

ahead unto the reducing of the *wholeness* in our inner heart.

For example, pressure of finance may argue that I fragment my tithe—reduce it to less than the biblical 10%. I may do this, but the compromise puts me outside the promise of God's blessing when my heart-felt, trusting obedience allows *Him* to compensate for tough economic hands by *His* hand of provision, not my calculated reduction. Or, I may leave a portion of the *whole* truth out of a conversation—refusing the "ping" which directs me to "come completely clean." Such moments of how we may fractionalize the heart's integrity are wrapped in the intended idea of *integer* as it relates to "integrity."

The Hebrew *thom* specifically means, "complete, whole." The Greek counterpart is in the idea of *eirene*, which is usually translated "peace." The essence of "peace," between parties for example, is that they are "one"; thus the picture of the *wholeness* in integrity. The heart at peace is the heart that keeps tuned and responsive to the "pings" mentioned above; the life that is *integrous* (i.e., is the one which is *completely* and *entirely* focused on God's Word, values, and will).

Of further help in grasping the meaning of "integrity" are the commonly used terms,

"integrate" or "integration." All of us immediately recognize the societal implications
of these terms: ethnic or racial groups are
brought together and interspersed as
one—as the *one* race of mankind, rather
than separated as competing "races" motivated by competition or bigotry. The concept of "all together" is clearly present, and
when applied to your heart or mine, current
slang says it all: "Man, you need to get it all
together!!" Integrity means "I'm getting it
all together" on God's terms. Whether it's
how I use my time, serve my employer, love
my wife, care for my kids, keep my mind
occupied—whatever; instead of *dis-inte-
grating* under the fiery pressure of the
world-spirit, I am finding things "fitting
together"—integrating—in God's good order and way. It's a lifestyle summarized in
the words of an old gospel song, which
asked:

> "Is your *all* on the altar
>   of sacrifice laid,
> Your (whole) heart does
>   the Spirit control.
> You can only be blessed
>   and have peace and sweet rest,
> When you yield Him
>   your (whole) body and soul."

Integral is an interesting English cog-

24

nate to *integrity*, which refers to "that which is essential or necessary to completeness." In demonstrating its application to our study, perhaps the most insight might be found by my relating the most exciting discovery I made that day I was desperately racing to prepare my message on "integrity."

As I was paging through my Hebrew resources, I suddenly was electrified to find the plural form of the Hebrew word *thom* had been left untranslated in most Bibles. In many places the word *thummim* simply appeared in exactly those letters. You probably recognize it, for any reader of the Old Testament has encountered the description of the breastplate of the High Priest of ancient Israel. Besides the jewel-bedecked chest-cloth which hung from his neck, with each magnificent stone representing one of Israel's twelve tribes, there is mention made of the presence of "the Urim and the Thummim" (Ex. 28:30; Lev. 8:8; et. al.).

The interesting thing about the Urim-and-Thummim, is that even though we are told *what* it was used for, we are not specifically introduced to *how* it was used.

The "What"

The Urim (meaning "lights") and the Thummim (meaning "perfections" or "completenesses") were "consulted" (see

25

Ezra 2:63). In short, when the people of the Lord needed a special sense of guidance or discernment, which only God could give, and human wisdom seemed undependable, they would have the High Priest inquire of the Lord "by the Urim and Thummim."

The "How"

While the scriptures only mention *that* this was done, *how* the priest did it is only known from reports which have been transmitted to us in the rabbinical writings. It is said that the High Priest would go into the Holy Place, past the Lampstand and Shewbread Table, and stand between the Altar of Incense and the Veil which separated this area from the Holy of Holies. And there—as near as he could move in drawing near to God on all but one day of the year—he would ask the Lord for Israel's directions from Him, and God would answer "by the Urim and Thummim."

Because the word "lights" is mentioned, some believe that a kind of "holy glow" shone, signaling God's will or pleasure, by some order of "yes" or "no" system. But there is a great practical truth in the fact the breastplate was over the heart and that the word "completeness" (*thummim*) was used. It would seem there was a combination of a supernatural signal, blended with an inner sense of God's peace, wholeness, composure, and assurance to the heart of the leader. And it is very instructive for us today.

You see, brother, while Jesus Himself is the only High Priest there is today—He's ours, Hallelujah!—there remains the fact that He has called and equipped us to be priests under His leadership (1 Pet. 2:5, 9; Rev. 1:6; 5:10). He has also given us "the breastplate of righteousness" (Eph. 6:14), which in a very real sense is a priceless gift of a heart-covering which will signal "right and wrong" to us—if we'll accept the signals!! The Bible says to us all: "Let the peace (*eirene*) of God rule in your hearts" (Col. 3:15).

Can you hear it! Just as the "lights and completenesses" were sensed by the ancient priests, so we are to live in the *light* of God's Word with the *peace* (complete integrity, wholeness) of God's Spirit assuring us when we are walking wisely, and correcting us when we are not. It's God's present-day "Urim and Thummim," provided by the ministry of the Holy Spirit who will open our understanding through the Scriptures and guard our heart through the comfort of His "completing" Presence. This is His "peace" *ruling in our hearts*!

That "peace" is not just a state of

tranquillity—not just a "feel good" on a sunny day when the sky is blue and clear. It's to guide us into all truth and truthfulness for daily living and decisions we need to make. If we allow the Lord, He will cause His "completenesses" or "perfections" to keep us from fragmenting our lives through compromise or folly—known or unintended.

I'll tell you, brother. There isn't a day that goes by that at some point I have to listen to that "internal umpire" saying, "That's out of bounds. Steer clear of that—go here instead." It's not so much an issue of my being tempted to do something stupid or to say a wicked thing, but rather it relates to and assists with issues of discernment and refinement. And it works wisdom in a life when the heart's integrity level is maintained through sensitivity and obedience.

But it's not without struggle. I'm sure that every person reading this has experienced the same temptation I have at one time or another, whether it is the Spirit of God or your own conscience speaking to you. You were warned, challenged, or corrected—and you closed your inner ear to that Voice. I fear I, too, have at times done this, for unfortunately that inner Voice of God's dealing with our hearts can be squelched.

There are many things that can cause us to become completely numb to the guidance of our conscience, to God's Voice, or to the wisdom that comes from abiding in integrity. The results of a numbed soul will too easily bring a fragmented heart which will entertain bitterness or unforgiveness, or worse yet, introduce spiritual blindness and deafness to the way and word of God's Spirit.

• Only integrity of heart can guard against these blights on our soul.

• Only integrity of heart will decide "even though this feels good right now, I'm going to submit to what I know is better!"

Maintaining our integrity by "complete and full-hearted" responses to the Holy Spirit's "still, small voice" will keep us instead in line with God's full, whole, perfect, complete, and entire will.

It's wise to beware concerning the relatively small things which will seek to invade this life of integrity. For example—being in a conversation where the quality of content takes a sharp dip below advisable integrity levels, and an internal Voice says, "Don't continue along that line of talk." There's enough fallen nature in any one of us to allow a short, minor transgression—"just a toe over the line." Maybe we're mid-sentence with something we suddenly sense we shouldn't be saying. But then, we think "it'd be too embarrassing to stop and say to those we're addressing, 'Hey, I shouldn't be saying this.'" It can seem awkward, or pretentiously pious, or—well, just plain make you "look dumb." Hey, I understand that feeling! And I've had to do that very thing.

Not long ago I was speaking with a brother on the phone and I blurted out something I shouldn't have said. It wasn't a lie, profane, or impure, but I had spoken something unworthy, careless, exaggerated. I stopped: "John," I said interrupting myself. "Wait a minute—I've got to go back.

"You know me well enough to know I'm not trying to appear to be some 'supersaint' or 'holy Joe,' but I shouldn't have said what I did a moment ago."

I went back, recited the comment to him, and then continued, "Just let me pray a minute, John." And I said:

"Jesus, please neutralize those careless words. Forgive me for sloppy speech and for in any way polluting my brother's ears with it. I put those words under Your Blood for covering, cleansing, and release. Thank you, Lord."

Then, I resumed. "Sorry, John, for interrupting—now, what were you saying?"

And that was it.

He knew where I was coming from, and we proceeded with our conversation with my integrity of heart repaired and intact.

Racing with God

Paramount to walking in integrity is to pursue our "race course" of faith in a *way* that does not disqualify us. The Apostle Paul uses two metaphors from the field of athletics—running and boxing. In both figures his objective is to point out the danger of "disqualification"—not of losing citizenship, not of death, not even of consuming dishonor—simply being "out of the running." The sacrifice of our heart's integrity can disqualify us from "running our race" faithfully with God.

Do you not know that those who run in a race all run, but one receives the prize? Run in such a way that you may obtain it. And everyone who competes for the prize is temperate in all things. Now they do it to obtain a perishable crown, but we for an imperishable crown. Therefore I run thus: not with uncertainty. Thus I fight: not as one who beats the air. But I discipline my body and bring it into subjection, lest, when I have preached to others, I myself should become disqualified.

1 Corinthians 9:24-27

Disqualified. That's a chilling term. It doesn't mean condemned to hell. But what does it mean?

I heard a pastor once describe this with a simple illustration. He said that in his desk he had many pens; but that one section in his drawer was for pens which no longer worked. They were no longer able to write or function properly, having been dulled or broken through misuse or uncleanness.

When asked why he kept these pens that didn't write, he noted they were either gifts from loved ones or commemorative pens from special events. Thus, he kept them as his—they were valuable to him even though they didn't write, but they had become "disqualified" for use.

So it is, God may not reject us from His family because we fall from His highest purposes through self-will or uncleanness. But the "disqualified" category can render us unfit for the Master's use, just by leaving us "laying in a drawer," instead of being fruitful, inscribing new words of life on the scroll of other human lives.

Listen! The Apostle Paul announces his own program of self-discipline: "I bring my body into subjection." The literal figure he uses employs the ancient Greek term for a boxer's knock-out punch. He is literally saying, "I deal my flesh a knock-out blow—putting it down for the full count of ten!" The reason? He wanted to be an instrument in the Master's hand—one who would win the match against the flesh and the devil. He determined to keep his heart tuned—to be integrated, all the pieces fitting together—walking in integrity.

Let's follow Paul as he followed Christ, doubtless in the spirit of David's words: "With my whole heart have I sought You; Oh, let me not wander from your commandments!" (Psalm 119:10).

Chapter Three:
Integrity of Heart—
A Study in Contrasts

There are two unforgettable personalities in the Old Testament which provide a pointed insight into the meaning of "integrity of heart" when they are studied in contrast. They are David and Solomon— father and son: two dynamic kings who shaped the history of a nation, bringing it unto breadth of boundaries and unto beauty of regality.

From the time of David's early beginnings, God anointed him with success after success in battle. So it was by the time David's throne was established in Jerusalem, the boundaries of the twelve reunited tribes stretched over a vast domain which came as close to fulfilling Abraham's vision as at any time in Bible history.

It is in this setting that it seems David must have written the words in a song celebrating the power-potential of a heart of integrity. Listen:

Consider my enemies for they are many; and they hate me with a cruel hatred. Oh, keep my soul, and deliver me; let me not be ashamed for I put my trust in You. Let integrity and uprightness preserve me, for I wait for You.

34

Redeem Israel, O God, out of all their
troubles!   *Psalm 25:19-22*

As you listen to this song, a heartcry is
sent forth to the Lord pointing out the
surrounding presence of enemies which
would seek to encroach upon David's
kingdom—to smite, to smash, to smother!
The king is painfully aware of a peculiar fact:
He has been blest with such broad boundaries, that there is no way he can secure
them with any number of troops. He is
vulnerable to the secret attack of an
enemy—unless. . .

"Oh God, keep me. . .deliver me. . .pre-
serve me."

Unless the Lord guards the boundaries,
there is no hope of detection—no early warning signals of an advancing host. And so
David makes an agreement with the Lord:
"Lord, let my integrity (the completeness of
my devotion to You) and uprightness (my
commitment to *do* right as You teach me
Your way—Lord, let those things become
my defense under Your hand!"

Do you understand, brother, what this
man is saying to God—what he is making as
the bond of His trust, dependence, and
covenant? David is saying, "Lord, YOU BE
MY DEFENSE!! I'll walk with a pure heart
before You, and let THAT be my means to

know that You'll keep me alert, prepared, and will direct me when I need to take action."

In short, David is pointing to a lifestyle that comes to terms with the fact, "I can't be everywhere, doing everything, all the time—trying to preserve my hindparts, trying to verify my worth; trying to win by the power of my scheme and hand.

"But, I *can* keep a right heart before the Lord, and let Him teach me, show me, lead me, and instruct me at any time, concerning anything where I need to take action that will keep the boundaries of blessing tended."

This isn't an argument for sloth or laziness, as though a pure heart doesn't need to pay attention to life's duties. But it is to note that, for example:

• I can't, as a businessman, "cover" every conversation of people who might try to oppose me or denigrate my work;

• I can't, as a parent, be everywhere my kids are and know every influence that's being brought to bear upon them;

• I can't, as a busy person in an informationally-exploding world, keep up with every new thing that might impact my well-being—either as a threat or as a blessing.

But I *can* do this: I can do my best at my

job, my family life, and my daily enterprise—but *then*, I need to be able to cast myself on the Lord's adequacy *in the knowledge I've not violated any trust with Him or others that would prohibit His free and powerful hand defending, providing for, and protecting me*! Like David, we can then say:

Vindicate me, O Lord, for I have walked in my integrity. I have also trusted in the Lord; I shall not slip.

Psalm 26:1

This is the David of whom the Lord spoke: "He's a man after My own heart!" And the heart of God was moved by the heart of a man committed to keep trust with Him. (It's another study, but even in David's most miserable failures—when heart-trust and integrity were grossly violated, we find his repentance pressing back into this heart-to-heart, close-walk with God [Psalm 51].)

Another King

Through the best and worst of times, God kept His covenant with David; David's boundaries were preserved, and his son Solomon inherited a broad and wealthy kingdom. Solomon was appropriately humble at the time he received this heritage:

Then Solomon stood before the altar of the Lord in the presence of all the assembly of Israel, and spread out his hands toward heaven; and he said: "Lord God of Israel, there is no God in heaven above or on earth below like You, who keep Your covenant and mercy with Your servants who walk before You with all their hearts. You have kept what You promised Your servant David my father; You have both spoken with Your mouth and fulfilled it with Your hand, as it is this day. Therefore, Lord God of Israel, now keep what You promised Your servant David my father, saying, 'You shall not fail to have a man sit before Me on the throne of Israel, only if your sons take heed to their way, that they walk before Me as you have walked before Me.' "

1 Kings 8:22-25

Solomon was saying, "Lord, keep this kingdom by the power of Your hand and promise." Only a few days later the Lord spoke to Solomon in answer:

And the Lord said to him: "I have heard your prayer and your supplication that you have made before Me; I have consecrated this house which you have built to put My name there forever, and My eyes and My heart will be there perpetually. Now if you walk before Me as your father David walked, in integrity of heart and in uprightness, to do according to all that I have commanded you, and if you keep My statutes and My judgments, then I will establish the throne of your kingdom over Israel forever, as I promised David your father, saying, 'You shall not fail to have a man on the throne of Israel.' But if you or your sons at all turn from following Me, and do not keep My commandments and My statutes which I have set before you, but go and serve other gods and worship them, then I will cut off Israel from the land which I have given them; and this house which I have consecrated for My name I will cast out of My sight. Israel will be a proverb and a byword among all peoples."

1 Kings 9:3-7

Here is God's answer: "I will perpetuate your kingdom, your boundaries, your family, your enterprise *if you will walk before Me in integrity of heart as your father David!!*" It's a clear pattern that holds promise for you and me: God will repeat protecting and providing acts He has shown in the past to those who walked with Him, but we enter into that covenant by moving on the same pathways of walking with Him as those who were so protected and provided for before.

This works in business, in your relationships, in your family, in your decisions, in your problems, in your opportunities, in your times of pain, in your high challenges, *in all your ways*!! BUT—it works *only* where a heart of integrity can be found at the center of a man's life and thoughts.

Solomon's Mistake

Solomon adopted a different strategy than his father David did for preserving his kingdom's boundaries. Instead of the pathway of trust (sealed with a heart of integrity), he took the pathway of treaties—sealed with the covenant of marriage to pagan princesses whom he married as a part of making alliances with neighboring nations.

But King Solomon loved many foreign women, as well as the daughter of Pharaoh: women of the Moabites, Ammonites, Edomites, Sidonians, and Hittites; from the nations of whom the Lord had said to the children of Israel, "You shall not intermarry with them, nor they with you. Surely they will turn away your hearts after their gods." Solomon clung to these in love.
1 Kings 11:1-2

This was not merely a matter of carnal passion. This is a man who is surrendering to "business savvy" instead of the "wisdom of God." It seemed wise to strike treaties, marry the neighboring kings' daughters, and thereby preserve the boundaries through the supposition that conceding to earthly wisdom would secure his throne. But it became his downfall.

"They turned away his heart," the Bible says; the same way that seemingly minor concessions of a man's personal integrity can do. While seeming insignificant at the moment—

- a slight indulgence,
- a "white" lie,
- a passing flirtation,
- a small compromise,
- an "adjusted" dollar figure,
- an unpaid-for stamp or office resource,
- a "fudged" expense report,
- an accepted "gift" for "special" services rendered—

The list of potential "princesses" welcomed to secure your own boundaries is endless.

Sir, Solomon didn't set out to have 1000 wives! He became the victim of a pathway that supposes that self-preservation and self-advancement are obtained by human manipulation. Instead, the Lord says:

OF PROTECTION: "Unless the Lord guards the city, the watchman stays awake in vain." (Psalm 127:1)

OF PROMOTION: "Promotion comes neither from the east, west, or south. . .for God puts down one and exalts another." (Psalm 75:6, 7)

The perpetuation of God's purposes in our lives is assured on the grounds of our simple, childlike openness and obedience to Him. Integrity of heart is *not* attained through a legalistic attention to ritual law. Integrity of heart is *not* the result of having mastered eerie spiritual discipline. But integrity of heart IS the result of a man who will (1) keep tuned to the "pings" of Holy Spirit correction prompting his soul, and who will (2) keep wholly, completely, entirely dependent upon the Lord.

Little children, keep yourselves from idols.   *1 John 5:21*

Keep your heart with all diligence, for out of it spring the issues of life.   *Proverbs 4:23*

Chapter Four:
Men Learning Integrity in the Business Place

Some of the most dynamic insights we ever gain come straight from the experience of others who tell of their learning, however imperfectly, to apply God's Word to the practical details of their lives. I've invited nine men from among the hundreds I've watched grow into men of integrity, to briefly relate tension points which became triumph points. These faced very real "integrity" issues, and each in different circumstances overcame an assortment of obstacles that would have rendered them "disqualified," had they not applied biblical principles.

Sensitivity to these brothers, who have been willing to share their weaknesses and strengths with us, recommends that I refer to them by profession only. The testimonies are theirs. They are true. And the integrity issues dealt with in realms of business, morality, relationships, and spiritual leadership will, I hope, inspire you just as those brothers have inspired me.

The Business Deal
An investment real estate broker with a large Los Angeles firm.

It was the first week of 1990. I would

later call this season the "financial winter of my life." There was no fruit, no leaves, no indication of anything particularly good about to "bud" forth in our lives financially speaking. Things looked bleak, but we stood fast waiting for the blessing of the Lord.

Then a very large deal came into the works. It was a $5 million sale that promised to yield a *huge* commission! Needless to say, this was an exciting prospect.

But suddenly the heart-rending news came. It was discovered that the buyer was engaged in a "double escrow," which meant that although he was buying it at $5 million, he was turning around to sell it at $7 million to a controlled buyer with a "rigged" appraisal. What he was doing was dishonest, and I knew I couldn't participate in this scam. So, I handed the sale over to another broker, refusing to handle the deal—and knowing I was giving away an easy-money windfall.

That was tough. For it was a *lot* of money.

Two years later at our church, the Holy Spirit had declared the New Year to be "The Year of the Lord's Redeemed." My wife and I reached back in faith and prayed that God would redeem that large sale that went bad at the last minute. Because we had acted *in the integrity of our hearts*, we believed that the Lord would repay us.

There were a number of business deals that surfaced throughout the year which looked like they might be God's "redemption" of that horrible disappointment two years before, but each one of them, for one reason or another, fell through.

On December 21st—nearly the last week of "The Year of the Lord's Redeemed"—as I was leaving with my family for a Christmas trip, the phone rang. It was a bank who owned a large property upon which, earlier that year, one of my clients had made an offer. But his offer had been declined in favor of a higher offer made by someone else. Now the caller apprised me that that higher offer had fallen out of escrow, and as a result, this was a "panic" call from the bank, which needed to sell the property before the year ended. My client's offer of $5.2 million was accepted, and precisely on December 31st—the last day of the "Year of the Lord's Redeemed"—the escrow closed. The commission it yielded was the largest I've ever had the pleasure of receiving—and all the more gratifying for it was received with a *free* heart, unencumbered by anything less than a fullness of integrity.

A Subtle Issue of Discrimination

A vice-president for a major financial institution who manages a portfolio of real estate investments for pension fund clients.

For many years I've subscribed to the belief that the "good" and the "right" courses of action in business are the same—whether I'm dealing with believers or non-believers. Unfortunately, with disturbing frequency, I have experienced a problem when dealing with other Christians who didn't grasp or apply this principle. It seems that once they found out I was also a believer, they would expect me to give them special concessions or render to them preferential treatment just because they were believers. While I often enjoyed business-related fellowship with other Christians, it seemed to me that *right* dealings were *right*, no matter what the other party believed in terms of their spiritual commitment. Why should I treat a Christian with "more fairness" and a non-believer with less? Without my consciously realizing it, these experiences with other Christians made me progressively reluctant to openly proclaim my faith to other believers whom I might encounter in the course of my business. But with time, the Lord began to deal with me about this issue.

Several years ago I had a group of commercial properties in Texas added to my portfolio, including a notable shopping center in Austin—a property which was in serious trouble. My first order of business was to select and hire a local real estate broker to assist me in leasing the property, preferably one with a reputation for being the "best in town." During my first couple of trips there I talked with as many people in the business as I could, gathering referrals for my file. Interestingly enough, the name of one particular broker kept coming up with notable frequency. Jill had a reputation for high integrity and great effectiveness in her work. So I arranged a meeting with Jill, and in the course of casual conversation, we discovered that we were both Christians.

At first, I was tempted not to hire Jill. I was afraid that someone might accuse me of favoring her because she was a believer (and an outspoken one, at that). And I was concerned that I might have the same problem with her that I'd so often had with other Christians in the business—that she would expect me to somehow give her firm some special allowances because of our mutual faith in Christ. However, I realized that since I'd made up my mind to hire Jill *before* I knew she was a believer, to *not* hire her now would mean I'd be making a decision based solely on her Christianity—a violation of my own heart integrity. I would be doing the very same thing I had felt so strongly against—the very thing I didn't want people to do to me: act differently towards me because I was a Christian. And so I made my decision. I engaged Jill to be my Austin broker.

Over the ensuing three years, God both blessed our business enterprise and expanded my personal experience with Kingdom power at work in the business place. I'd never before prayed with a business-partner to accomplish specific business objectives. A little more than a year after praying together that God would help us lease the project's anchor tenant space (vacant for five years), Jill and I stood in the exact same place where we had prayed—only now we gazed not at a vacant space, but at the grand opening of the project's new anchor department store!

In another situation, our decision to lean on the generous side in calculating another broker's commission rights ultimately resulted in Jill leading that broker to the Lord.

Through these experiences I have learned a rich lesson not to be an "undercover" Christian in the workplace! The genuine exercise of Kingdom principles and the dynamics of agreement in prayer with other Christians has made for broader horizons of triumph in my business world—much more than I ever expected it would.

Taking An Offensive Stance

An international business consultant specializing in information systems architecture for Fortune 500 companies and mega-corporations.

It never goes away. The Lord deals with me all the time about issues of integrity. It's not because I'm weak or lukewarm in my commitment to Jesus. But the opportunities to compromise are ever-present. This is accentuated by the fact that as an international consultant, I'm traveling about 40% of the time. During many weeks of the year I'm away from home four days out of seven. I know from personal experience that business trips can be tough on Christians!

But the Lord has taught me how to approach this difficult way of life: I've learned how to put temptation on the *defensive*.

I no longer turn on the TV while in a hotel room. When I check into a hotel room I lay hands on the bed, the walls, the doors, and the windows, and I engage in spiritual warfare. I bind up any negative spiritual influences that may be present in that room. I pray against any spiritual residue that may be left over from sin that could have been committed in that room—spiritual influences that would seek to creep into my life. Another important part of my spiritual arsenal, especially in hotel rooms, is worship and praise to the Lord.

As a guest speaker on the road, I also go down to the large hotel conference rooms long before people arrive and I pray over the seats, over the podium—and in short, I storm the gates of heaven seeking God's Kingdom to come and be established in that place. I ask that God's will would be done on earth—in the arena of my business dealings—as it is in Heaven. I seek the Lordship of Jesus to rule in my sphere of influence.

I realize this may sound radical to you, but I assure you, I'm *not* a religious zealot! I simply love the Lord. And this kind of spiritual offensive not only keeps my integrity in check—at every level—but it has spiritual impact on others. It influences people who don't even know the Lord because they are being prayed for diligently.

As men living in the age of super computers, stock market realities, and marketing issues—whatever our line of work may be—we *have* to come to grips with issues of the invisible spiritual realm and how they affect our integrity.

For we do not wrestle against flesh and blood, but against principalities, against powers, against the rulers of the darkness of this age, against spiritual hosts of wickedness in the heavenly places.
Ephesians 6:12

Our human frailty must constantly face spiritual forces of temptation that seek to undo us. If we don't take an aggressive stand against issues of compromise, and pursue the Lord diligently in places where we might stumble, then our chances for success will be dramatically limited.

With the consequences of moral failure being so great, we are wise to keep temptation on the defensive. Try it. Go on the *offensive* against sin. It works—and victory *can* be realized!!

Chapter Five:
Men Learning Integrity in the Face of Moral Temptation

Having a "Single" Eye

Logistics Manager who has worked on NASA's Space Shuttle program. He's been married for over 30 years.

How many of you are TV channel flickers? By that I mean a person who is constantly changing channels with a TV remote so you can watch bits of many programs almost simultaneously. To the chagrin of my wife, I must plead guilty to this practice, but never did I imagine that this would have such a negative impact on my role as priest of my home. Let me explain what happened.

Recently, my wife and I subscribed to a basic cable system with some 72 channels to flick through ("hog heaven" for a bonafide "flicker"). We didn't want any of the premium channels or the decoder box that comes with them. That way, when you flick through unwanted channels the image appears as a series of wavy lines that makes it unviewable. That's what we understood, anyway.

One night, while flicking my way through TV land, I came across one of the premium channels. For some reason, the wavy lines were minimal and I could see clearly what was going on: men and women engaged in sex. I was surprised and shocked at what was on the screen. Even so, I allowed 20-30 seconds of observation to pass—feeling upset and disgusted at such garbage— nevertheless, I watched. I finally turned it off. There was a "yucky" feeling in my spirit for I knew I had done wrong by letting that junk enter the lamp of my soul, even though it was only a half a minute. I should have repented right then and there, but I didn't. I just shrugged it off and vowed to myself not to do that anymore. I didn't think much more about it, nor did I tell my wife what happened.

That night at 2:30 a.m. my wife and I were abruptly awakened by the ring of the phone. Since the phone is on my wife's side of the bed, she answered it. On the other end of the line was an obscene caller, whom my wife interrupted with words something like, "God loves you and He has a much better plan for your life than this kind of stuff," and she hung up the phone.

While all this was going on, the Lord was speaking to me. *So very clearly* He was telling me that what I had done had "uncovered" our home. I was responsible for letting that evil—in the form of a perverted phone call—come into my house and into my wife's ears. Because of what I allowed my eyes to see, I had, by my actions, "given permission" to the hosts of spiritual darkness to invade my dwelling—to arrange that call. My heart sank at the reality of knowing how true that was. I groaned at the thought of disappointing the Lord. Right then—after repenting before the Lord and confessing my sin to my wife—I settled the matter. And we went back to sleep. But what a vivid lesson.

I learned that my maintaining purity and integrity before the Lord will affect everything in my family's lives. Walking purely will prevent the enemy from having any inroads through which he can attack my family or me. I was reminded that as priest of my home, I needed to let my mind dwell on the words of Philippians 4:8, which urges us about monitoring our minds:

> *Finally, brethren, whatever things are true, whatever things are noble, whatever things are just, whatever things are pure, whatever things are lovely, whatever things are of good report, if there is any virtue and if there is anything praiseworthy; meditate on these things.*

Wrestling with Pornography

A former student who now serves on a church staff.

My introduction to pornography was as a little boy. My friend's father had a whole collection of pornographic magazines which I had the opportunity to look through on a couple of occasions.

That was the starting point of my many years of bondage to pornography. I would sneak peeks at the girlie magazines in drug stores and would get my hands on them whenever I got the chance.

Over the years, that escalated to hard-core magazines and X-rated movies. I could never seem to get enough of it. I really loved looking at that stuff.

There was one thing that made this part of my life rather difficult. I was a Christian, and had been for several years, but I found I had become *"blinded"* by my constant staring at pornographic material. Eventually, however, through involvement with men's gatherings at our church, I began to break through the blindness—I began feeling true guilt over looking at the pornography, and with the beginnings of these convictions, the wrestling match began.

I would weep before the Lord for my sense of shame and helplessness. I would stand on the Word of God and declare, "No temptation has overtaken you except such as is common to man; but God is faithful, who will not allow you to be tempted beyond what you are able, but with the temptation will also make the way of escape, that you may be able to bear it" (1 Cor. 10:13). I would quote Romans 6:14, "For sin shall not have dominion over you . . ."

I don't mean to (nor do I) minimize the power of the Word of God. And I don't mean to make light the power potential in speaking God's Word into situations that you face. But it wasn't making the difference in my life. I would go through seasons of victory where I would not yield to temptation, or feel very tempted. In my early 20's I even went more than two years without looking at pornography. But self-sufficiency—trusting in my own strength—was about to catch up with me.

One day, opening a magazine, I opened the door "just a crack." But to my embarrassment, I got "bashed in the head" as I began stumbling again. It was not with the same frequency as in the past, but it was enough to keep me feeling guilty and feeling like a hypocrite. Why? Because here I was, "Mr. Mature Christian"—having been a Christian more than half my life, and now even working in a church, and *still* not walking in the victory of a Christ-filled life in the Spirit.

But a new day dawned. And I began to experience a new level of deliverance as I began to OBEY the scripture in James 5:16:

> *Confess your trespasses to one another, and pray for one another, that you may be healed. The effective, fervent prayer of a righteous man avails much.*

It took a great deal of humbling myself to open up to someone else, and to—with integrity of heart—share the "crud" that was in my life. But I knew if I obeyed God and went beyond my own feelings, He would meet me there and do the work in me that needed to be done. And He has, PRAISE GOD!

As long as I kept the sin only "between God and me," I could not gain the victory.

I knew I was forgiven.

I knew I had been cleansed by the precious Blood of Jesus.

But as long as nobody else knew about it, it was easy to sin again. While I didn't *plot* to keep on sinning, it seemed I couldn't get beyond a certain place as long as I kept it to myself.

Opening my heart in confidence with another brother in the Lord became a God-ordained strength for me. Whenever I would feel weak, I knew there was somebody there I could talk with and pray with. And even when I would succumb to the temptation, I would share that with my prayer partner and not allow the Adversary the old place of dominion in my life by keeping it between me and God only.

There is also the feeling of not wanting to have to confess the same old sin to my prayer partner again, so I often withstand the temptation based on that. It's not that he would have any negative thoughts toward me, but I want to behave accountably—I don't want to have to always keep mentioning old things!!

Brother, there is victory when you partner with another brother or brothers. It's powerful to learn to trust one another, and grow in strength with one another as you walk together with them and with Jesus—in integrity of heart.

Lessons Regarding
Sexual Temptation

As a film director, this brother was hired to make a motion picture about the people and culture of France for a popular theme park. Sexual temptation was something he least expected to encounter while doing this family entertainment project.

I was working on a film which required significant location scouting, which meant that before I ever shot any film, I had to go on extensive tours of the cities and country-sides of France—the real "star" of the film. This film required the full cooperation of the French Government, so as I embarked on this 5-week tour of France, my personal escort was a French Government official, who turned out to be a very beautiful woman. This was a big problem because my attraction to this woman was immediate, and I would have to work closely with her in order to make this multi-million dollar project happen.

Before I proceed, let me point out the strengths and weaknesses I carried with me into this situation.

Strengths:

• I rarely have problems with lust;

• I was raised in a godly home so the concept of sexual purity was deeply in-grained in me throughout childhood (I was a virgin until my wedding night);

• I'm happily married to a woman I find extremely attractive;

• I'm determined to never let the Lord or my wife down.

Weaknesses:

• At that time, my wife had just given birth to our first child . . . and as many men know, that's a season of abstinence which can enhance one's vulnerability.

• This was my first trip overseas. Nobody over there knew me. I was totally separated from accountability.

• I was rising fast in my career. This can produce an euphoric and foolish feeling of power that sometimes makes you feel like all "the rules" don't apply to you.

• This woman—my key government contact—to whom I was strongly attracted, was *also* attracted to me.

Added to all of these liabilities was the fact that this woman and I were touring the most romantic country on earth. It was "first class" all the way with chauffeurs, the best hotels of Europe, four-star restaurants—just like a $100,000 dream vacation.

During this whole time she made verbal invitations toward me. She would continually reserve adjoining hotel rooms with one thin door separating the two rooms. To say the least, it was important for me to stay in touch with my wife by phone during this trip.

One night, as part of our scouting circuit, we were sitting in a restaurant in a romantic port village. The hotel was just upstairs. After dinner this woman hit me with a direct proposition. I responded as I did to all the other advances she'd made before: I again simply affirmed with a smile, "I just can't. I'm a happily married man." I strove to be diplomatic, but direct.

That night in my hotel room, I experienced tremendous inner conflict. Here I was, a Bible-believing Christian, absolutely committed to serving the Lord in purity, madly in love with my wife, yet I was shocked at how overwhelming the force of temptation was. While praying earnestly to God for help, it occurred to me to confront myself in the mirror. I looked into my own eyes and said out loud all the reasons why it would be absolutely wrong and disastrous to commit adultery. I took out a picture of my wife. And into the mirror, I reaffirmed my love for her and the scriptural truth of walking in obedience to God.

So that evening, as well as throughout the entire trip, I escaped the clutches of disaster. I'm happy to say that we didn't even touch beyond our first handshake.

I should also point out that the old adage about cold showers is accurate. They work. I took several during the trip.

Here's what I learned through the entire experience:

(1) Regardless of how great our holy zeal may be or how strong our Christian upbringing was, we all have "fallen flesh" that

is extremely vulnerable to temptation.

(2) Never play with infatuation. The early stages of temptation are fun. It is such an ego-boost to have a woman be "interested" in you. But don't even think about flirting, i.e., getting too friendly.

(3) Avoid tempting situations. Now that I've been through that experience in France, I've been more careful than ever. In recent years I've had to interview potential secretaries for my business. On two occasions, I had a very frustrating time finding anyone qualified for our unique demands. Yet, on both occasions, the only women perfect for the job were particularly good looking and a bit "forward." So I felt it would be best to keep searching for qualification without potential temptation.

(4) Be accountable. On my French tour I tried to be accountable to a non-Christian associate, but he said, "Gosh, I hope you won't regret passing on this great opportunity!" (Thanks, buddy!)

That 5-week French tour came in two segments. So before the second segment began, I went back home to the States and was able to tell my Christian friend about the temptation I would be facing during the remaining three weeks. I told him that when I returned from the trip, he needed to ask me how well I did in resisting temptation. I asked him to "grill me." Knowing that I would be coming home to that interrogation really helped, in addition to diligent prayer, and—when the temptation reached dangerous levels—affirming to myself in the mirror the Truth of God's Word and the folly of sin.

Chapter Six:
Men Learning
Integrity in Relationships

Integrity with My Wife
A seminar speaker on tax law and who has an income tax practice.

Last year my wife and I were at a point where we needed to "tighten the belt" on our finances. I told her that we needed to stop any unnecessary spending for several months. She and I agreed that we would both postpone buying any "extras" for ourselves until our finances were in better shape.

One week after telling her this, I went with a friend to a special garage sale—one that featured baseball cards. This is an area of great interest to me because I have made significant investments in the baseball card market. (If a person knows what he's doing and is patient, it can be quite a lucrative instrument of investment.) At this sale I found a rare rookie card which I've wanted to purchase for quite some time. Not only that, but the seller had *two* of them and he made me a deal I *couldn't* refuse. I went to the bank and withdrew the money needed to buy the cards. It was such a *great* deal—I just *knew* my wife would understand!

When I arrived at home, my wife asked me, "completely out of the blue," if I had purchased any baseball cards. Suddenly, I remembered our agreement that neither one was to make any extra purchases that were not absolutely necessary. Caught with her question hanging in the air, I quickly changed the subject so I could avoid admitting that I had transgressed our agreement.

As soon as I dodged the issue, I knew that I had crossed a line in the spiritual realm. Truth and deceit are very spiritual issues. I knew that if I didn't confess the fact that I had transgressed our agreement, it would be the first time in our relationship that I had ever lied to her.

But wait, did I *tell* my wife a lie? Had I *uttered words* of deceit?

No!

I had avoided an answer and was "scot-free," I was tempted to argue to myself!

But I had deceived her by withholding information that was tightly hinged to a mutual agreement. I was ducking into the shadows, avoiding the light of exposure. And that's a lie. I knew if I allowed deceit to enter our relationship now, our marriage would never be the same. *I* would never be the same. I would carry that sin around with me and it would cast a shadow on every area of my life: my marriage, my career, and my leadership at church. That's why sin is like leprosy—it spreads . . . until we confess it and repent.

I knew the Lord wanted me to get this issue dealt with fast. So I went to my wife and explained what had happened. Although I was willing to resell those coveted cards, my wife didn't feel I should. It was actually a relief for her to see my commitment to "keeping a clean slate" in our marriage. If I had confessed my sin to the Lord, and promised to not repeat the offense, but had not been willing to be accountable to my wife by admitting my willful transgression, not only would my integrity as a husband have suffered, but I would have allowed a small issue to become a wedge between me and my best friend—my wife.

I've never regretted telling the truth to this day . . . not even if it hurts, not even if it meant that I might have to resell a 1968 Nolan Ryan rookie card!

Surprised by Idolatry

A student, currently pursuing his undergraduate studies with a goal of eventual pastoral ministry.

It was late in the summer of 1988 and she was no longer displaying around her neck the small diamond pendant which I had given her for her birthday.

This was not a good sign.

Ever since I had given it to her, that pendant had been the barometer of our relationship's health—or lack of it. When our relationship was "on," the pendant was on her neck; when we were "off," the pendant was off. Two weeks after it had come off her neck, she broke up with me for the third and "final" time.

I went into my prayer closet—literally kneeling over my shoes and hunched under my shirts—and cried. It was the only place in the apartment where the neighbors wouldn't hear me wailing before the Lord. With tears streaming down my face, I brought my case before the throne of God.

"What happened? God, you promised!"

And I waited.

Nothing.

"How could You let her become so callous?" I cried again. "I committed my life to her with no compromise! I was determined that she would become everything Christ wanted her to be. I was committed to work with You in that process! God, she means *everything* to me! *I live for her!* She's supposed to become my wife! Lord, I love only her. I *idolize* her . . . ! I . . . *IDOL*!!??"

It was at this point in my prayer that the

realization struck. Something had gotten way out of alignment. I became quiet in my closet. I finally heard the Father's voice. He reminded me of my first love: Jesus.

What had happened to me was that my eyes had become so fixed on God's *promise* that I lost sight of *God*, the Giver of all good promises. My original commitment to this woman was good. It started out in right alignment for I sought "that I might sanctify and cleanse her with the washing of water by the word" (Ephesians 5:26). I had once said to her, "You may break up with me, you may end up hating me, but I am committed to your growth in Christ."

However, as I felt her slipping away, my response was to clamor and compromise in an attempt to preserve the relationship. That's where my priorities got jumbled. Like Abraham, I clamored for an Ishmael. Like Esau, I had sold my birthright. And the more I clamored, the more contempt she displayed toward me until the necklace came off the "final" time.

But God came down into my prayer closet where I wept in repentance. He met me there and restored my soul. And once my priorities were straightened out and Jesus was once again the first-love of my life, God was then free to work mightily and redemptively in my circumstances.

I praise God for showing me how the integrity—the *totality*—of my heart had been compromised. For having repented and re-prioritized, things were restored.

I thank the Lord that today that woman and I are serving the Lord together, and this November she and I will celebrate our fourth wedding anniversary, as we are expecting a baby to be added to our home.

Relationship with
Spiritual Leadership

A consultant to young CEOs in the area of path finding, strategic analysis, and repositioning.

Leadership is not a foreign virtue in the realm of my profession. In fact, I've dealt with leaders and leadership consistently in my line of work. However, within the first year of having been made a deacon in my church, the spiritual side of leadership gave rise to a number of new questions I hadn't before confronted.

On one hand, I wanted to be submissive and loyal to church leadership. Most of us know that to be an effective leader you need to be properly submitted to the authority over you. But on the other hand, I had strong convictions about certain aspects of direction that our church leadership was taking. There were a couple of issues I was uncomfortable with. While I wanted to continue being a church deacon, I also knew I had to express certain points of view that might not be popular with the pastor.

However, an interesting battle was going on inside of me. It was like a voice was saying, "Just keep your mouth shut! You're a deacon, and you've finally gained a certain amount of respect, so don't blow it or you'll lose it all! Maybe someday, if you hang in there, you'll be in a position to change how things are done."

In conflict with this voice, was another Voice: the Voice I now know was the Holy Spirit. It seemed to me Jesus was impressing these convictions upon my heart. It was as if He were saying: "I didn't make you a deacon so you could sit by quietly and give up your own points of view in order to protect your church position. What would be the purpose of My putting you in a church position, only for you to pretend to be someone other than who I made you to be? I want you to submit your viewpoint to leadership. Don't be afraid to be the 'real you.' That's the only kind of deacon I can use. Be prepared to resign if they find your views aren't representative and supportive to the direction of the church."

So, I sent a letter to my pastor telling him my views and offering my resignation if he felt my views were not representative of the type of leadership our church required. He then asked if I wanted to discuss my opinions. I agreed to meet with him and he later spent several hours answering my questions. During our conversation, God gently showed me how much I didn't know about what was going on at the church and why things were being done the way they were. I was humbled.

After coming to a greater understanding of our church's focus and the purpose for their mode of operation, I withdrew my resignation. And later, I became more involved than ever in building ministry within the church. Had I buried my convictions or just become cynical and unsubmissive, I would not have been able to move into more authority in God's plan. Leadership in ministry grew out of lining up my beliefs with my actions and walking in the responsibility in which God had placed me. It involved integrity of heart toward (1) my convictions, (2) the Lord's corrections, and (3) my deeper call to committed service.

Expressing conflicting convictions to people, especially people in authority, isn't comfortable for any of us. And to express our opinions does not mean we are necessarily being rebellious or unsubmissive. It's all in the motivation of the heart and the spirit in which it is shared.

True submission is also uncomfortable at times.

It was ironic that as I submitted to God and expressed myself, my pastor took me seriously enough to submit himself to me! This had a profound impact on my understanding of God's authority and how God wants us to follow willingly, and learn the true spirit of servant-leadership. He desires to remove any impediments to our unbelief or obedience. But that removal must start with a recognition and dealing before God with the conflict in our hearts. By obeying God's leading to speak, although it was difficult, I understood the deacon role and responsibility at a deeper level. Although the truth seemed to hurt at first, in reality it healed.

Chapter Seven:
Integrity of Heart—
In Front of Jesus

For over twenty years I have been privileged to be the invited guest of conference after conference where either hundreds or thousands of pastors would gather for edification and inspiration toward ministry. It is safe to say that I've ministered to a half-million pastors in one way or another—having travelled to over 20 nations, and time and again across the United States, not to mention via cassettes, radio, and television.

I refer to this fact, not as a point of pretension or pride, but because it might help you, dear brother, grasp the number of times I have been asked a certain question. It is phrased in many ways, but the essence of the inquiry is a desire to know a "secret" or a "key" to effective life and growth as a servant-leader under Jesus Christ.

Many want to know the number of hours I pray daily—the number of hours I read the Word—the number of hours per week I prepare sermons—the number of personal calls I make on people. . .Always, always, always, the question is—"How MUCH DO YOU DO to assure God's blessing on your life?"

It's the human mistake we all are inclined toward. It's based on the idea that the achievement of *some* quantity of *something* is a guarantee of success, whatever a person's life goal or vocation.

But my answer has always been the same; pointing to the fact that the *only quantity* God is really interested in as far as our lives are concerned is that *our whole heart* be His.

The subject of this small book has focused on the matter of "integrity of heart," noting that true integrity—by definition—involves the whole, the complete, the entire, the undiminished, the unfragmented, the totality of our heart being opened *to* Father God, shapeable *by* the Holy Spirit, and growing *in* Jesus Christ.

To conclude, I want to relate a story which I think may summarize *how* such a walk with the Lord may be perpetuated.

I Was About Eleven Years Old

When I was a boy, I was early introduced to a means my mother would use in dealing with each of us children—my brother, my sister, and me. Whenever Mama thought any of us might be tempted to be less than truthful because of the pressure of a situation where possible correction may follow an honest confession, she would take a precautionary step.

Instead of simply asking, "Did you do (such and such). . .?"; she would precede the question with a statement. This statement had a very sobering effect on me, because it so vividly evidenced the reality of

74

my accountability to be truthful in the eyes of God. Mama would say, "I'm going to ask you a difficult question, Jack. But before I do, I want to say, I'm asking it 'in front of Jesus.'"

She wasn't playing games.

She wasn't threatening.

She wasn't using a religious ploy.

Rather, in our house we took the Lord seriously. Our home was a happy place to live, but we really believed in the genuine things about God's love, His kindness, His blessing, His salvation in Christ, and the beautiful truth of His Word. And when Mama would say, "In front of Jesus," a powerful image would come to my mind.

We all knew God is everywhere, all the time. But there was a unique sense of the immediacy of the Living Lord when those words were spoken. I could imagine Jesus seated on a throne immediately to my left as I stood face-to-face with my mother and prepared to hear whatever question she had.

A Visit to Dicky's House

I had come home from a friend's house one afternoon, having been most of the morning at Dicky's—a kid a few months older than I who lived across the street. We played together a great deal of the time, so there was no reason for anything unusual to be thought when I, an 11-year old boy, came home that day.

But I discovered the next morning as I

was about to leave for school, that my mother had "felt" something about my return home that day.

I had just finished my breakfast and was about to leave the kitchen and get my school things so I could head out. But I was stopped before I left the room, when my mother turned from the kitchen sink, and while drying her hands said, "Jack—I want you to wait a minute. I need to talk with you."

Her voice had that tone which children recognize of their parents when the issue is sobering and the consequences might be undesirable. I stood there, nervously waiting for what she was going to say.

"Son, when you came home from Dicky's yesterday, I had a very strange feeling go through me." She paused, thoughtfully. "At first, I didn't know what to do about it; then, I prayed last night, and I believe the Lord showed me simply to do what I'm doing right now."

"Jack, I want to ask you what happened at Dicky's house yesterday. And I'm asking this—*in front of Jesus.*"

I was frozen to the floor. The moment was one of those crystalline ones which seems as though it could be shattered by a whisper. On the one hand, I *knew* what happened at Dicky's house and knew I didn't want anyone else to know. And on the other hand—there to my left—the Throne of my Living Savior, Jesus Christ, was as real to me as though I were in heaven itself.

I began slowly. . .awkwardly. . .guiltily.

"Well, Mama," I said rather quietly and with hesitation. "When I was at Dicky's, after we'd been playing in the living room for a long time, he said to me, 'C'mon into my room a minute.'

"When he said that, he kinda laughed, and looked around to see if his mom or dad were anywhere they could hear. Right then I felt something bad was about to happen, but I went with him anyway.

"When we got in his room, he closed the door and then opened one of the drawers in the chest there. He reached way back and brought out a little tiny telescope."

I hesitated all the more, feeling the embarrassment of the confession I was about to make.

"But Mama, it wasn't a telescope." I paused again. Waiting. Not wanting to go on. "Instead, Mama, when you looked into it, there was. . .a naked woman." My eyes were moist. I looked into the face of my mother, feeling ashamed.

"What did you do, Son?" she inquired.

"We laughed," I admitted.

"How did you feel then?"

"Mama," I said with sincerity, "I felt bad."

" Then, Son. What do you want to do now?"

I walked toward my mother, whose arms opened to me as I did, as I said, "I want to pray, Mama."

And we did.

And although that event took place over four decades ago, at its root is a truth that has always continued to be just as alive and present today as it was then. *I am living my life in front of Jesus.*

I'll never know how many things that morning's confrontation and confession may have saved me from in my yet-to-be-realized future as a teenager and young man. Just as surely as I don't really know "how many" of anything I do or have done may have contributed to some degree of fruitfulness in my life and ministry, as others have asked me to quantify human efforts.

But I do know this.

I know that there are no limits to what God can do *in* a life, what He can do *through* a life, and what He can grow *around* and *within* a life, when it's lived—*in front of Jesus.*

That's the place where integrity of heart will always be sustained. For our consciousness will be on Him, not on things. And with Jesus in view, all life, fruitfulness, and fulfillment are certain to be realized with time—however tempting or trying the path.

Let's live our lives out that way.

In front of Jesus.

DEVOTIONS

IN THE FIRST EPISTLE TO
TIMOTHY

Contributed by Bob Anderson

With this epistle, the Apostle Paul was seeking to encourage Timothy, a young pastor, as he led the congregation at Ephesus through a number of difficult problems. Timothy had a significant amount of work cut out for him: false teaching needed to be effectively fought with the Truth; church leaders needed to be chosen with wisdom; different social classes in the church required extra sensitivity; and church worship needed to be brought into order. All of this was to be accomplished while maintaining an exemplary life, accurately teaching the apostolic faith!

This epistle has not only served as a universal handbook for pastors and leaders throughout the ages, but it is a particularly relevant book for any man pursuing deeper spiritual maturity.

(It is suggested that this devotional be used for stimulating discussion and prayer within a small group of men meeting regularly.)

☐ **Today's Text: 1 Timothy 1:1-4** *(key v. 3)*

1 **Today's Truth:** Paul's first order of business was to charge Timothy to confront false teachers—an issue Paul had previously discussed with him. In addition to the spreading of erroneous doctrine that mixed law with grace, there were those who expanded Old Testament genealogies, making up names that didn't exist and stories to go with them.

Today's Thoughts: _____

_____

_____

☐ **Today's Text: 1 Timothy 1:5-7** *(key v. 5)*

2 **Today's Truth:** For those who love "bottom-line" conclusions, verse five is a treasure. God's commandment doesn't stimulate debate or the wrestling with words as human philosophies do. Rather, it produces within people an unhypocritical faith, a conscience free of guilt, and a heart that flows with pure love.

Today's Thoughts: _____

_____

_____

☐ **Today's Text: 1 Timothy 1:8-11** *(key v. 8)*

3 **Today's Truth:** The law is designed to instruct the ignorant and to judge the ungodly, not to condemn those who walk with Christ in faith.

Today's Thoughts: _____

_____

_____

☐ **Today's Text: 1 Timothy 1:12-14** *(key v. 14)*

4 **Today's Truth:** Paul describes the Lord's grace as "exceedingly abundant." The Greek phrase is very strong, conveying the idea that the grace of God "super-abounded" toward Paul.

Today's Thoughts: _____

_____

_____

☐ **Today's Text: 1 Timothy 1:15-17** *(key v. 16)*

5 **Today's Truth:** At times, we are all woefully aware of our own unworthiness and sinful depravity. But Jesus provided a "showcase" of grace in Paul, "the chiefest of sinners," so that we may take heart. None of us is out of God's reach to save. (cf. Isaiah 50:2a)

Today's Thoughts: _____

_____

_____

☐ **Today's Text: 1 Timothy 1:18-20** *(key v. 18)*

6 **Today's Truth:** It's interesting that Paul's charge to Timothy to "wage the good warfare" was predicated upon "prophecies previously made" concerning him. In order to fight effectively, we need to be confident of God's personal direction for us.

Today's Thoughts: _____

_____

_____

82

☐ **Today's Text:** 1 Timothy 2:1-4 *(key v. 1)*

7 **Today's Truth:** Paul's words are challenging yet very comforting at the same time. Regardless of who sits on human thrones, there is One to Whom we can bring our government in prayer and see dramatic results. Because all earthly thrones exist in the shadow of His, we can pray with confidence.

Today's Thoughts: _____

_____

_____

☐ **Today's Text:** 1 Timothy 2:5-7 *(key v. 5)*

8 **Today's Truth:** Jesus is the ultimate Mediator between man and God because He is both. We do not come to a "representative" of God, we come to God in human form—the Son of Man.

Today's Thoughts: _____

_____

_____

☐ **Today's Text:** 1 Timothy 2:8-10 *(key v. 8)*

9 **Today's Truth:** The physical expression of up-raised hands can be a difficult step for someone new to this pattern of worship. It cuts deep into human pride, and by its very posture acknowledges human surrender and dependence upon God. But that's what makes it so powerful! When our worship is lifted *up* in such childlike openness, that's when God sends *down* His power!

Today's Thoughts: _____

_____

_____

☐ **Today's Text:** 1 Timothy 2:11-15 *(key v. 11)*

10 **Today's Truth:** This verse is not a prohibition of women speaking in church, but rather has to do with quietness of demeanor; a call to not being "mouthy," pushy, brash, or haranguing.

Today's Thoughts: ——————————

——————————————————

——————————————————

☐ **Today's Text:** 1 Timothy 3:1-7 *(key v.3)*

11 **Today's Truth:** A key word describing a man who "rules his own house well" is *gentle*. The Greek word conveys someone who is "fair, reasonable, and considerate," not legalistic or harsh.

Today's Thoughts: ——————————

——————————————————

——————————————————

☐ **Today's Text:** 1 Timothy 3:8-11 *(key v. 11)*

12 **Today's Truth:** When Paul says the wife of a spiritual leader is to be *reverent*, the Greek conveys that she is to be "worthy of respect"—a decent and honorable person—just as husbands are also to be *reverent* in their demeanor.

Today's Thoughts: _____

——————————————————

——————————————————

☐ **Today's Text: 1 Timothy 3:12-16** *(key v. 16)*

13 **Today's Truth:** When Paul proclaims "great is the mystery of godliness," he's not saying, "Boy, who could EVER understand this?" The word *mystery* in the New Testament means "something once hidden which is now revealed." It's "great" in its *significance and power*, not in its *obscurity*.

Today's Thoughts: ⎯⎯⎯⎯⎯⎯⎯⎯

⎯⎯⎯⎯⎯⎯⎯⎯⎯⎯⎯⎯⎯⎯⎯⎯

⎯⎯⎯⎯⎯⎯⎯⎯⎯⎯⎯⎯⎯⎯⎯⎯

☐ **Today's Text: 1 Timothy 4:1-5** *(key v.1)*

14 **Today's Truth:** Nobody begins their faith-walk intending to fall away. And nobody who walks in faith with Jesus needs to walk in tormenting fear of eventually falling away someday. As long as we live in submission to those in spiritual authority over us and we're accountable to one another, we have a great safeguard against backsliding.

Today's Thoughts: ⎯⎯⎯⎯⎯⎯⎯⎯

⎯⎯⎯⎯⎯⎯⎯⎯⎯⎯⎯⎯⎯⎯⎯⎯

⎯⎯⎯⎯⎯⎯⎯⎯⎯⎯⎯⎯⎯⎯⎯⎯

☐ **Today's Text: 1 Timothy 4:6-8** *(key v. 8)*

15 **Today's Truth:** Paul's not rejecting the virtues of physical exercise. He's putting it all in perspective: godliness is forever, affecting our entire being.

Today's Thoughts: ⎯⎯⎯⎯⎯⎯⎯⎯

⎯⎯⎯⎯⎯⎯⎯⎯⎯⎯⎯⎯⎯⎯⎯⎯

⎯⎯⎯⎯⎯⎯⎯⎯⎯⎯⎯⎯⎯⎯⎯⎯

☐ **Today's Text: 1 Timothy 4:9-11** *(key v. 10)*

16 **Today's Truth:** Why do we give the Lord our personal best, hard work, and we keep on serving Him even in the face of tribulation? Because, Paul says, "we trust in the living God" who is the Savior of everyone who will believe!

Today's Thoughts: _____

_____

_____

☐ **Today's Text: 1 Timothy 4:12-14** *(key v. 14)*

17 **Today's Truth:** We've all had desires to be more gifted like this person or that. But God has placed in each of us a unique giftedness (Eph. 4:7-8) for a special destiny nobody else has (Jer. 29:11). Our job is to simply receive His gifts and use them.

Today's Thoughts: _____

_____

_____

☐ **Today's Text: 1 Timothy 4:15-16** *(key v. 15)*

18 **Today's Truth:** Do you want to be a success? "Meditate on these things . . ." In Joshua 1:18 the Lord promises that if we meditate on God's Word and obey it all, then we will be prosperous and have good success. 1 Tim. 4:15 also urges that we give ourselves totally to what God has spoken.

Today's Thoughts: _____

_____

_____

☐ Today's Text: **1 Timothy 5:1-4** *(key v. 2)*

19 Today's Truth: We are to regard "younger women as sisters, with all purity." So much of what determines whether we are tempted or not towards the opposite sex is our mindset. If we learn to see Christian women as sisters and non-Christian women as souls in need of Jesus, the potential for sexual lust rapidly dissipates.

Today's Thoughts: _____

_____

_____

☐ Today's Text: **1 Timothy 5:5-8** *(key v.8)*

20 Today's Truth: Someone who does not provide for his own family has not only ignored the basic principles of the Christian faith, he's transgressed the common sense held by most non-Christians.

Today's Thoughts: _____

_____

_____

☐ Today's Text: **1 Timothy 5:9-12** *(key v. 10)*

21 Today's Truth: For a widow to receive financial support from the church, she must have a reputation for good works and must have had a faithful marriage.

Today's Thoughts: _____

_____

_____

☐ Today's Text: 1 Timothy 5:13-16 *(key v. 14)*

22 Today's Truth: Though this verse is given in respect to young widows, the caution is universally valuable: that we "give no opportunity to the adversary to speak reproachfully." Since he is the "accuser of the brethren"—and a diligent one at that—we should avoid *all* appearance of evil.

Today's Thoughts: _____

_____

_____

☐ Today's Text: 1 Timothy 17-20 *(key v. 20)*

23 Today's Truth: The public correction of leaders who are in public ministry, occasioned by the failure of integrity, is not an act of cruelty. The goal is to cleanse the wound in the Body of Christ, instill godly fear in other leaders so they won't fall, and help the congregation learn about the tragedy, together at one time, rather than allow rumors to distort the truth and harm "the sheep."

Today's Thoughts: _____

_____

_____

☐ Today's Text: 1 Timothy 5:21-23 *(key v. 22)*

24 Today's Truth: Paul warns against haste in the appointing of elders. Choosing leaders with solid integrity is a crucial responsibility.

Today's Thoughts: _____

_____

_____

☐ **Today's Text: 1 Timothy 5:24-25** *(key v. 25)*

25 **Today's Truth:** So much of our labor for the
Gospel which nobody presently sees will one day
be open before all eyes. That's not what motivates
us to serve, of course, but it can greatly comfort us
in seasons when we feel unappreciated or at times
when we see little harvest for so much sowing.

Today's Thoughts: —————————————
_____
_____

☐ **Today's Text: 1 Timothy 6:1-2** *(key v.1)*

26 **Today's Truth:** Christian slaves serving unbe-
lieving masters were to do so with honor and
thereby be effective witnesses. Although none of
us serve as slaves, we do serve bosses—some not
easy to respect. Yet we're to "work as unto Christ."

Today's Thoughts: —————————————
_____
_____

☐ **Today's Text: 1 Timothy 6:3-6** *(key vv. 5, 6)*

27 **Today's Truth:** Any person who views godliness
as a means to selfish gain will be fruitless and
disappointed. But if the equation is turned around
where godliness and God's kingdom is sought
first, God's blessing and provision will abundantly follow (cf. Mt. 6:33, John 10:10, Ps. 16:11).

Today's Thoughts: —————————————
_____
_____

☐ **Today's Text: 1 Timothy 6:7-10** *(key v. 10)*

28 **Today's Truth:** Who doesn't enjoy financial prosperity? Let's admit it! Is it fair to say it's "nice?" But what's the *real* issue here? If we maintain a relationship with Jesus in which He is our first love and top priority, other issues in life will tend to find their proper place. God gives us the power to enjoy what we have (Ecc. 5:19), but if money is priority one, sin and sorrow will result.

Today's Thoughts: —————————————

—————————————————————————

—————————————————————————

☐ **Today's Text: 1 Timothy 6:11-12** *(key v. 12)*

29 **Today's Truth:** "Fight the good fight of faith!" Having faith in this world is not without conflict, but we are assured ultimate victory: "Many are the afflictions of the righteous, but the Lord delivers him out of them all" (Psalm 34:19).

Today's Thoughts: —————————————

—————————————————————————

—————————————————————————

☐ **Today's Text: 1 Timothy 6:13-16** *(key v. 16)*

30 **Today's Truth:** Jesus dwells in "unapproachable light." No wonder our countenances are changed when we spend time with Him and our integrity is renewed in His Presence! (cf. Psalms 17:15 & 34:5)

Today's Thoughts: —————————————

—————————————————————————

—————————————————————————

☐ **Today's Text:** 1 Timothy 6:17-21 *(key v. 20)*

31 Today's Truth: Paul's final charge to Timothy, and hence to us, is that we should guard the Gospel as a rare treasure, making sure that our message is clear, pure, and without the pollution of human philosophies.

Today's Thoughts: _____

_____

_____

Additional Resources for
Biblical Manhood
Available from Jack Hayford and
Living Way Ministries

AUDIO CASSETTE MINI-ALBUMS (2 tapes)

Honest to God	SC122	$8
Redeeming Relationships for Men & Women	SC177	$8
Why Sex Sins Are Worse Than Others	SC179	$8
How God Uses Men	SC223	$8
A Father's Approval	SC225	$8
Resisting the Devil	SC231	$8
How to Recession-Proof Your Home	SC369	$8
Safe Sex!	SC448	$8
The Leader Jesus Trusts	SC461	$8

AUDIO CASSETTE ALBUMS (# of tapes)

Cleansed for the Master's Use (3)	SC377	$13
Becoming God's Man (4)	SC457	$17
Fixing Family Fractures (4)	SC217	$17
The Power of Blessing (4)	SC395	$17
Men's Seminars 1990-91 (10)	MSEM	$42
Premarital Series (12)	PM02	$50
A Family Encyclopedia (24)	SC233	$99

VHS VIDEO ALBUMS

Why Sex Sins Are Worse Than Others	WSSV	$19
Divorce and the People of God	DIVV	$19
Earthly Search for a Heavenly Father	ESFV	$19

Add 15% for shipping and handling.
California residents add 8.25% sales tax.
Request your free Resource Catalog.
Living Way Ministries Resources
14820 Sherman Way • Van Nuys, CA 91405-2233
(818) 779-8480 or (800) 776-8180

A MAN'S IMAGE AND IDENTITY

*A study in a
man's pathway
to Christ-likeness
in today's society*

Jack Hayford

THOMAS NELSON PUBLISHERS
Nashville • Atlanta • London • Vancouver

Published in Nashville, Tennessee, by Thomas Nelson, Inc., Publishers, and distributed in Canada by Word Communications, Ltd., Richmond, British Columbia, and in the United Kingdom by Word (UK), Ltd., Milton Keynes, England.

Unless otherwise noted, Scripture quotations are from the NEW KING JAMES VERSION of the Bible. Copyright ©1979, 1980, 1982, Thomas Nelson, Inc., Publishers.

ISBN 0-7852-7794-3

Printed in the United States of America

1 2 3 4 5 6 7 - 01 00 99 98 97 96 95

*This message was originally brought at
The Church On The Way.*

*It has since been edited and revised
for publication by Pastor Hayford,
in partnership with Pastor Bob Anderson,
Director of Pastoral Relations.*

TABLE OF CONTENTS

Chapter One
THE POWER OF IMAGES

Images.

They're everywhere.

While living on this high-concept, visually-oriented techno-planet, we're virtually suffocated by images of all kinds.

- From advertising;
- from TV;
- from movies;
- from billboards and newspapers and magazines . . . a deluge of images pours daily into our lives.

And they stick with us. From the image factory of entertainment and news, images of faces and events scorch the memory for years and years. That's verified by the fact that it takes no effort for any of us to recall the exact images of:

- The explosion of the space shuttle Challenger at take-off;
- John F. Kennedy clutching his throat while riding in a Dallas motorcade;
- Neil Armstrong's first step onto the lunar surface;
- The eerie luminescent missile contrails raining on Baghdad during the first eve of Desert Storm.

Images have the power to live on in our minds for a lifetime.

But that's not all.

Images also have the power to shape us.

Complete image systems like those architected by advertising agencies and styled by society's values forge their own icons that affect us by their persistent tutorial nature. They continually spew forth informally announced but very real social standards by which we tend to measure our lives--standards which determine how well we are conforming to everyone else; standards which determine things from what is "politically correct," to what is "acceptable behavior" in this "brave new world order." If image competition doesn't compel us to have a car nicer than the neighbors, then it will motivate us to subtly inform a lunch gathering about the social "note-worthy" we had to dinner last night. Or it may incite us to go out of our way to let people know just how well our kids are doing at their Ivy League school. Or maybe it's falling to the temptation to spend more than we should on the latest fashions with money that should have gone into ministry.

Teenagers, for example, have suffered with some of the most severe and blatant degenerations of peer-image-pressure ever. The simple label of the clothing they wear to school is often a critical factor which establishes their worth as human beings among their peers. Worse, in recent years, the image of being "cool" is now sometimes secured in urban high school social circles by having a condom tucked away in the wallet--ready for action. Even if it was never used, the "illusion of coolness" is still sought--and obtained--by nothing more than the possession of so unworthy a symbol.

At every age of life, the pressurized process that comes from a world filled with images is basically the same. It's a cyclical process. We're not only drawn to *ingest* those images from the world around us, we're also being programmed to *project* those same images in our living in order to be accepted as "one of the crowd." The world spirit of comparison and competition is fierce, virtually compelling us to wear the label, look the look, talk the talk, join the pack--and so often, to compromise our morals. In short, "look" just like the world-image dictates.

The real stinger is, *image* is not just a *look*.

It's a design of *thought*.

It's a pattern of *values*.

Image is not just surface layering--what we look like--it's substantive stuff. It touches the core of our being.

For example: If a person said they opposed abortion in *any* way, in most secular circles scorn and ridicule can be guaranteed. The reason: you aren't conforming to the "correct" way of thought; you aren't taking on their *image*. The point is that hosts of issues today are ground into the fabric of our minds--whether we like it or not. And it's crucial to identify, because the issue of *image* in our lives extends to that which governs the *way we live* and *what we think* and *who we are.*

Illustration:

Picture a digital watch. Instead of mainsprings and gears, it runs on a very tiny circuit of computer-technology origin. That circuit was literally a photograph--*an image*--before it ever kept time. First, the pathways of logic were drawn with ink on paper; the circuit was designed as an image. This image determined how the electrical current would flow and what it would do throughout all the intersections, avenues, roads, and courses that would eventually form the electronic circuit. This *image* was designed to *DO something*; in this case, it was designed to keep time.

Next, the design of this circuit image was photographed on high resolution film and reduced to a micro-sized version. Taking the multiple components of that tiny film image, it was then layered into a *physical* composite imprint, i.e., a computer chip. This imprinted "circuit" then became the works of the watch. So what started out as a mere *photographic image* ended up being a *functional machine.*

Similarly, if I choose to take, for example, a pro-life stand on the moral issue of abortion, it's because my view of God's image in each human has imprinted a circuit of behavior which, to use our illustration, has made me a "functional machine" in the interest of the unborn. The reverse is true, as is the application to anything shaping the thinking of people in our society. Each mind is a kind of working logic system similar to a computer chip: it generates a pattern of behavior, a circuit of response, a network of conclusions--all according to the *image* burned into the circuitry. (And most of us learn early, if we don't conform to the world's *image* on a subject, we are certain to meet with disapproval.) Therefore:

• *Image* is more than surface, pretense, showy stuff.

• *Image* generates decisions every hour.

• *Image* can determine a person's future.

As the Bible says, "As a person thinks in his heart, so is he." A paraphrase might read, "According to the circuit image in a person's heart, that's how he or she will make decisions in life."

Image is potent stuff. And it's quite an expansive topic, but with very critical and specific applications to a man's life in Christ.

So how do we, as men of God, approach the topic of *image* as it pertains to our lives in Christ, and how do we conform to the right image in the most effective way while resisting the world's image? The initial step requires us to analyze the chief forces that stand at the ready to either conform us into God's image or to hinder that process. Understanding those forces and the full impact of the word "image" is the beginning

11

point of our study.

In approaching the topic of A MAN'S IMAGE, we're pressing deeper than simply denouncing materialism and immorality while puffing-up high-toned religiosity. We're saying *more* than, "Let the *world* take their yachts and latest Rodeo Drive fashions, Mercedes logo on the hood, arrogant walk and air of sophistication, immoral conquests, and filthy films." And we're saying more than contrived religious images--pretentious fastings, displayed generosity in offerings done before the eyes of man. Instead, our focus is simple and direct: it's on Jesus! And Jesus has everything to do with *image.*

When Genesis 1:26 announces that "God created man in His own *image,*" *image* suddenly becomes a very spiritual topic which deserves to be understood and must be reckoned with. The Bible makes it clear: *Image* is more than making a good impression; more than having certain clothes or a new hairstyle; more than a shallow facade of acceptability, as if social acceptance were the equivalent of substance and character.

Image conveys:
• likeness and resemblance
• functional behavior
• decision-making dynamics

Therefore, image is:

- *identity*
- *character*
- *destiny*.

Unfortunately, as we'll see, God's original blueprint for us as men--His Chief Designer *image*--has been distorted, mangled, and continues to be transmitted in a damaged condition. We'll discuss several diverse forces that impose failure upon God's intended image for humanity, but the initial and instigating one is common to every human being: Sin. The Fall. The ruined circuitry.

In even greater power than sneezes or shoe sizes, Adam's DNA--with his fallen image--envelopes us. Cast millenniums ago when Adam chose not to heed God's voice, but instead confirmed allegiance to the lying serpent, the devil, his fallen image is still as fresh today as it was back then in the Garden--reproduced now with every newborn baby emerging from the womb. Bequeathed to us through inheritance, this is an image of sin, brokenness, and failure that produces our:

- irresponsibility to obey God's holy laws;
- incapacity to fulfill our God-ordained destinies;
- inability to enjoy life as God intended it to be.

Consequently, we live in a society, a race, that needs massive amounts of repair.

There are broken images of lives everywhere. How things appear in the human race, the image of how life is in this present world, is not how God originally designed it to be. Life as it is now isn't according to the original circuit image designed for man in Heaven.

There's been a short-circuit of that design.

Augmenting this negative influence of Adam's fallen nature in us are several other forces which have an image system all their own. They are seeking to establish their circuitry as the image-making device in our personality. Some of those forces come at us from the mere nature of the human condition; other forces come from a contrived, strategic, intentional effort of hell to ruin lives--sometimes by subtle means, other times by the bold and brash. Put all these dynamics together in the same lifetime of experience and you've got a struggle on your hands.

The good news is, we aren't locked into a fatalistic pre-determined destiny. The bad news is: we have two destinies awaiting us, both of which are in conflict with one another, both vying for our allegiance by reaching to us with their *images*; (1) the natural out-working of all our inheritance in *Adam's fallen image*; and (2) the destiny dynamically unfolding to us through the *image of Christ*--a potential for us all when we received Him as our Lord and Savior.

Christ's Person, powerfully growing within us, can restore the image of God in our manliness, and a circuitry which is diametrically opposed to the fallen image of Adam can be ours.

Exposure to the Imprint

But in order for the image of Christ to be successfully imprinted upon us and within us, *we* must participate in the process. *We* have to do something. We have to *commit* to an ongoing, sufficient *EXPOSURE to the living God.* Let me explain by means of a simple but beautiful analogy.

The first known photograph was made in 1816 by Joseph Niepce. But long before that, it's almost as though we're listening to a description of the photographic process in the Old Testament, three thousand years before Niepce produced his first image!

> *They looked to Him and were*
> *radiant, and their faces were*
> *not ashamed.   Psalm 34:5*

A friend pointed out the photographic process in this verse to me. Let me share it.
- *"They"* (the film--that which would receive an image)
- *"looked"* (exposure)
- *"to Him"* (the source of Light)
- *"and were radiant"* (bore a resemblance to that to which they had been exposed).

And the resulting photographic exhibi-

15

tion was successful: *"their faces were not ashamed."*

Here is another 3,000-year-old "Kodak moment" from King David:

> *As for me, I will see Your face in righteousness; I shall be satisfied when I awake in Your likeness.   Psalm 17:15*

It's divine photography. *Image* produced by Light. (Some things never change!) And God's Spirit is yearning to engage us in a whole new reshaping process: to transform us from the broken image incurred by the Fall and propel us toward the liberating, glorious image of Christ, the Founder of the Original Image. But this process requires that we let God's light--the truth of His Word--shine into our souls. It's *that* exposure:

- an open heart
- a receptive attitude
- a mind alive to *Him*
- a humbled soul

There's where the new image can be imprinted.

Chapter Two
MEN RESISTING
THE WORLD IMAGE

It's one of the Top 10 Stories of all time!

All the elements are present. The episode of The Fiery Furnace, taken from the pages of God's Word, not only commands our attention by its raw excitement, but it's loaded with insight into how the "world" seeks to impose its image on *any* man in *any* generation. Although the story takes place in Babylon--the ancient world's image of cultural and commercial success--and though it's distanced from us by nearly twenty-five centuries in time, it's as contemporary as today's newscast.

To get it all, it's best to read the first three chapters of the prophetic book of Daniel. But for inclusion here I'm only presenting that portion of the text which provides the essential support for the key points we're studying.

OVERVIEW: The time was 606 B.C. World power was in the grip of Nebuchadnezzar, Emperor of Babylon. This City was the essence of cultural advancement, military power, economic dominance, and spiritual idolatry. Located near today's Iraqi Capital of Baghdad, it commanded a realm reaching from today's Persian Gulf to the Mediterranean Sea.

When the Babylonian troops lay siege to

Jerusalem, Capital of Judea, the Judean Kingdom collapses. As part of the spoils of war, Nebuchadnezzar takes some of the nation's finest, most intelligent young men back to Babylon, to train them for service in the King's Court. The best known are Daniel, Shadrach, Meshach, and Abednego.

There are three steps in unfolding the story: The Capture and Training; The King's Dream and Interpretation; The King's Image and Confrontation. These three steps issue in the fiery furnace event and the miraculous deliverance of the committed young men. Here is the abbreviated presentation:

    I.   The Capture and Training (Daniel 1:1-21)

    II.   The King's Dream and Interpretation (Daniel 2:1-49)

    III.   The King's Image and Confrontation (Daniel 3:1-18)

    Conclusion: The Fiery Furnace and Miracle Deliverance (Daniel 3:19-30)

The Abbreviated Text: Daniel 1-3

CHAPTER 1: In the third year of the reign of Jehoiakim king of Judah, Nebuchadnezzar king of Babylon came to Jerusalem and besieged it. And the Lord gave Jehoiakim king of Judah into his hand . . . Then the king instructed Ashpenaz, the master of his eunuchs, to bring some of the . . . young men in whom there was no blemish, but good-looking, gifted in all wisdom, possessing knowledge and quick to understand, who had ability to serve in the king's palace, and whom they might teach the language and literature of the Chaldeans. And the king appointed for them a daily provision of the king's delicacies and of the wine which he drank, and three years of training for them, so that at the end of that time they might serve before the king.

Now from among those of the sons of Judah were Daniel, Hananiah, Mishael, and Azariah. To them the chief of the eunuchs gave names: he gave Daniel the name Belteshazzar; to Hananiah, Shadrach; to Mishael, Meshach; and to Azariah, Abed-Nego. But Daniel purposed in his heart that he would not defile himself with the portion of the king's delicacies, nor with the wine which he drank; therefore he requested of the chief of the eunuchs that he might not defile himself . . .

And the chief of the eunuchs said to Daniel, "I fear my lord the king, who has appointed your food and drink. For why should he see your faces looking worse than the young men who are your age? Then you would endanger my head before the king."

So Daniel said . . . "Please test your servants for ten days, and let them give us vegetables to eat and water to drink. Then let our appearance be examined before you . . ."

So he consented with them in this matter, and tested them ten days. And at the end of ten days their features appeared better . . .

As for these four young men, God gave them knowledge and skill in all literature and wisdom; and Daniel had understanding in all visions and dreams.

Now at the end of the days, when the king had said that they should be brought in . . . the king interviewed them, and among them all none was found like Daniel, Hananiah, Mishael, and Azariah; therefore they served before the king.

CHAPTER 2: Now in the second year of Nebuchadnezzar's reign, Nebuchadnezzar had dreams; and his spirit was so troubled that his sleep left him. Then the king gave the command to call the magicians, the astrologers, the sorcerers, and the Chaldeans to tell the king his dreams. So they came and stood before the king. And the king said to them, "I have had a dream, and my spirit is anxious to know the dream." Then the Chaldeans spoke to the king in Aramaic, "O king, live forever! Tell your servants the dream, and we will give the interpretation." The king answered and said to the Chaldeans, "My decision is firm: if you do not make known the dream to me, and its interpretation, you shall be cut in pieces, and your houses shall be made an ash heap."

The Chaldeans answered the king, and said, "There is not a man on earth who can tell the king's matter; therefore no king, lord, *or ruler has ever asked such things of any magician, astrologer, or Chaldean . . . and there is no other who can tell it to the king except the gods, whose dwelling is not with flesh." For this reason the king . . . gave a command to destroy all the wise men of Babylon.*

Then with counsel and wisdom Daniel answered Arioch, the captain of the king's guard . . . he answered and said to Arioch the king's captain, "Why is the decree from the king so urgent?"

Then Arioch made the decision known to Daniel. So Daniel went in and asked the king to give him time, that he might tell the king the interpretation. Then Daniel went to his house, and made the decision known to Hananiah, Mishael, and Azariah, his companions, that they might seek mercies from the God of heaven concerning this secret, so that Daniel and his companions might not perish with the rest of the wise men of Babylon. Then the secret was revealed to Daniel in a night vision. So Daniel blessed the God of heaven.

Then Arioch quickly brought Daniel before the king, and said thus to him, "I have found a man of the captives of Judah, who will make known to the king the interpretation."

Daniel answered in the presence of the king: ". . . there is a God in heaven who reveals secrets, and He has made known to King Nebuchadnezzar what will be in the latter days . . .

"You, O king, were watching; and behold, a great image! This great image, whose splendor was excellent, stood before you; and its form was awesome. This image's head was of fine gold, its chest and arms of silver, its belly and thighs of bronze, its legs of iron, its feet partly of iron and partly of clay. You watched while a stone was cut out without hands, which struck the image on its feet of iron and clay, and broke them in pieces.

"This is the dream. Now we will tell the interpretation of it before the king. You, O king, are a king of kings. For the God of heaven has given you a kingdom, power, strength, and glory . . . you are this head of gold. But after you shall arise another kingdom inferior to yours; then another, a third kingdom of bronze, which shall rule over all the earth. And the fourth kingdom shall be as strong as iron, inasmuch as iron breaks in pieces and shatters everything; and like iron that crushes, that kingdom will break in pieces and crush all the others.

"And as the toes of the feet were partly of iron and partly of clay, so the kingdom shall be partly strong and partly fragile. As you saw iron mixed with ceramic clay, they will mingle with the seed of men; but they will not adhere to one another, just as iron does not mix with clay. And in the days of these kings the God of heaven will set up a kingdom which shall never be destroyed... and it shall stand forever . . . the great God has made known to the king what will come to pass after this. The dream is certain, and its interpretation is sure."

Then King Nebuchadnezzar fell on his face, prostrate before Daniel . . . and said, "Truly your God is the God of gods, the Lord of kings, and a revealer of secrets, since you could reveal this secret." Then the king promoted Daniel and gave him many great gifts; and he made him ruler over the whole province of Babylon, and chief administrator over all the wise men of Babylon. Also Daniel petitioned the king, and he set Shadrach, Meshach, and Abed-Nego over the affairs of the province of Babylon; but Daniel sat in the gate of the king.

CHAPTER 3: Nebuchadnezzar the king made an image of gold, whose height was sixty cubits and its width six cubits. He set it up in the plain of Dura, in the province of Babylon. And King Nebuchadnezzar sent word to gather together . . . all the officials of the provinces gathered together for the dedication of the image . . .

Then a herald cried aloud: "To you it is commanded, O peoples, nations, and languages, that at the time you hear the sound of the music, you shall fall down and worship the gold image that King Nebuchadnezzar has set up; and whoever does not fall down and worship shall be cast immediately into the midst of a burning fiery furnace."

Therefore at that time certain Chaldeans

came forward and accused the Jews. They spoke and said to King Nebuchadnezzar, "There are certain Jews whom you have set over the affairs of the province of Babylon: Shadrach, Meshach, and Abed-Nego; these men, O king, have not paid due regard to you. They do not serve your gods or worship the gold image which you have set up." [Daniel was apparently away on a court mission at this time.]

Then Nebuchadnezzar, in rage and fury, gave the command to bring Shadrach, Meshach, and Abed-Nego. So they brought these men before the king. Nebuchadnezzar spoke, saying to them, "Is it true that you do not . . . worship the gold image which I have set up? If you do not worship, you shall be cast immediately into the midst of a burning fiery furnace. And who is the god who will deliver you from my hands?" Shadrach, Meshach, and Abed-Nego answered, "O Nebuchadnezzar, we have no need to answer you in this matter. If that is the case, our God whom we serve is able to deliver us from the burning fiery furnace, and He will deliver us from your hand, O king. But if not, let it be known to you, O king, that we do not serve your gods, nor will we worship the gold image which you have set up."

Then Nebuchadnezzar was full of fury, and the expression on his face changed toward (them) . . .

And he commanded certain men of his army to bind and cast them into the burning fiery furnace. Then these men were bound in their garments, and were cast into the midst of the burning fiery furnace.

Then King Nebuchadnezzar was astonished; and he rose in haste and spoke, saying to his counselors, "Did we not cast three men bound into the midst of the fire?" They answered and said to the king, "True, O king." "Look!" he answered, "I see four men loose, walking in the midst of the fire; and they are not hurt, and the form of the fourth is like the Son of God." Then Nebuchadnezzar went near the mouth of the burning fiery furnace and spoke, saying, "Shadrach, Meshach, and Abed-Nego, servants of the Most High God, come out, and come here." Then (they) came from the midst of the fire. And the satraps, administrators, governors, and the king's counselors gathered together, and they saw these men on whose bodies the fire had no power; the hair of their head was not singed nor were their garments affected, and the smell of fire was not on them. Nebuchadnezzar spoke, saying, "Blessed be the God of Shadrach, Meshach, and Abed-Nego, who sent His Angel and delivered His servants who trusted in Him, and they have frustrated the king's word, and yielded their bodies, that they should not serve nor worship any god except their own God! . . . There is no other God who can deliver like this." Then the king promoted Shadrach, Meshach, and Abed-Nego in the province of Babylon.

In every way this is a story *of* men *for* men to *shape* men!

• It begins with four men caught in the vice of circumstance, being called to conformity to a human system governed by the then-most-powerful man in the world, King Nebuchadnezzar.

• It continues with men demonstrating a faith which determines to become *effective* within the system, but *not* to be *shaped* by it.

• The story turns a corner and we see a man dream of God's purpose for His life; a dream he at first doesn't understand.

• Answering his dilemma is another man; one who knows God and is able to speak into the life of a man (even his king) with the truth of God's purpose.

• At this point we discover a man (the king) who supposes that he is the one who can bring God's purpose about in his life by his own wisdom and power. His pride cultivates a self-image which he seeks to use to intimidate others.

• While the majority in the system bow to the image-intimidation, a distinct band of men refuses, knowing the call to *bow* to the system is different from *serving* in the system. Their faith and spiritual commitment is put to the test. They honor God first!

• When these men "face the heat," the

result is God's divine intervention, and the confounding of all onlookers as God steps into their situation and vindicates them.

*   *   *   *   *

I don't know that there is any incident in God's Word that more specifically or clearly addresses the pressures which a believing man will face today. The world system is structured by the same satanic spirit which motivated Nebuchadnezzar. That's the reason the Book of Revelation uses the name of ancient Babylon to symbolize and summarize the whole of all global commerce and corruption that will eventually come to its demise. Look at the parallels in the story which reveal the kind of "image-pressures" which a man faces today.

1. "Your only worth is to serve the system."

When the four young men are taken to Babylon for training, there is no regard for anything else than what they can bring to the king's program. There is no regard for any value other than the "meat on the hoof" value of each man's ability to serve the interests of the business.

IMPACT: *The world system will seek to reduce your view of your worth to your ability to succeed on its terms.*

2. "Your identity is not yours to determine."

The renaming of the four young men is powerfully significant. The abolishing of their born identity reflects the will of the system to not only *re*-locate (geographically) but to *dis*-locate (psychologically). Study also will disclose the fact that each of the four names contained a form of the Name of the God of Israel: Dani*EL*, Hanani*YAH*, Azari*YAH*, and Misha*EL*. Further, the names they were given were each related to Babylonian deities--demon gods worshiped in that culture. It's a classic ploy of our Adversary to seek to put his stamp on your life, your mind, your work.

IMPACT: *The world will seek to link your identity with its operations and remove your association with anything remotely related to God, His way, or His will.*

3. "Feed and feast on our delicacies."

Imagine, if you will, the heaping "training table" which was set before the team of young men which had been gathered from the several nations Nebuchadnezzar had conquered. They were not only survivors from their separate cultures, but they were given preferred treatment and the opportunity to "make it big in the big city." The table set before them--a menu which contained food prohibited in the Jewish culture from which Daniel and his partners had come--becomes a testing point. Will they let their tastes be determined by the society around them, or will they keep their self-control intact and trust God to make them successful anyway?

IMPACT: *Whether it's the call to employ the devious methods used in the corporation, the three-cocktail lunch, or the feast at the office party, today's man faces the decision as to what forces will shape him: the "spread" on the outside, or the "Spirit" on the inside.*

4. "Is there anybody here who really has touch with God?"

The second chapter of Daniel is a dual study in God's dealings with men. On the one hand, His unfolding of His sovereign purpose to Nebuchadnezzar tells us:

A. God speaks to any and every man, even though the man may himself not have a true knowledge of Him. God's imprint seeks to register truth on every human soul, and each man must determine what response he will show to the Creator's revelation to his mind and being (see Romans 1:18-2:11).

B. God uses the man who is faithful to Him to penetrate the confusion of the world's inability to understand His purpose, and to make him an interpreter of His ways, His truth, and His power.

IMPACT: *When a man resists the world system's shaping him, but still serves within that system with wisdom, he is destined to become a shaper of thinking in that realm which couldn't shape him. The world is seeking men who really have touch with God!*

5. "Face the music and dance or you'll face the heat and die!"

When the king builds the image and calls everyone to worship at his command, we have the clearest picture possible of the world system's seeking to pour a man in its mold. And it's all being spearheaded by a man who depicts the world system's way of a man demonstrating his authority. Nebuchadnezzar is the picture of the typical man who (a) has an inner sense of destiny but who only thinks it can be fulfilled by *mastering* other people, rather than *serving* them. And he equally depicts any of us men who (b) become infuriated whenever our will or whim isn't bowed to by those we seek to dominate. There are considerable issues for us to confront in ourselves if we find either of these world-traits in our lives as believers.

But foremost at this point of the biblical narrative is the incredible faith of the three young men. (Daniel's absence doesn't suggest he surrendered to the system. You can read of his own personal response to a similar situation in Daniel 6.) Here, this trio "faces the music," but refuses to bow to its call. Their response brings intense fire upon their heads, but amid their fiery circumstance the Lord Himself comes to walk with them and to deliver them.

IMPACT: *The truth within you, incarnated in your commitment to its moral and spiritual demands, will outlast any flame of human fury or fashioning.*

What "Worldliness" Is

The real evil of worldliness is that the world spirit is committed to trying to stamp its image upon and within us. Worldliness means world*like*ness. It means adopting the world's value system.

And we're all vulnerable.

The temptation to succumb to the world's image is often severe. Sometimes the circumstance of your associations or employment *demands* that you conform to its image or your very survival in the system will be threatened. That's what happened to these three men who stood before the king in ancient Babylon, but they "faced the music," survived the flames, and wouldn't buy into the world image. They refused conformity to the "circuit" of values and behavior the system sought to "imprint"--to *image* them with.

When the Scripture reports they were commanded to "worship" the golden image, it does not mean they were to just fall down before a golden spike and salute. Rather they were to yield to the image's system, *swear allegiance* to it, to accept a "circuit" engraved inside them--to worship a spiritual icon of an alien kingdom.

Don't miss the picture! Nebuchadnezzar is a type of Satan--the arch-manipulator of the world system. He's the one that sits at hell's Master Controls and from that location exerts massive pressure throughout the globe to conform mankind--one at a time--into his own image. The plan is well-coordinated and administrated efficiently, as hosts of spiritual powers move invisibly among mankind to enlist "buyers" into the system.

People who are without God have the universal human proclivity to worship, a desire to "know" *something* or *someone* in one form or another which gives life meaning and fulfillment. However, more often than not, the worldling ends up in a worship of self-will and self-protective interest, following anyone who makes pride and self attainment an object of homage as an image to be served.

Satan, of course, is the arch-proponent of pride and self-will's self-serving way. His style is to so smoothly arrange the "music"--the call to *his* system's values--that each person thinks he has chosen this course on his own: "I did it *my* way."

There are custom-made approaches, too. If a man isn't assailed by the pressure to participate in a world-system of worship born out of *pride* (self-righteousness, in-

flated ego, or a sense of macho superiority),
then the Master Manipulator has other tactics. He'll lure the soul to worship a system
that gives rewards, pleasure, or "freedom
from threat" if you just bow down to the
system's image. In one form or another, the
world's system of "worship"--requiring obei-
sance to its image--is either seductive, coer-
cive, or blinding. It *never* has in mind the
ultimate blessing of its devotees. Its intent
is solely on their destruction, for Satan, as
the prince of this world, hates the prospect
of any man bearing God's image, and with
vitriolic wrath seeks to control people and
remove any hope for that true image's recovery.

There's a marvelous added lesson which
we must not miss amid the triumph of faith
this episode reveals. Read again the response of the three to the king's threat of the
furnace:

> *If that is the case, our God*
> *whom we serve is able to de-*
> *liver us from the burning fiery*
> *furnace, and He will deliver us*
> *from your hand, O king.*
>
> *BUT IF NOT, let it be known to*
> *you, O king, that we do not*
> *serve your gods, nor will we*
> *worship the gold image which*
> *you have set up.*
> *Daniel 3:17-18*
> (emphasis added)

33

I love the way they phrased that challenge. "Our God is going to deliver us from the fiery furnace. BUT IF HE DOESN'T ... we're *not* going to serve you anyway!"

There's a beauty in the humility manifested by these men.

Listen, these are great men of faith! But they don't pretend omniscience. They acknowledge they're just like you and me-- human and vulnerable. They feel no need for bravado: "Hey, Neb! You pagan dingo!! Let us show you what REAL power is!!"

No sir! They admit they have no guarantee on the outcome of their boss's decision, but they're going to serve the Lord. Can you see how this liberates you and me to say, "The Lord's going to see me through, *but if He doesn't do it the way I might expect* Him to, or the way I hope He will, or on my timetable--I'm *still* going to trust Him anyway!" It reminds me of Job's words, "Even if God Himself slays me, I'll still trust Him!"

There is a place of trust where any man can rest in the Lord . . . *no matter what!*

• Knowing God's beyond-genius and omniscient wisdom is supporting you;

• Convinced of His beyond-computer design of His redemptive purpose in you; and

• Comforted by His beyond-imagination eternal love for you, commit yourself to such eternal faithfulness and let male ego and self-reliance take a back seat.

A Set-Up

I can't escape this recurrent phrase, "he set it up": "the king had set up" (3:2); "Nebuchadnezzar had set up" (v.3); "the king had set up" (v. 5); "the king had set up" (v. 7).

Listen to it. *The image situation was a "set-up"!* It's the colloquial term we use for scams, conspiracies, and traps. So it is we'll find the adversary's plan is always "set up" to put you down, trip you up, or topple you over; set up to force your compromise. We face a world of set-ups which are set up:

• to come down at times with intimidating force;

• to seek to etch a different image on our souls;

• to define our identity on the system's terms;

• to compel conformity to behavior alien to our highest call in life.

But three men--living in an era exactly like yours and mine--did more than survive. They impacted and imaged the society which was trying to stamp its image on them! A furnace, heated up to a blinding blaze and intended to reduce them to ashes, was mastered by the might of the Master who walked with them through the flames. Please note this, brother: It's *in* the fire you'll often find the nearest and dearest fellowship with Jesus!! And note also, when it was all over, Nebuchadnezzar could only admit: "There's no god like the God of these men!"

Chapter Three
DECODING THE ENCODED EFFORT AT RECODING THE FIRST CODE

The title's a mouthful, I admit. But it touches the nerve of an idea that needs to be central to the understanding of every man, and that sentence--serving as title to this chapter--says it all. You and I are living out our lives in a setting where two powers wrestle to control us: God, to *restore* us; Satan, to *destroy* us. The key for each of the two is to communicate to us--to get the message through that says, "Everything's better if you do it my way." The problem in our communication with God is that our human receiving unit has been jumbled, and doesn't receive as clearly from the Manufacturer (God) as it does from the Manipulator (Satan).

Let me "decode" the title.

First, by proper definition, a code is "a systematically arranged, comprehensive set of laws"; and also, "a set of signals used to transmit messages." In a word, there is an imprinted "image" of the world's "laws and signals" which has been burned into the mind of each soul which has ever lived in sin--and we all have. This was not the original circuitry (which now has been damaged)--the original "image" of clarity in understanding God's "laws and signals."

Consequently, (here comes the " Title" explanation) we need:

> To *discern* ("to decode"), what has been *burned into* our thought processes by the world spirit ("encoded"), so that the Holy Spirit of God may *restore* ("recoding"), the *Father's will and way* as the governing circuitry of our life and thought ("the first code").

The Bible puts it in these words:

> *And do not be conformed to this world, but be transformed by the renewing of your mind, that you may prove what is that good and acceptable and perfect will of God.*
>
> *Romans 12:2*

The *re*-conforming of our minds from the world's order of thinking is central to a man's finding his IMAGE in God again. Before we examine any of this process further, I want to be clear in our definition of "the world's image." The terminology itself can sound so petty and nitpicking: "the world's image" can sound like a puritanical, self-righteous, petty dart game waging an "Us vs. Them" or "The Churchy" versus "The Nasty" contest.

My concern about this clarity of definition is because as I was growing up, it seemed I heard the words "worldly" and "worldliness" in church constantly. This usually involved mentioning a list which included about a dozen *"don't do's."* So, generally, it was assumed if you *didn't* do those things, you were a "good Christian." It seemed much like a 4-year-old's "star chart," as when a child is being taught to, "Clean your fingernails (check), comb your hair (check), tie your own shoes (check)-- Hey, Gold Star!"

As adults, some believers have carried that mentality into the spiritual arena. They suppose that any "worldliness" or "world image" is outside the question if they have their "stars" for "not doing any of the bad things non-Christians do." But such legalistic propositions of righteousness are not the way of the Lord. The inner issues of the heart are far more significant than any list of "don't do's," for the heart is the source from which our actions spring. However, lest we smugly overlook "outside" issues, it would be reckless if you or I totally discounted the wisdom of personally watchdogging even those items on traditional lists of do's and don'ts. Because it *is* true that our habits, our appearance, and the ways we recreate and entertain ourselves DO reveal something of our heart attitudes to God's ways and will. So don't be too quick to trash "lists," because behind such legalism, you can still find something of a true *heart*-righteousness intended. Valid discernment was probably present at the inception of what may have now become a legalistic program.

But our focus on "world image" transcends any alienating, damning, separatist, or performance-oriented mind-set. Our quest for "A Man's Image and Identity" on God's terms has to do *not* with turning up the heat, twisting the screws, or making lists and condemning. We're seeking what the Incarnation of Jesus Christ *as a man* has opened for us; the door to, *"Christ in you, the hope of glory"* (Col. 1:27). His presence is the ultimate agent which can dissolve the world's image in us and imprint His.

Image, Imaging, Imagineering, Imagination.

They are more at the core of everything life contains than we probably perceive. From the *creation design* of "man in the image of God," to the *creative designs* of Madison Avenue's "image-making" of personalities and corporations for the purpose of mass-marketing, the concept of "image" surrounds us.

"Imaging" is the word often used to describe the impact of initial experiences upon our psyche. In short, when a specific encounter takes place, say between two people, the power of that encounter is such that it tends to set the grid over all future relationship, unless, of course, something changes the initial "imaging" impact of that encounter. This, for example, is why many men withdraw from either the *desire* to be a "spiritual man" or from the *belief* they could ever become so.

So often the "image" of what a "spiritual man" is has been shaped by encounters with fanatics on the one hand and godly giants on the other. To the first "image" the response is, "Not for me, no way, no how, if that nuttiness is what it means to be 'spiritual'!" To the second "image," usually seen in a spiritual leader whom the man respects, but who is so advanced in maturity and leadership the man feels a hopeless comparison, the response is passive. Most men would feel it was little use to even *think* of becoming so remarkable a person, and the positive "imaging" serves only to summon their respect because no relationship exists with the man to discover *how* such maturity or growth came about.

This brings us precisely to the heart of this study. I want to break in on the impact of any and every "image" that would hinder faith or that would obstruct growth. To do this I'm inviting you to join me in studying the idea of "image" as it is threaded throughout the Word of God. Some form of that word occurs about 200 times in the pages of Scripture. That doesn't include another 180+ times in which a form of the word "idol" occurs, and the two words must be fixed firmly in association if we're to think clearly about "A Man's Image and Identity." Idolatry--the substituting of an alternate image (or "circuit") for God's image (or intended purpose/plan/character) *in our lives*--is more of a fundamental problem than we often realize. So, let's look into the central concept of "image." Join me in an exciting survey.

First, I want to make a quick SIX-POINT TOUR of the Old Testament, and at each point post a principal issue concerning God's intended image for us as His own. So take your Bible in hand and prepare to mark these key points. And one other thing: Would you also prepare to think through each point--take ACTION, letting the Holy Spirit assist your meditation on each point's focus.

POINT 1: The Original Image--Gen. 1:26

> *Then God said, "Let Us make man in Our image, according to Our likeness; let them have dominion over the fish of the sea, over the birds of the air, and over the cattle, over all the earth and over every creeping thing that creeps on the earth."*

The Bible reveals our humanity to be the direct result of plan and purpose on the part of an almighty, all-knowing Creator. This contrasts sharply with the world-mind notion that man's existence is the chance result of primitive electro-chemical interactions at mankind's beginning, or that our personal being is only due to a chance sexual encounter by our own parents, bringing about our introduction to life as an individual. There is no way to exaggerate the importance of emphasizing the difference of these approaches, because everything spins in opposite directions from that juncture of understanding.

When the Bible says that we were made *"in the image of God,"* the matter of physical appearance is hardly in view. The essential element of sound-mindedness we're to gain from this revelation is that "in His image" means that God created us:

- With a capacity to relate to Him.
- With a potential for everlastingness.
- With a sovereign will of free, self-choice.
- With a mind to think and emotions to feel those thoughts and feelings which would produce actions that would profit us, fulfill our intended purpose, and rejoice both God's heart and ours.

The "Fall of Man"--the entry of sin into the race (Genesis 3)--damaged and twisted this image. With that, man's capacities and potentialities all remained intact. The problem was they all became *self*-centered rather than *God*-centered, and the now-blinded mind of man too entirely focuses on his own ego, and his soul too readily becomes a playground for demonic manipulation and extortion.

ACTION: Pause and review the original

"image" intent in the four statements above. What does each one mean to you, personally?

POINT 2: The Multiplied Defect--Gen. 5:3

> *And Adam lived one hundred and thirty years, and begot a son in his own likeness, after his image, and named him Seth.*

This may be the most tragic verse in the Bible. It reports the beginning of the *compounding* effect of sin now damaging the original image and intent of God for man. In direct terms the Scripture states that man, who had been made in GOD'S image, not only has fallen but is reproducing his offspring in HIS OWN image. In contrast to the earlier set of traits, when man was "in the image of God," we see each generation passing to the next these traits:

• A distancing from God, produced by fear and uncertainty.

• A lost view of "everlasting" values, replaced by a shortsighted view of "this moment" which prompts unwise urgency or wearying desperation.

• Free will, but one that makes choices motivated by a blinded mind and dulled, jaded emotions. Thus most choices are the product of a viewpoint--and image--being "sold" by the Arch-Deceiver, rather than from a clear-headed view of ultimate reality.

• The result is that whatever profit is gained or purpose fulfilled, it has limited-at-best satisfaction, and God's intent is not only never realized--*it is not even perceived!*

The essential factors above are described in Ephesians 2:1-3. It's the status of all of us until God's grace rescues us and sets forward the process of redemption in our lives.

The crux of the "image" problem is in the fact that every one of us has been born with a scrambled "discerner," and we tend to not even recognize the world system's values being imprinted upon us. We become "conformed to the world image" by forfeit, and learn to think of distorted patterns of behavior and values as normal.

ACTION: List some matters in your own life that "seemed" normal, until the Holy Spirit pointed out to you the "world-image" in those practices. (Examples: How often we tolerate anger--"Dad was that way, so I guess it's normal that I am." We absorb prejudice and hatred--"I know I'm not perfect, but they're sure worse than I am and they deserve what they're getting." We learn socialized lying and dishonesty-- "It wasn't really the truth, but it wasn't a lie that'd hurt anything"; or, "Those few stamps I used from the office aren't that big a deal, and besides, I stayed late last night and I didn't get anything for it.") Think this through. The matters brought to your mind may vary in apparent significance, but learning to let the Holy Spirit re-sensitize our inboard computer is key to our being "re-imaged."

POINT 3: The Spreading Impact--Gen. 9:6

Whoever sheds man's blood,
by man his blood shall be shed;
for in the image of God He
made man.

It would be easy to pass by this reference to man's being made in the image of God, presuming it to be only a divine declaration concerning capital punishment. But besides the fact that the rare and infinite value of the human personality is asserted by this edict of Heaven's Sovereign, the very *need* for its being stated tells us something. It forcibly brings to view the progressively deteriorative power of the world image on the human personality. In other words, once the divine image is broken, things do not stagnate at a "broken image" level, but they grow worse. The whole context of this verse displays this fact.

Murder was never approved by God, yet when Cain slew Abel, God's mercy permitted Cain to live (Genesis 4:1-15). But the capacity of fallen flesh to further erode the basic divine order, once the original image has become distorted, is seen in Genesis 4:16-24. Here, Cain's offspring, Lamech, not only kills in retaliation, but considers himself to be a candidate for a reward for having killed (vv. 23, 24). Genesis 6:11

further reveals how such violence spread. So the message is clear: The fallen image not only *replicates* itself, it *multiplies* and advances its capacity for evil and goes on to excuse its corruption. And so it was that following the Flood, God gave the command concerning capital punishment; not as a vendetta against murderers, but as a preventative against the fallen human drift toward violence and presumption and its lost perception on the value of life.

ACTION: Can you think of any example of how you tolerated one dimension of carnal indulgence, and later found it leading to an even deeper violation of God's values? What evidences are apparent that our society is characterized by this kind of fallen image impact? For example, have you found yourself becoming more passive toward our culture's casual or passive value on human life?

POINT 4: The Image-Making Prohibition--
Ex. 20:4; Lev. 26:1

> *You shall not make for yourself a carved image, or any likeness of anything that is in heaven above, or that is in the earth beneath, or that is in the water under the earth . . . You shall not make idols for yourselves; neither a carved image nor a sacred pillar shall*

you rear up for yourselves; nor
shall you set up an engraved
stone in your land, to bow down
to it; for I am the Lord your God.

It's amazing how applicable these commandments are today, especially remembering that almost every idol in the ancient world glorified either power or sensuality. These ancient "graven images" were far more than mere depictions of human beings. They were either (1) objects intended to summon the deification of human passions for power, prominence, or raw force; or (2) they were pornographic images designed to incite lust and motivate toward prostitution as a form of worship! But the awesome power of such images is not in the outward form, it is in the inner shaping that occurs in the personality. God's command was not merely some narrow-minded anti-artform or ban-the-statues cult. He was prohibiting His people's pursuit of surrounding themselves with things which engrave themselves on the psyche, which dehumanize and obliterate moral discernment.

ACTION: Have you ever found your inner mental speech habits impacted by exposure to profane language in the workplace or by films you've watched? Have you ever noticed that even if you didn't *speak* foul language, your mind revealed an imprint of its presence? What implications might this have on our thinking that we are supposedly immune to videos where we enjoy the comedy and pretend we are blanking out the profanity the script employs?

POINT 5: The Destruction Mandate--
            Deut. 7:1-11

> *When the Lord your God brings you into the land which you go to possess, and has cast out many nations before you . . . Thus you shall deal with them: you shall destroy their altars, and break down their sacred pillars, and cut down their wooden images, and burn their carved images with fire ...For you are a holy people to the Lord your God; the Lord your God has chosen you to be a people for Himself, a special treasure above all the peoples on the face of the earth.*

These few words from the longer passage of the Lord's command to Israel are as important to us today as to them when they entered the Canaanitish culture to conquer it. The "No Covenant--No Mercy" mandate (Deut. 7:2) sounds so brutal, we are tempted to rise in defense of those things before which God Almighty was so biting in His absolute commands. But a full reading of the text brings us to these words:

> *Therefore know that the Lord*
> *your God, He is God, the faith-*
> *ful God who keeps covenant*
> *and mercy for a thousand gen-*
> *erations with those who love*
> *Him and keep His command-*
> *ments.*

Let us be strongly reminded that God's
call to destroy the images which His people
encountered was motivated by His knowledge that if they didn't, those images would
eventually destroy them!! Hear it, please:
God's "No mercy" clause is an expression of
His mercifulness! And when we grasp that,
we'll understand all the more what horrific
impact there is in the world's image system.
Such idolatry--i.e., mind/habit control
through "images"--can take any number of
forms.

Ed was a football hero whose scrapbook
recorded his exploits as a national sports
figure. As a Christian he was faithful in his
stand for Christ, a position he never reverted
from--he was a good witness! But a strange
thing happened.

At a time of weakness and weariness, he
fell into a moral slippage which nearly cost
him his marriage and his job. As he repented, the Holy Spirit directed him to burn
his scrapbook. Ed later tells how the literal
"images" of his accomplishments, reported
and depicted on the news clippings, had

preserved the notion of his being a "sports jock." So it was, when he was in a time of weakness due to worthy labor and other involvements including serving publicly the cause of Christ, a "hook" in the old image of himself drew him to a place of unwittingly trying to prove "I still have the old stuff," and it led to the edge of moral destruction.

ACTION: While Ed's experience doesn't require a legalistic response that everyone burn their memorabilia, it's amazing how frequently our attics hold mementoes that prompt memories that tug us toward repeating past failures. Where in your life do you need to allow God's Spirit to deal with such matters and to mold you into one who resists *any* facet of the world image?

POINT 6: The Self-Defined Image--
           Judg. 17, 18

> *In those days the tribe of the Danites was seeking an inheritance for itself . . .*

The entire book of Judges is a disgraceful display of the lengths to which even God's own people may revert in unworthy ways when a clear vision of GOD'S IMAGE is lost to their eyes. (We'll see later that there *is* a revealed "image of God.") The brief text above is taken from the center of a two-chapter passage that involves a man named Micah, who isn't to be confused with

50

the prophet whose book bears his name. There's a powerful warning in this extended portion of the Bible: It's a warning about the potential death-dealing force of self-defined religion--what happens when a person *thinks* he's tapped into God via some privileged pathway, even though it's a path God prohibits to everyone else.

The more memorable cases--such as Jim Jones and the Guyana tragedy--are usually supposed to exhaust the way this deception occurs. But Micah's cultivating *his own image* and then calling it God, can happen as quickly in the secret recesses of an individual soul as in a group which is destroyed as it mindlessly follows a religious madman.

Note that not only was Micah deluded by his self-developed image, but he also became the instrument for leading a whole tribe of Israel into idolatrous confusion. Their vulnerability is hinted at in words which might be spoken about many people you and I meet *and influence* today: "They were seeking their own inheritance."

I have to listen carefully here, for it's a solemn reminder that if I fall into defining my own ways and standards as "the image of correctness," there are many who are seeking *something* and may settle for what I represent, however false my example or leadership.

ACTION: Let's ask these questions: Even if the example I present is right, is it

51

possible that personal pride in my example could poison its spiritual power potential? What is self-righteousness, and how does Micah's case represent its destructive power? Dad, what does your church attendance pattern model to your kids--all week long? In what way might a well-intended man pollute his potential for good by creating his own standard of discipleship as a substitute for God's?

This study of the Old Testament's development of the idea of "images" traverses the span from God's image to man's self-constructed substitute. We've seen:

• The original image FOR MAN as God conferred it upon him.
• The fallen and multiplied image OF MAN as sin relays it.
• The reminder how images THROUGH MAN become further debased.
• The command of God TO MAN to give no place to world-images.
• The instruction of God THAT MAN destroy world images in his possession.
• The warning from God as to HOW MAN can delude himself by self-contrived images.

Perhaps this study would merit recurrent review or conversational interaction with another brother in Christ. The lessons don't end here, nor does the biblical revelation of human folly generated by world-images conclude with these few key examples.

As we've earlier observed: With the subject of images, we're at the core of our call to be men of discernment who know WHAT we're about, HOW we're being shaped, and WHO we are.

Where do we go from here?

Chapter Four
TRANSFORMED INTO HIS IMAGE

It was a disgusting revelation of my own inner smallness. It surfaced a horrible flaw in my sense of security and confidence in my person--my identity. I failed at both points: (1) feeling threatened by a comparison with another man's achievement, and (2) feeling submerged by his apparent excellence when statistics showed his work exceeded the fruit of my efforts. Let me tell you about it.

It began with a tour of a new church facility. You would think I would be thrilled: "Look, God's Kingdom advancing!" But not so--at least, not *that* day! For the further I went as I was being led by our host, the more I found myself fighting to be honestly *glad*. After all, this man was in the same vocation as I, and the expansive, marvelously developed, brand-new-church-campus was vastly more beautiful and grand than where I serve.

I labored to quench the detestable surge of the spirits of comparison and competition--they're ferocious when those demons assail a man's identity! I thought I might be winning over the temptations, until we turned a corner and entered the area where the tapes of this pastor's messages were duplicated and shipped to all parts of the world. Granting myself the carnality of inquiring, "How many tapes are shipped each month?" (privately and sinfully hoping it was fewer than the number distributed of mine), I was suddenly sorry I'd asked. The numbers were astronomical by comparison with mine. I winced inwardly, and minutes later almost slinked away. When I might have rejoiced in the gifting of a dear man of God, when I might have praised the Lord for the marvelous evidence of divine grace bringing about tremendous fruit, I was tinged by jealousy and ashamed before the Holy Spirit's convicting me of such pitiful smallness of soul.

Please answer me, Sir. Do you recognize *anything* of yourself in my sad response?

I'm happy to say I wasted little time in repenting that day, but the fact I felt such intimidation, such erosion of my own identity, is due to an *image* problem--resulting in an *identity* crisis. You see, brother, at the root of my failure was a two-step mistake:

1. Yielding to comparison, I was looking at the IMAGE OF MAN, rather than seeing the IMAGE OF GOD in the creative uniqueness of God's grace in him. In effect, I was making myself an enemy of the Creator by beginning to resent what He had done through my fellow-pastor friend.

2. Yielding to competition, I was bowing to the IMAGE OF A MAN's accomplishment, rather than rejoicing in the IMAGE OF GOD's mightiness at work in powerful productiv-

ity. In doing so, I put myself in competition with God's sovereign choice and divine almightiness. How senseless and stupid! To attempt competing with God is to name yourself a loser in advance!

I ended up winning that day--winning because I returned my identity to its proper place: in Jesus Christ my Lord. And I confessed my sin of becoming so wrapped up in the IMAGE OF A MAN that I missed worshiping the manifest evidence of GOD HIMSELF at work in a wonderful way. The *quick* transformation came about because the *truth* of God's transforming my mind had found a place long before, even though the place of that truth in practical application suffered a momentary lapse that day.

Let's pursue this great truth of "transformation into Christ's image" as it unfolds in the New Testament.

The Image Of God

Jesus came not only to save mankind's *eternity* from destruction, but He also came to save mankind's *identity* from confusion. In His sinless life and death we are provided with forgiveness of sin and given the hope of heaven. But in His matchless person and nature we see the revelation of all that man-the-creature was meant to be. And we are provided with a hope--"the hope of glory"--by the promise that this matchless One has not only come *to* us to save, but is ready to dwell *in* us, to bring life:

• *Life* with a sense of destiny, bringing *confidence*;

• *Life* with a sense of adequacy, bringing *joy*;

• *Life* with a sense of His abiding, overthrowing *fear*,

. . . *Confidence* that walks without a strut and doesn't need to prove itself.

. . . *Joy* that lives with a satisfaction in God's sufficiency, removed from the carnal need to prove oneself equal to anyone.

. . . *Fear* that is overthrown, giving pride no place to gain a footing, for pride is only the false constructions pushed into position to compensate for whatever we fear "isn't enough" in ourselves.

Brother, pause to think on these things because the starting place for our securing a continual sense of adequacy, confidence, and fearlessness is to not only *see* God's image in Jesus, but to experience our being *transformed* into that same image. Look at the Scriptures with me.

Just as the Old Testament Scriptures reveal God's original image and plan for us, and describe the sorry process of deterioration that occurred by reason of man's pursuit of false images, the New Testament opens with hope. Defining that hope is seldom done in a thorough way.

Usually, the Gospel is summarized in a "get-saved-and-go-to-heaven-some-day" statement, which is true as far as it goes, but it leapfrogs right over the powerful *present* purposes of God in a man's life. *Besides* our receiving forgiveness of sins and the promise of eternity in heaven through our Lord Jesus Christ, we are *also* promised:

1. The daily enablement of the Holy Spirit for every practical detail of our life and living.

2. The wisdom of God for growth in our marriage, raising our kids, and conducting business on our jobs.

3. The increase of God's grace deepening into the fabric of our nature and strengthening our character.

4. The provision of God's promises for our physical strength and health, and our material and financial blessing.

5. The unlimited power of prayer to avenue through us by the Holy Spirit's power and to impact and change circumstances in the world around us.

While this summary doesn't elaborate all the abundance promised us in the *here and now*, it's enough to incite any thinking man's question: "How can I grow in this order of living?" And the answer is, *"Christ in you, the hope of glory"* (Col. 1:27). A THREE-POINT trip through key New Testament scriptures shows why--and *how*!

NEW TESTAMENT STEP ONE:
The Penetration

And the Word became flesh
and dwelt among us, and we

*beheld His glory, the glory as
of the only begotten of the Father, full of grace and truth. No
one has seen God at any time.
The only begotten Son, who is
in the bosom of the Father, He
has declared Him.*
                    John 1:14, 18

Because mankind had a dual need, God
became flesh to address *both*--the need of a
REDEEMER and the need of a RESTORER.

As *Redeemer*, Jesus became one of us
because His *death*, as a human being, was
a legal requirement of God's justice. There
is no other Way (John 14:6) and there is no
other Person (Acts 4:12) by which this could
be done.

As *Restorer*, however, Jesus became
one of us because His *life*, as a human being,
provided a spiritual demonstration of God's
ability to reinstate His image in human
flesh. In other words, God not only makes
a way to *save* mankind, but He also reveals
His plan to repenetrate mankind with His
image.

That's the reason the Scriptures are so
meticulously clear on this point: Jesus was
the Image of God *as* a man to reveal that
image again, *among* mankind to display
that image again, and *unto* mankind to offer
that image again!

Read these thoughtfully:

• **God's glory (image) is promised to "all flesh."**

> *The glory of the Lord shall be revealed, and all flesh shall see it together; for the mouth of the Lord has spoken.*
> *Isaiah 40:5*

• **God's glory becomes incarnate in His Son, Jesus.**

> *And the Word became flesh and dwelt among us, and we beheld His glory, the glory as of the only begotten of the Father, full of grace and truth.*
> *John 1:14*

• **God's Person (image/character) is displayed in Jesus.**

> *He who has seen Me has seen the Father . . . The words that I speak to you I do not speak on My own authority; but the Father who dwells in Me does the works.*   *John 14:9, 10*

• **Satan fights this reentry of God's revealed image.**

> *. . . The god of this age has blinded (the minds of those) who do not believe, lest the*

> light of the gospel of the glory
> of Christ, who is the image of
> God, should shine on them.
> 2 Corinthians 4:4

• As the "repenetrating" image of
God to mankind, Jesus Christ is called
"the firstborn"--that is, the beginning
point of a new race of the Redeemed.

> He is the image of the invisible
> God, the firstborn over all cre-
> ation.   Colossians 1:15

• Now, our Savior--the Redeeming
Man who has come to be the Restoring
Man--is enthroned. He has initiated the
path   of God's desire for all who are
saved--to remake the image of God in us,
and to restore us to the high destiny
intended in our creation.

> Who being the brightness of
> His glory and the express im-
> age of His person, and uphold-
> ing all things by the word of
> His power, when He had by
> Himself purged our sins, sat
> down at the right hand of the
> Majesty on high . . . For it was
> fitting for Him, for whom are all
> things and by whom are all
> things, in bringing many sons
> to glory, to make the author of
> their salvation perfect through

sufferings.
Hebrews 1:3; 2:10

The summary testimony of these texts is that God's plan to *redeem* man included more than recovering from sin and death. God's purpose is to reinstate His image in each of us--to recreate *in* us the very thing which will complete our intended being: *both* to KNOW God and to SHOW His Person and Presence through our lives by reason of His fullness indwelling us.

NEW TESTAMENT STEP TWO:
The Transformation

The beauty of the Gospel plan for our experiencing God's image restored in us is that the same grace that *re-penetrated* is poured out to us by the Holy Spirit to see that image *reinstated* too! Look at these clear-cut statements of that expectation offered to us:

- **Paul prayed for this image to be formed in people.**

    My little children, for whom I labor in birth again until Christ is formed in you.
    Galatians 4:19

- **God is totally committed to seeing His image in us again.**

    For whom He foreknew, He

62

also predestined to be con-
formed to the image of His Son,
that He might be the firstborn
among many brethren.
                    Romans 8:29

• Our walk and worship of Christ pave the way to this.

I beseech you therefore, breth-
ren, by the mercies of God, that
you present your bodies a liv-
ing sacrifice, holy, acceptable
to God, which is your reason-
able service (literally, 'your
spiritual worship'). *And do*
not be conformed to this world,
but be transformed by the re-
newing of your mind, that you
may prove what is the good
and acceptable and perfect will
of God.   Romans 12:1, 2

The evidence is there and the promise is contained within it. Dear brother of mine, we're offered the chance for a reinstatement of God's image in each of us. What a towering possibility! What a removal from the relentless "push" to establish our own status, verify our own worth, build our own image, secure our own identities!!

If it could happen, it would (1) break the human desperation to "be someone," for God's dwelling within us in fullness would cause us to be satisfied that we ARE complete in Him.

> *For in Him dwells all the fullness of the Godhead bodily, and you are complete in Him who is the head of all principality and power. Col. 2:9, 10*

If it could happen, it would (2) break the human pattern of sin, with its manifold expressions of anger, lust, dishonesty, and coveting, for God's dwelling within us in fullness would remove the insatiable quest to "have things" or "control things."

> *Therefore, let no one glory in men, for all things are yours ...the world or life or death, or things present or things to come--all are yours. And you are Christ's and Christ is God's. 1 Cor. 3:21-23*

> *But seek the kingdom of God, and all these things shall be added to you. Do not fear, little flock, for it is your Father's good pleasure to give you the kingdom. Luke 12:31, 32*

And the glorious part of God's program of rescuing and restoring mankind is that it CAN happen: God's image CAN be restored in us. And here's how.

*NOW THE LORD IS THE SPIRIT;
AND WHERE THE SPIRIT OF
THE LORD IS, THERE IS LIB-
ERTY. BUT WE ALL WITH UN-
VEILED FACE* (i.e., fully open
to His work in us) *BEHOLDING
AS IN A MIRROR* (i.e., God's
Word) *THE GLORY OF THE
LORD* (i.e., Jesus' fullness,
character, and revelation of
the Father's image), *ARE BE-
ING TRANSFORMED INTO THE
SAME IMAGE FROM GLORY
TO GLORY, JUST AS BY THE
SPIRIT OF THE LORD.*
   2 Cor. 3:17,18

   Would you join me, Sir? Let's rise for a
moment in praise to the wisdom and grace
of the Living God! For with these texts and
in this truth we are being told, "Your identity
problems, your image-making quests, can
be put to rest if you'll hear Me!" God has
given His Son and sent His Spirit--to *recover*
and *reinstate* us and to so *fully reveal His
image in us*--that we are given His "hope of
glory!"
   • Hope that the "glory" of His presence
will grow His purpose in us as we give place
to His Spirit;
   • Hope that every vestige of carnal
surrender to fear, lust, or pride can eventually be removed from our life-patterns;
   • Hope that the depth of Christ's work

in our lives will evaporate the need for self-verification, as He verifies His work in and through us.

• Hope that "Christ in you" will crowd out all smallness and pettiness and wrestling with human comparisons and competitiveness--for *now* our manhood is secured in His!

The Obvious Question: How Now?

The promise of "Christ in you" is to be received. But it's a promise we begin to *live out*, not an electric switch we *turn on*. The confession I made at the beginning of this chapter--my struggle with smallness when visiting another church site--is the reminder that we're called to a *growth* program, not an *instant-action* one. My temptation to regression was overcome quickly. But that quick comeback was a different thing from earlier traits of (1) not being aware at all of my entrapment in self-image making (during earlier years of my experience); and (2) my beginning lessons at confronting such temptations to smallness or false masculinity (which I didn't overcome quickly--and at previous times I stumbled completely). But if I've learned any lessons, they are these:

FIRST: Believe in the *promise* of the Holy Spirit to restore God's image in you.

SECOND: Receive the *power* of the Holy Spirit to fill you daily, enabling obedience and faith as you walk with Jesus.

THIRD: Respond to the *presence* of the Holy Spirit when He speaks, giving instruction or correction at points where *your* image-making or struggle with identity may be occurring.

FOURTH: Rest in the *process* of the Holy Spirit's indwelling. He isn't going to go away!! He's come to abide, and as long as you remain committed to the first three points, the fourth will assure His fulfillment of the word--

"CHRIST IN YOU . . . THE HOPE OF GLORY!"

Early in this chapter I said there are three New Testament Steps in the "transformation process" bringing us back into the image of the Creator through our Redeemer Jesus Christ. I've intentionally left the third step as a P.S. to this book. You'll find it later on page 77.

Chapter Five
CIRCUMCISION:
THE SEAL OF HIS IMAGE

There is only one way for us to fully enter into the Lord's design for us as men: Circumcision . . .

The *circumcision* of our *hearts*!

There is probably no more masculine image in the Bible than the powerfully pictured truth typified in the ancient rite of circumcision--the surgical removal of the excess flesh from the foreskin of the male sex organ. But the New Testament applies this to the *heart* of a man, and thereby we're introduced to a dynamic truth.

It began with Abraham and the covenant that released his promised life-begetting capacity (Gen. 17). Then the covenant was transmitted to successive generations, as the Lord proscribed to the nation of Israel that they circumcise every male on the eighth day.

I want you to see with me how this was the Lord's mark, an *image*, that He placed on His people. For example, with the application of this image in Joshua's time, God said, "I have rolled away the reproach of Egypt from off you." Point: You're no longer bound by the slave-image of your past, but you're now cut loose to the promise of your future! "The reproach of Egypt" is a figure of speech that speaks to us about the image of this world, and as such it represents many things:

- Patterns of the past dictating the present.
- World-worship and materialistic pursuit.
- Intimidation, fear, and carnal competitiveness.
- Conformity to compromising expectations.
- Being trapped or leashed to empty tradition.
- The pressure to perform to verify worth.
- Self-concepts of limitation and restriction.

. . . All rolled away--rolled away because the Lord is instituting a new economy of things. It's not the Lord supplying us with more carnal currency to attempt buying into the world's vain "economy" of values. Rather, He gives us a new economy--a new sense of Kingdom worth. It's a real and exceeding wealth which is based on an economy rooted in the spiritual currency of Christ's work on the Cross; an economy driven by the quickening of the Holy Spirit inside us. His transforming power within you and me has enormous purchasing ability; buying us a new life-power that's *first* born *in* us, and *then* can be cut loose *through* us.

The image of circumcision is powerfully instructive, because it depicts a man's call to let God determine which image will mark him.

In Genesis 17, the Lord first calls Abraham to receive circumcision as a mark and seal of the covenant.

> *And he received the sign of circumcision, a seal of the righteousness of the faith which he had while still uncircumcised, that he might be the father of all those who believe, though they are uncircumcised, that righteousness might be imputed to them also.*   Romans 4:11

Have you ever wondered how Abraham might have responded when the Lord told him this was to be the seal of his agreement with Him? It must have been startling! To begin, it was a new practice. And further, it not only was a sensitive subject by reason of the anatomy involved, but the world around thought the Jews foolish for circumcising themselves, and they were mocked by the rest of society as "body-mutilators."

The world will always mock the image God designs for a man. (In the case of physical circumcision, it's only been in this century that the practice has received confirmation from the medical community as to its value in personal hygiene. But until now, the Jewish community bore the brunt of scorn because they were not of the same image--the world's.)

Circumcision does come with a price. The physical rite teaches spiritual lessons in a very personal way.

First, in circumcision there is no recourse to privacy. The mechanics of the surgery involve *exposure*. Spiritually applied, our circumcision of the heart involves our allowing--indeed, welcoming--God to deal with our hearts; willingly exposing to Him the private matters of our soul. While there are no secrets unknown to Him, there are places where He knows surgery is essential to imprint His image on us, but upon which He will not work without our trust and submission. Thus, the circumcised heart admits that there is no private reserve withheld from God. Openness before Him--a nakedness of soul--keeps everything exposed. We stand as *His* alone; in the blaze of His presence daily.

Second, in physical circumcision there is no escape from pain. The process cuts. In the book of Joshua we read that it took three days for the men to recover from the pain of circumcision when administered in adult years rather than early in life as intended. This isn't some form of spiritual masochism. It's simply dealing with things that should have been dealt with sooner--yielding to the application of God's Word as the Spirit's sword, in circumcising action, slices away the surplus, the unnecessary, the excess. Flesh is pared that God's glory might be revealed in us--a new identity. And *identity*

71

is the central issue, for *thirdly*--

Circumcision cuts to the core of a man's identity.

The physical act of circumcision impacts that very member identifying a man's manhood. "It's a boy," was one day proclaimed, and this physical member provided identity. Now God cuts away at the heart of a man's false quests for recognition, shallow programs of ego-centeredness, every self-dependent enterprise at securing my own identity. And it's all that God Himself might declare of you--of me: "It's a *man* now!"

The benefits of circumcision impact a lifetime . . . and an eternity.

> *In Him you were also circumcised with the circumcision made without hands, by putting off the body of the sins of the flesh, by the circumcision of Christ, buried with Him in baptism, in which you also were raised with Him through faith in the working of God, who raised Him from the dead.*
> *Col. 2:11-12*

. . . Resurrection power and a changed life replace the momentary pain of circumcision.

Circumcision of the heart affects specific outworkings; manifestations of God's paring back the superficial. By this inner process of circumcision, He can bring us to our true identity in Him.

Remember years back when long hair and beards gained stylish acceptance? It was in that context that my friend, Jerry Cook, a fellow-pastor, told of a young man in his church who was a dedicated partner in ministry. Buck genuinely loved working with the young people in Jerry's congregation and he had a strong love for Jesus. He also happened to have very long hair and a beard. The latter is what occasioned Buck's becoming a tender illustration regarding "image" and a man's "identity."

One day, as Buck was walking downtown, he passed by the local barber shop. He later admitted that as he did, a kind of sneer rose up within him; smirking to himself, "Man, nobody's *ever* going to get me into a place like that! Thank you, Lord, I'm a *free spirit*, unbound by anybody's social conventions!" But almost instantly the Holy Spirit pierced his soul. The Heavenly Voice whispered, "Buck, are you willing to get your hair cut?"

"Lord, you know I don't need to do that! No way! I'm free!"

And it was then--then and there--that the Lord stopped him in his tracks: "Buck, you *could* have kept your hair long. But now, because you said, 'No,' I'm calling you to do it. Get a haircut, and do it now." And the holy punchline completed Buck's own testimony of this circumcising encounter: "Buck, I'm asking you to get your hair cut because *the roots of your hair have grown into your heart.*"

The incident thunders with practical insight and revelation. God wasn't mocking the man, He was being *merciful* to him. He was identifying a point in a man where his identity was confused with "image," and where the *real* man needed to be redefined. It involved circumcision--God touching a point where Buck's fruitfulness in ministering to others was in jeopardy because he could no longer distinguish between the value and sufficiency of Christ's image in him and the empty value of wearing a costume of individuality.

Whenever my liberty begins to become a pridefully-carried thing, I'm in danger. When I replace God's values with my own situational ethics, I'm in trouble. If I see in myself an insistence for my own way; if I rationalize it and tell God, "it's okay because I still love You"--even though I'm not meeting Him eye-to-eye and heart-to-heart--then I'm trading my real identity for a false one.

Please understand me. I'm not talking about *hair*. I'm talking about *heart*. Buck's hair was a part of his past values--values now in transition. A new identity was now being unfolded in Christ. However, a residue of false-identification with the world's image remained and needed to be addressed by God. It's at that point when God confronts us with the need to let Him change our image that our decision needs to be made.

A heart-check is in progress.

And the image into which we have allowed our hearts to be molded into over the years and months--whether it is the computer-chip circuit of the Holy Spirit's creation or the circuit design of this world--will yield a decision compatible with that image.

Until the Lord starts doing a work in the heart, the exterior elements have little significance. But as soon as He points something out to you or me, then we become responsible. Matters may be tolerated by reason of our own immaturity or deafness of soul--until *now*. Then, the Lord will speak to us about forms of habit; about attitudes; about things we eat, drink, listen to, watch--and how much. But He *never, ever* does this to diminish our pleasure or joy. The Bible says, "At your right hand there are pleasures forever more," and Jesus said, "I came that men might have life and have it more *abundantly*." And that will always be the consequence of heart circumcision: greater joy--greater abundance of grace in our lives. He shapes us as a tree is pruned so that *the fruit will increase*, not so our potential will wither up and die.

Listen please, Sir. You can:

. . . be saved and be filled with His Spirit;

. . . pray for hours daily and win souls to Christ;

. . . touch lives, give to the poor, fast consistently; and

. . . love people, serve greatly, and even give time to the PTA.

But all the while the Lord may be saying to you, "There's this *place* in your heart where I need to shape My image--through surgery." The most mature among us will periodically find new areas where the Father wants to reshape, refine, or renew His image in us. So never cease that availability to His ongoing transformation. It's the pathway to fruitfulness, dear brother. And it's the path to gaining an unshakeable certainty of who He is. And who you are.

PS: A Final Word . . .
OUR ULTIMATE HOPE

It's been a happy task to walk beside you, my brother.

These pages, directed toward pursuing the pathway of our growth, as men who care about God's way, as we seek a way past "world-image" entrapment, self-security, and false-identity systems, has been a pleasure to pursue. I hope it's been that for you, too.

But I didn't want to conclude without inviting you to look *beyond* the present; to look to the ultimate tomorrow, and the Coming of our Lord Jesus Christ.

It's not only good to keep His Return on our mind as a daily point of joyful expectation, but there are also wonderful references to His Coming which bear on our subject of God's image in us.

NEW TESTAMENT STEP THREE:
The Ultimate Transformation

In Chapter Four, I state there are three New Testament Steps to a man's full transformation into the image of God. Then, I concluded the chapter by saying I would not deal with the last one until this closing note in our study.

My reason for waiting is my awareness that too many believers put so much anticipation in the Return of Jesus as the answer to every personal or earthly dilemma, that they don't bother to give attention to their own responsibility for growth in Him *now*--before His Coming.

Though we have studied the massive potential of "Christ in you--the hope of glory--NOW!", I still don't want to sign-off without pointing you toward a high promise in God's Word which lifts our eyes to the glorious hope of Jesus' Return; to the *ultimate transformation we'll experience.*

Whatever we realize of God's restored image in us during this lifetime--and there's *much* awaiting us--let's make no mistake; the *consummate* transformation will occur when Jesus appears to receive His people unto Himself:

> *Beloved, now we are children of God; and it has not yet been revealed what we shall be, but we know that when He is revealed, we shall be like Him, for we shall see Him as He is. And everyone who has this hope in Him purifies himself, just as He is pure.*
> 1 John 3:2-3

Please notice the wisdom in the tension this text keeps before us. It's the very truth that has prompted my leaving this part of our study for now.

The Apostle John writes to say, "There's a GREAT transformation coming--WE WILL BE LIKE HIM--EXACTLY AND COMPLETELY!" But then he adds, "If you have this hope, then expect the refining, renewing ('purifying') process to be operational *now.*"

This same concept is presented in the Apostle Paul's letter to the Corinthians:

> *And as we have borne the image of the man of dust, we shall also bear the image of the heavenly Man.*
> *1 Cor. 15:49*

The surrounding text points to the ultimate day of our Lord when, at His Return, all the residue of human corruptibility and mortality will be *transcended* by the glory of our *translation* (the Rapture); and we'll be *transformed* totally--completely and eternally changed to enter eternity with our Savior.

There's not a man alive who has the slightest notion as to what the eternal future holds for us. But we can count on this: It's something worthy of God's creativity! Don't lock heaven down to the size of our tiny minds. It'll be more than a long-term vacation, more than an eternal retirement home, more than an endless party.

God created us in His image because He has imagined timeless wonders for our enjoyment with and beside Him, forever. So now that salvation has brought us back on track toward that destiny, let's grow in our true identity, as His present grace *progresses* the reinstatement of His image in us. And then, Sir--

Keep your eyes heavenward, for the day of our consummate and final transformation is near. Join me in:

> *Looking for that blessed hope*
> *and glorious appearing of our*
> *great God and Savior Jesus*
> *Christ.*   *Titus 2:13*

Let's keep growing in Him until then, brother. And though you and I may never meet until that Day, I'll see you there.

With Him.

DEVOTIONS

IN THE LAST EIGHT CHAPTERS OF

ROMANS

Contributed by Bob Anderson

The second half of the Book of Romans divides up into five main topical sections:

• Issues regarding God and Israel are discussed in 9:1-11:36;
• Rich applications of the Christian life are supplied to us in 12:1-15:13;
• Paul talks about his own ministry and plans in 15:14-33;
• Paul's personal greetings are found in 16:1-24; and,
• Paul gives his personal benediction in 16:25-27.

In the majority of these verses (12:1-15:13) Paul deals with the issue of Christian conduct, i.e., how we should live out our faith. He stresses that spirituality should be concretely expressed and evidenced by our actions in daily life.

(It is suggested that this devotional be used for stimulating discussion and prayer within a small group of men meeting regularly.)

☐ **Today's Text: Romans 9:1-5** *(key v. 3)*

1 **Today's Truth:** Here is a staggering display of compassion on Paul's part toward his countrymen. His love for them was so great that he was willing, if it were possible, to be condemned to hell himself if somehow it might provide salvation for the Jews. Of course, such an ambition is impossible, but the heart of the Savior is seen in Paul.

Today's Thoughts: _____
_____
_____

☐ **Today's Text: Romans 9:6-13** *(key v.8)*

2 **Today's Truth:** The outward image of being a Jew doesn't ultimately profit a man in God's Kingdom. It is the internal image being born of faith that makes one a "child of the promise"--one who is a Jew *inwardly* (Rom. 2:29).

Today's Thoughts: _____
_____
_____

☐ **Today's Text: Romans 9:14-19** *(key v. 18)*

3 **Today's Truth:** This verse doesn't mean that God prevents the unsaved from believing. It means that God uses both mercy and wrath to accomplish His redemptive purposes, and His heart does not desire *anyone* to perish.

Today's Thoughts: _____
_____
_____

☐ **Today's Text: Romans 9:20-26** *(key v. 22)*

4 **Today's Truth:** "What about God making people vessels of wrath!--*that's* not fair!" But the old saying is true: "the same sun that melts wax, hardens clay." God's miracles performed right under Pharoah's nose couldn't soften him because of his predisposition to hardness. So God used Pharoah's rebellion to show His glorious might.

Today's Thoughts: ————————

—————————————————————

—————————————————————

☐ **Today's Text: Romans 9:27-33** *(key v.29)*

5 **Today's Truth:** "Unless the Lord of Hosts had left us a *seed*, we would have become like Sodom"! God's DNA, the image-making power of Christ in us, preserves us from the moral decay and degradation of our Adamic sin nature.

Today's Thoughts: ————————

—————————————————————

—————————————————————

☐ **Today's Text: Romans 10:1-10** *(key v. 9)*

6 **Today's Truth:** How sweet and simple the knowledge of eternal salvation is! Paul could not have said it more succinctly than he did in verse 9.

Today's Thoughts: ————————

—————————————————————

—————————————————————

☐ **Today's Text: Romans 10:11-15** *(key v. 14)*

7 **Today's Truth:** There are times when a silent witness is important--when people can *see* Christ in us instead of just get an earful of words. But ultimately, salvation only comes through *hearing* and responding to the Gospel.

Today's Thoughts: _____

_____

_____

☐ **Today's Text: Romans 10:16-21** *(key v.16)*

8 **Today's Truth:** Israel cannot plead ignorance of the Good News or charge that God has been unfair with them--for they *refused* to believe the Gospel, though they were the first to hear it.

Today's Thoughts: _____

_____

_____

☐ **Today's Text: Romans 11:1-8** *(key v. 7)*

9 **Today's Truth:** The majority of the nation of Israel became blinded to the Gospel. The Greek word means that they literally had become callous or petrified against the truth. But verse 8 says "*God* has given them . . . eyes that they should not see." Why? Because that's what *they* had chosen. God simply induced a catalyst to speed up the process of manifesting *their own choice*.

Today's Thoughts: _____

_____

_____

☐ **Today's Text: Romans 11:9-14** *(key v. 14)*

10 **Today's Truth:** God's rejection of Israel is not final. For it is God's desire that the Jews eventually become jealous of the Gentiles' relationship with Christ, and thereby believe in the Gospel.

Today's Thoughts: _____

_____

_____

☐ **Today's Text: Romans 11:15-21** *(key v.18)*

11 **Today's Truth:** The human tendency toward racism and/or spiritual pride is addressed here. Paul reminds us that we must never forget that salvation is from the Jews.

Today's Thoughts: _____

_____

_____

☐ **Today's Text: Romans 11:22-29** *(key v. 26)*

12 **Today's Truth:** Paul is not saying that every Jewish person who ever lived will be saved. He is speaking in the collective sense, meaning that there will be a massive turning of the Jews to faith in Christ at some point in the future.

Today's Thoughts: _____

_____

_____

☐ **Today's Text: Romans 11:30-36** *(key v. 32)*

13 **Today's Truth:** Paul is touching on one of those truths that is extremely deep for the human mind. God began with the Jews, but included an era for the Gentiles, and then will soon embrace the Jews once more. And by this, He is doing everything possible to save as many people as possible throughout all of history, even though His dealings may appear, at times, to be quite severe.

Today's Thoughts: ———————————————
———————————————————————————————
———————————————————————————————

☐ **Today's Text: Romans 12:1-5** *(key v.2)*

14 **Today's Truth:** We are not to be *conformed* to this world. The Greek word for *conformed* is *suschematizo*. Recognize the word "schematic"–as in blueprints for an electronic circuit? We must not let our "circuitry" be programmed by this world's system of values.

Today's Thoughts: ———————————————
———————————————————————————————
———————————————————————————————

☐ **Today's Text: Romans 12:6-13** *(key v. 6)*

15 **Today's Truth:** Paul stresses that we should use the gifts God has given us. Have you asked God to show you your spiritual gifts and how to use them?

Today's Thoughts: ———————————————
———————————————————————————————
———————————————————————————————

☐ **Today's Text: Romans 12:14-21** *(key v. 17)*

16 **Today's Truth:** Verse 17 is one of a myriad of verses in Scripture defining in exact terms what the outworkings of the image of Christ are to be in our lives. "Repay no one evil for evil"–that certainly is contrary to the image of this world!

Today's Thoughts: _____

_____

_____

☐ **Today's Text: Romans 13:1-7** *(key v. 1)*

17 **Today's Truth:** "Oh no! Being conformed to the image of Christ relates to how honestly I pay my taxes? Does God really care about 1040s and 1099s? I mean, the Government is corrupt! I deserve to–" . . . Verse 7 tells us God's reply.

Today's Thoughts: _____

_____

_____

☐ **Today's Text: Romans 13:8-14** *(key v.14)*

18 **Today's Truth:** If any one of us "makes provision" for our flesh, something of corruption–in one form or another–will grow. To "make provision for" means to "plan ahead or make preparation for" gratifying the carnal nature; not stumbling into sin, but premeditated action.

Today's Thoughts: _____

_____

_____

☐ **Today's Text: Romans 14:1-6** *(key v. 1)*

19 **Today's Truth:** The image of Christ in us will cause us to put loving receptivity towards a brother or sister above debate and striving to be right about non-essential issues, i.e., those things which are neither commanded nor forbidden in the Word.

Today's Thoughts: ―――――――――――――

_____

_____

☐ **Today's Text: Romans 14:7-13** *(key v.10)*

20 **Today's Truth:** Paul mentions that we will all stand before the Judgment Seat of Christ. He presents this as a motivator so that we will love one another without contempt. This is not a threat of hell--the Judgment Seat of Christ determines the believer's rewards in heaven, not his salvation.

Today's Thoughts: ―――――――――――――

_____

_____

☐ **Today's Text: Romans 14:14-23** *(key v. 19)*

21 **Today's Truth:** When tempted to argue with a loved one over a petty issue, remember verse 19: "Pursue things which make for peace." We are to actively seek ways we might build up others.

Today's Thoughts: ―――――――――――――

_____

_____

☐ **Today's Text: Romans 15:1-6** *(key v. 5)*

22 **Today's Truth:** "Like-minded" is the blessed characteristic of believers who are being conformed into Christ's image. By grace, God grants this harmony to those who walk with their gaze fixed on the Prince of Peace.

Today's Thoughts: _____

_____

_____

☐ **Today's Text: Romans 15:7-12** *(key v.7)*

23 **Today's Truth:** If we all diligently applied to our family life and marriage those principles that govern our walk as Christians, divorce rates would plummet, and the home would be the happiest place on earth. "Receive one another" in this text is an *aggressive* act of acceptance.

Today's Thoughts: _____

_____

_____

☐ **Today's Text: Romans 15:13-19** *(key v. 13)*

24 **Today's Truth:** As Christians, we serve "*the* God of hope." He is able to enter any situation of apparent "hopelesness" and work miracles. Redeeming His people from despair is second nature to the Almighty.

Today's Thoughts: _____

_____

_____

☐ **Today's Text: Romans 15:20-26** *(key v. 20)*

25 **Today's Truth:** Paul sought to bring the Gospel to spiritually dry places; locations where people were ignorant of the Good News. For most of us, this doesn't require travelling to a foreign mission field. Think of one person at work or in your neighborhood who needs to hear about Jesus and target a lunchtime with them to share your faith.

Today's Thoughts: _____

_____

_____

☐ **Today's Text: Romans 15:27-33** *(key v.30)*

26 **Today's Truth:** When we see a spiritual giant such as the Apostle Paul *begging* for prayer, it is a reminder to us how dependent we all are on each other's spiritual support.

Today's Thoughts: _____

_____

_____

☐ **Today's Text: Romans 16:1-6** *(key v. 1)*

27 **Today's Truth:** Phoebe's name means "pure or radiant as the moon." This woman was obviously a brilliant reflection of the image and light of Jesus Christ. According to many scholars, it was this woman who carried this epistle of Paul to the congregation in Rome.

Today's Thoughts: _____

_____

_____

☐ **Today's Text: Romans 16:7-13** *(key v. 7)*

28 **Today's Truth:** The long list of Paul's greetings illustrates that he was not a leader who functioned in "authority at a distance," but he was one who cultivated intimate relationships with those he led.

Today's Thoughts: _____

_____

_____

☐ **Today's Text: Romans 16:14-20** *(key v.20)*

29 **Today's Truth:** The glorious promise of God to "crush Satan under our feet shortly" is predicated on our obedience and being innocent ("simple") with regard to evil (vs. 19). Note the teamwork involved: God will do the crushing but He will use our feet!

Today's Thoughts: _____

_____

_____

☐ **Today's Text: Romans 16:21-24** *(key v. 24)*

30 **Today's Truth:** There is power in pronouncing a blessing upon another person. Even the simplest words such as "the grace of our Lord Jesus Christ be with you" minister with a surprising degree of impact. This calls to mind that "Death and life are in the power of the tongue" (Prov. 18:21)

Today's Thoughts: _____

_____

_____

☐ **Today's Text: Romans 16:25-27** *(key v. 26)*

31 **Today's Truth:** It seems that Paul was almost able to close his letter in verse 24, but with one more final burst of praise and glorification of God, he pronounces his benediction. And with it, he reminds the reader that the glorious Gospel, amplified so magnificently in this Book of Romans, is commanded by God to be made known to every nation on earth in order that as many as are willing might know the Savior.

Today's Thoughts: _____

_____

_____

A MAN'S WORSHIP AND WITNESS

A study of how God's Kingdom comes to and through men

Jack Hayford

THOMAS NELSON PUBLISHERS
Nashville • Atlanta • London • Vancouver

Published in Nashville, Tennessee, by
Thomas Nelson, Inc., Publishers, and
distributed in Canada by Word
Communications, Ltd., Richmond, British
Columbia, and in the United Kingdom by
Word (UK), Ltd., Milton Keynes, England.

ISBN 0-7852-7797-8

Printed in the United States of America

1 2 3 4 5 6 7 - 01 00 99 98 97 96 95

TABLE OF CONTENTS

Chapter One
Right to the Center!

A Street-Level Application

There's a central core of pivotal possibilities in every man. This "center of being" so foundational in each of us is interchangeably called our "heart" or "spirit." It's called our heart because (like our physical heart) it is central to our life and effective functioning; and (like our emotional "heart") this "core" determines our primary focus, interests, and affections in life. This "core" is also called our spirit because it's central to touching God—the Source of our life and Resource of power to live it. Our worshiping the Almighty God is the key to activating and revitalizing this "core." Our worship "connects" us with Him:

• Like a "landsat" uplinks to capture a picture and message from a satellite in space.
• Like an elevator built into the hub of a high-rise, allowing contact and interaction at every floor level.
• Like a ski lift takes us from the plain of the mundane to the peak of adventure.

I had just finished a workshop on worship, and Jack had been one of the men present. You'd like him—a tough-but-gentle, strong-but-quiet guy—a contractor in the roofing business and a committed disciple of Jesus Christ. He had been there as I'd

7

outlined the principles of power in my message: *When a Man Worships.* Like so many of the hundreds of men I meet with monthly, Jack was getting hold of the fact that spirituality isn't mystical; that operating in continual touch with the Immortal, Invisible, Almighty God isn't a lapse into mindlessness or bizarre behavior.

We'd just looked at Abraham, who the Bible says "fathered" the way of faith for men like us, and among the power-principles we noted in Abraham's worship was the power of his footsteps. God told him, "Walk through the land I've promised you!" Abraham had done it because he believed his obedience was an act of worship, moving in to possess God's promised boundaries for his life. Jack's mind was gripped by this revelation in God's Word, reminding him that the worship of his heart was more than a meditative, devotional exercise—it was spiritually dynamic and impacting of a man's "outer" world as well as his inner thoughts. He was learning that as a man worships his Creator, his spirit—his inner being—is endowed with a "weight of glory." He saw how that "weight"—a pure vein of Heaven-born substance to his life, filling the core, or center of his being as he worships, is intended by God to be a means for pointedly dealing with practical daily issues and problems.

Jack and Julie had been having trouble

with their teenaged daughter, Cathy. A good kid had suddenly begun behaving strangely. A rebellion not present before was starting to stress the family's relationship with Cathy, and strained moments were crowding into a happy home.

Armed with this lesson on the power in the faith-filled footsteps of a worshiping man, Jack rose early the next morning before the family or neighbors were up and about. In the dim light of that predawn hour, he went outside and began to walk the property line bordering their home site. As he stood at each corner, he lifted his hands in praise to the Almighty, then strode forward with worship, doing two things:

• Declaring the might and glory of God, exalting His greatness, power, and love; and

• Calling on God's power to surround his home—to overrule any evil power seeking to penetrate the boundaries of his family's life.

Jack's worship-filled action was rewarded with incredible speed and precision.

Later that morning, right after Jack had left for work and Cathy for school, Julie, while washing the breakfast dishes, was impressed with a clear picture which came to her mind. She saw herself entering her daughter's room, opening a specific drawer, reaching to the back of the drawer under specific garments, and finding a small packet. She sensed God's presence prompting her and quickly dried her hands and did exactly what she had just "seen." As a result, she discovered a package of marijuana in that precise location, obviously hidden there by their daughter.

When Cathy arrived home from school, Jack and Julie lovingly, but pointedly, confronted her. Jack first described how God had moved him to walk in worship around their home, inviting God's power— "Thy Kingdom come!" Next, Julie related her experience at the kitchen sink, and her pursuant action. Then, laying the small packet before Cathy, they expressed their love for her and their desire to help—words that were instantly met with a teenager's tears and overflowing words of repentance. "Mom, Dad, I didn't really want this stuff. . .I don't know why I've been like I've been. . .but I know this is Jesus' way of stopping me. Thank you. . .Thank you. . . ." And amid more tear-filled eyes, a family was bonded closer than ever, and unknown, potentially devastating possibilities were averted.

It's just one example of the power of what I call "hardcore worship." If the core-like center of a man's being—his heart/his spirit—becomes filled with the solid gold of living praise, vital power will result. It's born through childlike humility in a man's worship before the Creator. It's the "praise with understanding" that brings the dimension of divine blessing into practical daily application. And it discovers and invites the power of God's Kingdom, over and above the efforts of the darkness to crowd out His glory-brightness from our homes or any part of our lives. Let's find out how we can each draw on this resource of power-through-worship.

Worship Defined

It's wonderful to hear the testimony of Jack's employing worship so effectively, but some people may be troubled by this "using" of worship. Aren't we supposed to worship God only for *His* sake, never for our *own*?

Of course, it's true that God Himself IS the object, the focus, and the centerpiece Personality of all worship—He Himself! But I believe He has made clear in His Word that He has more in mind and purpose through our worshiping Him than just Himself. He has *given* us His call to worship to release things both in us and through us as worshiping men. I contend that God instituted worship *for people*—not solely for *His* own enjoyment.

• I submit that worship is not intended by God for people to prove their own expertise in religious exercise, but that rather He gave us worship as a means for satisfying our hunger and thirst for Him.

• I propose that Sunday mornings were never designated as a weekly test to prove whether we love God or not, but that rather

11

He gave us His biblical call to worship together (Hebrews 10:25) to keep us in the mainstream of spiritual refreshing via worship, teaching, and fellowship.

• I contend that when worship focuses on "protecting God" from "unworthy" participants—disallowing participation by people who have not met some religious standard of desirability, sophistication, or compatibility—then its purpose is defeated. Such restrictive attitudes can never serve God's purpose as a means to bringing broken people into wholeness and fulfillment.

• I hold that worship is *for people*. You see, God did not first *receive* worship. He first *gave* it; creating man with this dynamic capacity, and it's very clear that God's mindset in "giving" worship as a potential exercise for mankind had man's best interests at heart. For example, the first gift given toward focusing worship was God's gift of the Sabbath (Genesis 2:3); a gift from God which Jesus made clear was *indeed* for the benefit (Mark 2:27) of mankind. Sabbath worship (including church life and fellowship in the New Testament) has been given for the restoration of the human soul, for the blessings which He releases to us in the context of our communion with and worship of God. And yet, to illustrate how quickly mankind can distort what God designs, the Pharisees wrenched the Sabbath into a legalistic ordeal that didn't bless anyone as God had intended, but only served to puff the pride of theological experts.

There have always been some who disagree that a key purpose of worship is to bless the worshiper. Such a concept has been viewed as a self-serving brand of "experience-oriented" spirituality. *Anthropocentric*, they would call it—which is a fancy, tongue-splitting way of saying, "centered in man."

"In worship," they would emphatically state, *"God* is blessed and God alone! How dare *we* presume to be beneficiaries of the act of worship which is, by its very definition, a consecration of devotion *heavenward to God!"* That sounds so holy. But listen:

I would certainly agree, and would resist any brand of pop-theology or worship practice if it is only configured to satisfy a man's quest for God *while at the same time* allowing him to continue pursuing his own indulgences. In this respect, I would heartily agree—God and His glory are the focus of our praise, and our obedience to Him is the evidence of our commitment to Him. I say, "Amen!" We should beware of any self-serving religious exercises which, though choreographed under the banner of "worship," transform no one and transcend nothing. Thus, the "man-centeredness" which others insist we avoid is indeed addressed. But, in settling that issue, let us not fall into the camp of anyone who would

13

fear the benefits of worship—people being "blessed" or holiness becoming too "happy" a lifestyle. Let's be sure to take into account the numerous scriptures which promise worshipers "blessings," "fruitfulness," and "increase" if we pursue the Lord with all of our heart:

> *I will sing a new song to You, O God; on a harp of ten strings I will sing praises to You. . .Happy are the people who are in such a state; happy are the people whose God is the Lord!*
>
> *Psalm 144:9, 15*

> *. . . I have come that they may have life, and that they may have it more abundantly.* *John 10:10*

We need to remember that in saying "worship is *for man*" does not mean that worship is *to him*. All worship, however benefiting it is to us, is directed to the Lord—we've made that clear. Even so, some may be disturbed at the thought that from God's perspective, the gift of worship He's given to us, His beloved creatures, is intended to *enrich, fulfill, bless,* and *benefit* the worshiper.

I want to emphasize that this is true.

Always.

And worship benefits us a lot.

Consider these biblical truths:

• When we give, it shall be given unto us (Lk. 6:38).

• God, like any good parent, is blessed

14

when His children are blessed (Mt. 7:11).

• Repeatedly, God calls His creatures to worship in His presence so that He might release, redeem, renew and restore them (Ps. 17:15; Jer. 17:14).

• The Bible virtually blossoms with such beautiful affirmation: God intends that in worship His people would find joy, blessing, fulfillment and purpose (Ps. 9:14; Ps. 43:4; Isa. 61:3).

A Dramatic Illustration

One of the most dramatic pictures of this principle is manifest in the way God delivered Israel and brought them to be a people who would learn to truly worship Him. The broken yoke of their Egyptian taskmasters opened the way to a meeting at Mount Sinai where they not only received God's commandments—He also gave them the tabernacle worship as a means of walking into a *life* of worship, which would *lead* to a *land* of His fulfilling purpose for them. When God called them forth so that they might "serve Me" (i.e., worship Him), He wasn't relocating them from one form of slavery to another—from Egypt's bricks to Sinai's rituals. No! He was leading them to a life of blessing; to a life of discovering that if you worship the Living God, you'll receive His promised purpose for you, and by that worship and its attendant blessing, you'll become a witness to the world.

He delivered His people out from bondage

and into worship, for it was only through worship that Israel could come to fully know God's heart and nature. Further, only through worship would they begin to grasp the far-reaching purposes of the One who had promised "I will bring you up and bring you in . . . to a land flowing with milk and honey." And their experience is a graphic picture of what it means, through worship, to know the God of your destiny, who designs His people to be great and to have real purpose on this earth. Just as Abraham, the Father of Faith, journeyed from altar to altar, worshiping the Lord through his lifetime as he was led by God, so Israel, and so we are called. See what He said to Abraham:

> *I will make you a great nation; I will bless you and make your name great; and you shall be a blessing.*
> *Genesis 12:2*

Capture the significance of that statement! It applies to you and me, revealing God's purpose for and through all who worship Him. God's original and ongoing design in redemption is not only to bless us who worship Him, but also to bless *through* us. Our worship becomes the pivotal point at which God not only meets us to minister to us, but where He transforms us and blesses us so He can minister through us. Our Father's high design is to bless the world through a "nation" of worshipers—

people who will become witnesses unto His glory:

Arise, shine; for your light has come! And the glory of the Lord is risen upon you. For behold, the darkness shall cover the earth, and deep darkness the people; but the Lord will arise over you, and His glory will be seen upon you. The Gentiles shall come to your light, and kings to the brightness of your rising.   *Isaiah 60:1-3*

But you are a chosen generation, a royal priesthood, a holy nation, His own special people, that you may proclaim the praises of Him who called you out of darkness into His marvelous light.   *1 Peter 2:9*

It is this understanding that will keep us motivated purely, sensibly, and openly in our worship. Our praise will never be a mere show of pretense in worship, as if we could somehow manipulate blessings from God. Our first and foremost reason to worship will be to fulfill our Lord's words:

Then one of the scribes came and . . . asked Him, "Which is the first commandment of all?" Jesus answered him, "The first of all the commandments is: 'Hear, O Israel, the Lord our God, the Lord is one. And you shall love the Lord your God with all your heart,

*with all your soul, with all your mind,
and with all your strength.' This is the
first commandment. And the second,
like it, is this: 'You shall love your
neighbor as yourself.' There is no
other commandment greater than
these."* Mark 12:28-31

See the direct relationship between *prioritizing* worship and *actualizing* our expression of God's love to those around us.
Vital worship to God transforms the soul
and brings a genuine concern for our
"neighbor"—the world around us. From
all these insights we distill these principles.

• Worship was and is our fulfillment
of God's foremost *commandment.*
• Worship was and is the touchpoint
of *relationship*—ours, both with God and
with man.
• Worship was and is the entrypoint to
finding and fulfilling God's intended *destiny* for one's life.
• Worship was and is the release-
point of great *blessing to us.*
• Worship was and is the power-point
by which we are transformed and empowered to become *witnesses* to the world
around us.

This perspective on worship is abundantly evident in the New Testament as
well. One of Jesus' most profound state-

18

ments about worship included reference to an immoral woman (John 4:7-29). He was clearly welcoming her to turn away from her emptiness, to be filled with the love of the Living God, Who is seeking the worship of honest hearts—even broken ones like hers.

Paul in his epistle to the Romans calls us to present ourselves as people of worship so we can come to know the goodness, the desirability, and the perfection of God's purpose in our lives (ref. Romans 12:1, 2).

Such illustrations from Scripture clearly show that IF we worship Him in spirit and in truth, esteeming Him worthy of all praise, all the benefits of worship are inescapable! In other words, God is SEEKING genuine worshipers, and wherever He can find them, you can be sure He will bless them and accomplish His purposes through them. How, then, should we think about our worship as men who are learning this wisdom?

He Is Worthy!

Get your tongue ready. Here comes a real twister: *weorthscipe.* Any serious word study of "worship" will ultimately bring you to this archaic word. It's Old English, meaning "to ascribe worth, to pay homage, to reverence or to venerate." The common ground between weorthscipe's definition and the word "worship," is the concept of *worth.* When we connect the idea of *worth* with the action of *worship,* a few interesting questions arise.

- What value or *worth* are we ascribing to God in our worship?
- Is our worship *proportionate* to God's actual character and glory?
- Do our worshipful *expressions* of devotion transcend mere intellectual assessments of God, and do they involve *heartfelt affection* and *expressed love* for the Lord?

It would be wise to take inventory of our worship, to assess it in the light of Scripture. For example, let's take a lesson from the ultimate earthly expression of worship—Solomon's Temple. On the day it was completed, God's pleasure with all that had been done was abundantly evident:

> *And they brought up the ark of the Lord . . . King Solomon, and all the congregation (were) sacrificing sheep and oxen that could not be counted or numbered for multitude. Then the priests brought in the ark of the covenant of the Lord . . . And it came to pass, when the priests came out of the holy place, that the cloud filled the house of the Lord, so that the priests could not continue ministering because of the cloud; for the glory of the Lord filled the house of the Lord.*
>
> *1 Kings 8:4-6, 10-11*

Don't miss the significance of this visitation of God's glory responding to a man's worship. What brought it about?

First, *immeasurable worth* was being ascribed to the Lord through the glorious Temple worship. No expense had been spared. It has been estimated that the entire project of Solomon's Temple cost approximately $4 trillion! Of course, Solomon was not confused by thinking that the shimmer of layers of gold and precious gems in the Temple WAS God's glory. On the contrary, he was awestruck with his God:

But will God indeed dwell on the earth? Behold, heaven and the heaven of heavens cannot contain You. How much less this temple which I have built!
1 Kings 8:27

Solomon recognized the incomprehensibility of the Almighty. He knew that God transcended any religious enterprise of man—that God could not be captured or contained inside a building or a method. But he also knew that God's presence would dwell richly wherever worthy worship was raised to His glory. In short, my brother, you and I can build a house of worship any place we decide, and it doesn't cost $4 trillion, $4 million, $4 thousand, or even 4 cents: it costs much more. A man's worship costs the full commitment of his heart—the core of his life and affection—unto God.

A Summary of Insights
God's visitation at the site of Solomon's Temple gives us a fivefold insight to the main

21

components of worship—a man's worship which makes a place for God's glory to manifest. These components include:

1. A *physical expression* of God's worth. This was evidenced in the very fact of His building the Temple. This represents a man's "making room" for the Lord to dwell where he is (1 Kings 6:1-38). This is the starting place: Make a place in your daily life, or build a place in any circumstance you face—give God "room" to work there.

2. A *conceptual grasp* of God's worth was expressed in Solomon's articulate, insightful prayer of dedication, extolling God's grandeur and majesty (1 Kings 8:22-53). When you worship, remember brother, we're worshiping an awesome God, Who is greater and grander than we can possibly imagine. Faith rises in such an atmosphere of worship and praise.

3. A *financial proclamation* of God's worth was declared by the huge investment made in the Temple, all of which came from free-will offerings presented by worshipers of the Lord (1 Kings 7:13-51). Never minimize the righteous wisdom of bringing tithes and offerings as you worship. We can't buy God's blessings, but disobedience in worship can prevent them.

4. A *spiritual statement* of worth was made by the countless sacrifices offered that day during the celebration of the Temple's dedication (1 Kings 8:62-66). Always remember that the heartbeat of all

living worship pulsates with the awareness that the Blood of the Lamb is (a) the means of our access to God's throne in worship, (b) the power which cleanses us as priestly men for worship, and (c) the promise of victory which overthrows the enemy as we worship.

5. A *divine visitation* resulted—the consequence of a man's worship opened the way for the entrance of God's glory and power, right there and right then (1 Kings 8:1-11). This same prospect is available today as you and I worship the Lord: He's ready to visit with transforming glory, to change our natures and to change our circumstance, right here—right now!

This is important enough for us to review and apply all these things again. As worshiping men, let's lay hold of the significance of each facet of the above.

Physical expression. Simply put, God's man gave God room. It was only a building—a Temple—but it symbolizes how each one of us may daily prepare a chamber of worship in our hearts—make room. Obviously, "to make room" will often require the elimination of clutter and obstructions. Even with the most sincere believer, worldly debris and carnal distractions can gradually crowd the heart. Suddenly, without ever having realized the quantity of these things, we find ourselves encumbered by the stuff of this world—"stuff" which seeks to suffocate the praises of God. Whether it's anxieties, sin, distractions—whatever would steal from God

His rightful place on the throne of our hearts—such obstructions are rightfully called "idols."

> *Son of man, these men have set up their idols in their hearts, and put before them that which causes them to stumble into iniquity. Should I let Myself be inquired of at all by them? Therefore speak to them, and say to them, "Thus says the Lord God: 'Everyone of the house of Israel who sets up his idols in his heart, and puts before him what causes him to stumble into iniquity, and then comes to the prophet, I the Lord will answer him who comes, according to the multitude of his idols, that I may seize the house of Israel by their heart, because they are all estranged from Me by their idols.'"* Ezekiel 14:3-5

Conceptual grasp. In J.B. Phillips' classic book, *Is Your God Too Small?,* he challenges the reader to come to grips with how often and how severely we each tend to minimize God in our own thinking. It happens naturally because our finite minds so easily tend toward thinking of God in human terms. Further, this happens frequently because the Adversary of our souls will constantly seek to undermine our faith by blurring our vision of the greatness of our God. But worship is the perfect opportunity to clear and to enlarge our vision, to let the Holy Spirit expand our perceptions, and to refresh our exposure to the Living God. David was diligent to remind himself Who his God was and how worthy He was of his continual trust.

When I consider Your heavens, the work of Your fingers, the moon and the stars, which You have ordained, what is man that You are mindful of him, and the son of man that You visit him?
Psalm 8:3-4

I will meditate on the glorious splendor of Your majesty, and on Your wondrous works.
Psalm 145:5

Financial proclamation. Our tithes and offerings affirm that God is worthy of our material sacrifice. When we give, we are saying in essence, "Lord, all that I have is from You to begin with. I trust You, and I freely and obediently give—not only because You command it, but because You are faithful and I know You will provide for all of my needs!" Simple obedience in this area of giving stems from God's Word, and it's rich with promise.

"Bring all the tithes into the storehouse, that there may be food in My house, and prove Me now in this," says the Lord of hosts, "If I will not open for you the windows of heaven and pour out for

you such blessing that there will not be room enough to receive it."
Malachi 3:10

Spiritual statement. Foremost, our worship magnifies the covenant of Calvary—the Blood of the Lamb. But Solomon's sacrifices, according to the Old Testament covenant anticipating Calvary, are instructive in additional ways. Look at the way he made sacrifices of innumerable offerings.

It may seem surprising that Scripture describes praise and worship as a "sacrifice." As men at worship, exactly what are we sacrificing, anyway? What are we losing?

Primarily, our "flesh." Just as animals' flesh was consumed on the altar with Solomon's offering of bulls and lambs, so our carnality ("flesh") may be consumed by the fire of God's Presence as we worship. Pride dies. Sophistication fades. Self-sufficiency is abandoned as we acknowledge our utter dependence upon God through worship and extol His worthiness to receive our thanksgiving and praise.

Therefore by Him let us continually offer the sacrifice of praise to God, that is, the fruit of our lips, giving thanks to His name . . . for with such sacrifices God is well pleased.
Hebrews 13:15, 16

Worthy worship ascribes all these things to the glory of the Lord. The result will always be a **Divine visitation**. We'll be changed and our circumstances, however restrictive, will be transcended by God's power. Those are the reasons He's "given" us worship; the reasons He's delivered us from our own "Egyptian" slavery. He's called us to be men of worship, but with the heart-qualities of a child. God is well pleased with such a spirit, for thereby the "core" of your being is becoming filled with the solid gold of His character and understanding. Such a childlikeness of this "hardcore worship" is not child*ish*. But it's that order of manly worship and tender-hearted trust seen in that no-nonsense roofing contractor, Jack. Though equipped with a workman's hands of granite, this man chose to be blessed with a heart as tender as a child's toward God; who, walking in the predawn hours with upraised arms around his property in worshipful dependence upon God, discovered the pathway for his family's deliverance.

Whatever our need,
whomever we're concerned for,
whatever we face—

Let's be men of worship like that.

TALK ABOUT IT! Chapter questions to discuss with a friend.

1. Have you ever had an experience similar to Jack's—where you felt the Lord called you to "walk the borders" of your home or apartment in prayer and worship? Share the results of your experience.

2. Do you think this is something men should do on a regular basis as priests of their homes? Decide when you will do this again, or for the first time, and find another brother to be accountable to regarding your commitment.

3. Do you still feel reservation about physical worship (raising hands, etc.)? Discuss your feelings about this with a brother.

Chapter Two
Your Body—His Temple

Do you ever feel like a spiritual "toad"?

That's the way I've often described my perception of myself on more occasions than I care to number. Even though I *know* it's right to worship, and even though I *love* the Lord with all my heart, I can feel as devoid of spirituality as a brass doorknob, as passionate for action as a tree sloth—that's what I mean when I describe my feelings as being on the order of a "toad."

Perhaps nothing challenges a man's worship more than coming to terms with the human inclination toward passivity. Presuming the barricades of pride have been overcome, and a child-like willingness to worship secured in my soul, any number of things can slow my readiness to worship like Jesus said.

And you shall love the Lord your God with all your heart, with all your soul, with all your mind, and with all your strength.   *Mark 12:30*

This text, summoning a man's worship of the Most High God with his total being—spirit, soul (mind, emotions, and will), and body, is matched with a similar summons from the lips of Paul:

> *I beseech you therefore, brethren, by the mercies of God, that you present your bodies a living sacrifice, holy, acceptable to God, which is your reasonable service. And do not be conformed to this world, but be transformed by the renewing of your mind, that you may prove what is that good and acceptable and perfect will of God.*
> *Romans 12:1, 2*

These verses are precious commands from God's Word, inciting us to worship expressively and tenaciously. But how often have "toadlike" feelings of inadequacy, weariness, guilt, or other human obstacles of mind or emotion hindered you? Private devotional times and public congregational meetings are equally blocked by such feelings. So, to become a man of worship, I've got to find the pathway to become dynamically equipped to worship God with an honesty toward my own feelings, but a willingness to exceed them by actions of my will and understanding.

Time and again, the psalms of David—certainly a man who learned the power of worship—declare "I WILL praise the Lord!" It's no secret that with many of the events in David's life, he was likely to often not "feel" much like worshiping. Alternately being chased by Saul—running for his life;

betrayed by his son—and running for his life again; desperately trapped at the hands of enemies; guilty of miserable failure as a victim of his own sin—such episodes hardly seem conducive to worshipful praise toward God. Yet David, as a man who knew the essence of adversity year after year, still continued praising God through it all.

It's a decision a man makes. So when the "spiritual toad" feelings beset us, whether due to weariness, discouragement, or failure, let's learn from David's example. The power of God's Word reporting David's overcoming praise can birth or renew a fortitude in us. Say with me, "I don't need to *feel* spiritual! I *will* to praise Your Name, O God!"

Join me as a partner in discovering what the Holy Spirit can do when such a posture of persistency in praise is taken. The Spirit of God will move into the moment, once you and I commit to praise irrespective of our feelings. He'll never view that action as mechanical or self-induced. He sees it for what it is—a will to exalt Jesus. . .a will to praise the Father. . .a will to live on the grounds of the Word notwithstanding circumstance or feelings. The Spirit of the Lord doesn't regard such assertiveness as hypocritical, as though requiring your feelings to bow before your will was somehow insincere because insufficient emotions were present. He can handle the fact that you're worshiping by reason of a determination to praise, and that you're not a man dependent upon "warm fuzzy feelings." In fact, God is possibly *more* blessed by such a "sacrifice of praise," coming from a man's sheer gut-determination, rather than by occasional praises that might arise "whenever I feel like it"!

Here are three key points we can apply to our personal times of worship that will help us praise the Lord more expressively and more meaningfully.

1. *Personalize your praise.*

To begin, it's certainly appropriate to bring high praise to God for His great wonders, His manifold graces of kindness, His mightiness in creation, the beauty of His attributes, etc. That's "personal" in terms of thinking on *His* personal nature and works. Further, there's no higher purpose in praise and worship than to magnify the Savior, to express thanksgiving for His death on the Cross, His saving grace shown to you, and for His goodness in walking with you day to day. These are personal reasons for praise that focus on Jesus Himself. And the most devout Christian will never fully grasp the immensity of these concepts.

However, there are other dimensions of personalizing your praise, and they can be tremendously transforming to our attitudes when we come in worship. Bring your praise "on home!" Whatever the setting, praise Him for where you live; praise Him for the things He has been doing in your life; express praise to God for your family members; and how about your job? Whether good things or bad things have been happening in your career, praise Him! The power of praise will begin to tower above the worst things you face and will pour a shower of added glory around the best things:

In everything give thanks; for this is the will of God in Christ Jesus for you.
1 Thess. 5:18

Every good gift and every perfect gift is from above, and comes down from the Father of lights . . .   James 1:17

Become a person given to *much* praise. Our absolute insurance against ever developing a bitter or perverse spirit, is for you and me as men of worship to be ever-thankful to God. A spirit of gratitude is heart-touched by even life's smallest blessings, and I remember being introduced to this grateful spirit by my Dad.

Indelible to my memory was one time, standing beside my father at a water fountain as he was drinking a glass of cold water. We'd both been working—I was giving it my teenaged best, while he was carrying the larger part of the load the task involved. As he finished, without pretended piety or any religious intonation, I heard him simply say, "Thank You, Lord, for this water." It was nothing loud or prolonged—he simply spoke the words. He noticed I was watching him closely at the moment, and turning to me, he said, "Son, I always thank the Lord for everything— including each glass of water. Not just on hot days in the middle of a job, but *every* time I take a drink." I don't know if it was because of the fact my father was a diabetic and thereby uniquely dependent upon the delicate chemical balance in his body, but somehow, some way, the Holy Spirit had touched a nerve of gratitude in him which touched my heart with under-standing: there's nothing too small for which to praise the Lord.

2. *Verbalize your praise.*

In some of my church background, I grew up in a spiritual environment where deep reverence was expected to be ex-pressed by one's silently bowing before God—and that's all. I learned the posture: eyes squeezed shut, hands folded, lips pursed silently in prayer. And I hasten to say, that such supposed requirements for the show of reverence certainly cannot be said to be "a bad thing." But frankly, it's worth asking the question, "How condu-cive is such silence to the expression of warmth and relationship?"

For example, if I come home from work and walk into the kitchen where my wife is cooking dinner, don't you imagine she'd be puzzled to see me stop, shut my eyes, bow my head, and with hands folded, expect her to "sense" I was bringing a loving greeting of my happiness to be with her and my gratitude for her care for home and family, not to mention her preparation of dinner? Of course, every couple has experienced moments of tender silence, simply sitting together, but love is essentially expressive and my dear lady, Anna, likes to hear me say, "I love you, honey."

Sure, I know that such a parallel of a husband-wife relationship with a worshiper coming before God may be an imperfect analogy. But it's not far off.

We were each created with a mouth, lips, and a tongue. We were given bodies to express and extend our communication. Could it be that God has no interest in their employment when we "commune" with Him? Would the Lord who formed our lips, tongue, and ears prefer our silence when we stand before Him?

Telling my wife about my love not only affirms her, it reinforces and deepens *my love* for her. Verbal confession is strong stuff.

So as you stand, kneel, or sit before the Lord, TELL Him your praise. SPEAK your worship! SING your exaltations! ARTICULATE your deepest feelings and thoughts. This isn't simply "making noise," but it's voicing biblical expressions:

My heart is steadfast, O God, my heart is steadfast; I will sing and give praise...

35

I will praise You, O Lord, among the peoples; I will sing to You among the nations. . . In the midst of the congregation, I will praise You.
                    Psalm 57:7, 9; 22:22

I assure you, brother, VERBALIZING worship can become like a drill bit that will plummet deeper into your being, tapping the possibilities of a new oil of anointing upon your life and the discovering of new riches of intimacy with your Creator.

3. *Mobilize your body.*

Telling my wife that I love her is much better than just thinking it. And better yet is to accompany my words of love with a tangible expression of it with a hug or a kiss. Likewise, engaging the emotions in worship means engaging my body in worship, too.

There are many ways to employ one's body in worship. But before we explore some of them, perhaps we need to address the matter of reserve along these lines. Unfortunately, even though the Bible is *very* pointed in its call to *physical* worship, some negate its importance. I appreciate the fears and the reserve which a few instances of fanaticism may have imposed on thoughtful worshipers. But to become biblical in the physical aspect of our worship is not a sectarian exercise, and a balanced view of physical worship can soon be seen as a logical, natural expression of our relationship with God. This is an added dimension of worship that the Holy Spirit will help us grow into. You don't want to be a fanatic and neither do I, but we can both trust the Holy Spirit. He is artfully gracious—always!—and can grow us into these expressions of worship without turning either of us into writhing weirdos.

Worship With Rededicated Bodies

Look closely with me at the fact the Lord sees your body and mine as a temple of His dwelling and as a literal, physical place not only for His occupancy, but as a center of His being magnified—glorified by what we do with our bodies as well as our spirits.

> *Or do you not know that your body is the temple of the Holy Spirit who is in you, whom you have from God, and you are not your own? For you were bought at a price; therefore glorify God in your body and in your spirit, which are God's.*
> *1 Corinthians 6:19-20*

Now let us reason together a moment. If *our **love*** for the Lord is to flow from ***all** of our entire being and strength*, should we be surprised that Scripture also directs our ***worship*** of the Lord to be expressed with ***all** of our being*—including our bodies? Biblical worship is powerful, not only because it involves every facet of our being, but also because it gloriously transforms us. Whatever part of ourselves or our lives we invest in worship becomes an instrument of ministry, receiving empowerment for becoming God's witnesses.

We've already made clear we're to worship the Lord with our minds, with pure emotions, with our spirits, and our bodies. But let's review in detail the Bible's "anatomy of worship," for it unsurprisingly brings us to the completion of a "grand tour" of our entire being at worship—mind, heart, soul, feelings. . .and body. Look with me at this catalog of scriptural directives which, text by text, call your and my whole physical being to respond in magnifying the Lord.

Knees

Few of us are unaware of the appropriateness of kneeling in prayer, praise, and worship to God, but how many understand the dynamic significance of the bowed knee? It's the symbol of submission—the spiritual indicator that I am yielding to the mastery of the Master. The Centurion who came to Jesus in Luke 7 recognized that a man *submitted* to authority becomes a man *endowed* with authority. **Knees** bowed in worship will become knees powerful in prayer. Interceding knees bring crowns of spiritual power upon the heads of those who pray—and worship paves the way.

Therefore humble yourselves under the mighty hand of God, that He may exalt you in due time.   *1 Peter 5:6*

*Therefore God also has highly exalted Him and given Him the name which is above every name, that at the name of Jesus every **knee** should bow, of those in heaven, and of those on earth, and of those under the earth.*
Philippians 2:9-10

Heads

As surely as it may be bowed in appropriate humility, the **head** of a redeemed man ought also to be lifted upward in praise. It's the posture of confidence. The head that is lifted up in worship becomes emboldened as it realizes it has been graced with authority. When the Lord lifts my head as I worship Him, I'll find new assurance to serve confidently in love, instead of exercising a pseudo authority that's "heady" in the human sense—brash, loud, pushy, inclined to intimidate others, or given to high-sounding religiousness.

*But You, O Lord, are a shield for me, my glory and the One who lifts up my **head**.*   *Psalm 3:3*

*Let us therefore come **boldly** to the throne of grace, that we may obtain mercy and find grace to help in time of need.*   *Hebrews 4:16*

Hands

Aside from the voice lifted in song or verbal praise, upraised **hands** are the most common physical expression of worship mentioned in the Bible. The Hebrew word for thanksgiving includes in its definition "the extension of the hands as with a choir of worshipers." The most natural expression any of us show when either grateful or rejoiced in our hearts is to extend our hands in appreciation or triumph. Further, hands lifted up to God in praise become hands that are willing to serve, and hands that are ready to touch with the healing power of Jesus.

*Therefore, I desire that the men pray everywhere, lifting up holy **hands**, without wrath and doubting.*
1 Timothy 2:8

*Thus I will bless You while I live; I will lift up my **hands** in Your name.*
Psalm 63:4

While there is not time to elaborate the biblical doctrine of "the laying on of hands" (see Hebrews 6:2), one thing is certain: worshiping hands can become direct extensions of Jesus' touch on this earth, and therein is great power.

*His brightness was like the light; He had rays flashing from His **hand**, and there His power was hidden.*
Habakkuk 3:4

Lips

Verbal praise is not simply an exercise of the mouth, tongue, and lips for the immediate moment alone. All worship expressions are not only to magnify the Lord, but to give place to His transforming work in you and me. If my lips are speaking from my heart, two things will happen: (1) My speech mechanisms will, through this act of dedication, be refined and equipped for better speaking to those around me in the spirit of God's love and truth; (2) My open declaration will have a way of sealing my commitments, breaking down doubt and neutralizing hypocrisy and the fear of man. The **mouth** that is opened with praise will be empowered by the Holy Spirit to declare God's Word to others with **lips** that speak the truth in love.

*O Lord, open my **lips**, and my mouth shall show forth Your praise.*
Psalm 51:15

*Because Your lovingkindness is better than life, my **lips** shall praise You.*
Psalm 63:3

*My **lips** shall greatly rejoice when I sing to You, and my soul, which You have redeemed.*
Psalm 71:23

Tongue

In league with my lips, the **tongue** tuned to the truth of worship will never fall prey to the duplicity of which James spoke:

41

*. . .The **tongue** is a little member and boasts great things. See how great a forest a little fire kindles! And the tongue is a fire, a world of iniquity. The tongue is so set among our members that it defiles the whole body, and sets on fire the course of nature; and it is set on fire by hell. For every kind of beast . . .has been tamed by mankind. But no man can tame the tongue. It is an unruly evil, full of deadly poison.*

James 3:5-8

But there is a means of transforming the tongue through worship. The tongue that extols the Most High will learn how to build up others, just as surely as it has learned to magnify God.

*There is one who speaks like the piercings of a sword, but the **tongue** of the wise promotes health.*

Proverbs 12:18

*And my **tongue** shall speak of Your righteousness and of Your praise all the day long.* *Psalm 35:28*

*My heart is overflowing with a good theme; I recite my composition concerning the King; my **tongue** is the pen of a ready writer.* *Psalm 45:1*

Deliver me from the guilt of bloodshed,
O God, the God of my salvation, and my
tongue *shall sing aloud of Your righ-*
teousness.   *Psalm 51:14*

Eyes

Jesus spoke of the eye of the heart or the soul—saying "the lamp of the body is the eye" (Matthew 6:22; Luke 11:34). At worship, the inner eye of the heart may be enlightened. Paul prayed for the Ephesians that "the eyes of your heart may see the Father's hopes for you" (Ephesians 1:17-18, author's paraphrase). There is no question that something transforming happens to the vision of a man at worship. Isaiah said, "I saw the Lord high and lifted up," and it changed the direction of his life from impurity to impassioned service for God (Isaiah 6:1-9). **Eyes** that behold the Lord transform the heart, and they become eyes that can see the lost, that perceive the pain of the broken, and envision ways to serve the needs of others.

Is it not to share your bread with the
hungry, and that you bring to your
house the poor who are cast out; when
*you **see** the naked, that you cover him,*
and not hide yourself from your own
flesh?   *Isaiah 58:7*

*My **eyes** are ever toward the Lord, for*
He shall pluck my feet out of the net.
                            Psalm 25:15

*I will lift up my **eyes** to the hills—from*
whence comes my help?

Psalm 121:1

*Unto You I lift up my **eyes**, O You who*
dwell in the heavens.

Psalm 123:1

Feet

The worshiping man is called to stand in
the Presence of the Lord. Psalm 134:1
speaks of those "who stand by night in the
house of the Lord" at worship before His
throne. To stand is to give full attention; to
stand is to realize you've been welcomed.
To stand is the opposite of a cowering,
groveling stance. While kneeling indicates
reverence, standing reflects understood acceptance and a readiness to be commis-
sioned. Ephesians 6:10-18 repeatedly instructs the believer to "stand" that we may
be equipped for victorious battle against
our adversary. Our **feet**, then, represent
our learning to take a stance by which we
magnify the Lord while at praise, and
commit to walk in obedience to follow
pathways of peace and carry the Gospel to
others.

*I have restrained my **feet** from every*
evil way, that I may keep Your word.
Psalm 119:101

How beautiful upon the mountains are
*the **feet** of him who brings good news,*

44

who proclaims peace, who brings glad tidings of good things, who proclaims salvation, who says to Zion, "Your God reigns!" Isaiah 52:7

*If you turn away your **foot** from the Sabbath, from doing your pleasure on My holy day . . . and shall honor Him, not doing your own ways, nor finding your own pleasure, nor speaking your own words, then you shall delight your-self in the Lord . . .* Isaiah 58:13-14

*You have turned for me my mourning into **dancing**; You have put off my sackcloth and clothed me with glad-ness.* Psalm 30:11

Come with me into His presence, Sir. Come with me often. Let's meet at His throne as men who worship and as men who offer complete worship.

With every aspect of our lives.

With every part of our bodies.

With the entirety of our whole being.

Bless the Lord, O my soul; And all that is within me bless His holy name! Psalm 103:1

TALK ABOUT IT! Chapter questions to discuss with a friend.

1. Discuss the reasons why worship can help you to overcome those "spiritual-toad" feelings. Share some experiences with a brother wherein you overcame a heavy or oppressive spiritual climate through worship.

2. Discuss the difference between *willing* to praise the Lord and *feeling* like praising the Lord. Do you feel hypocritical at times when you worship the Lord without the exuberance that others appear to be experiencing? How does this relate to your understanding of a "sacrifice of praise"?

3. Here's an interesting experiment: employ different physical posturings during your prayer times this month: kneeling, standing, walking, laying prostrate; head bowed, head lifted; hands upraised; etc. and speak your praise *aloud* to the Lord. Note the effects these various styles had on your worship experience. You may be surprised at the results of this experiment!

Chapter Three
Going Against the Grain

The *power* of biblical worship
 is explosive;
The *benefits* of worship
 are all-encompassing;
The *purpose* of worship
 is eternally profound; and thus,
The *opposition* to worship
 by the world-mind is fierce.

Simply put: hell's forces don't want you to be a worshiping man because they don't want you to become a dynamic witness for God.

We know that we are of God, and the whole world lies under the sway of the wicked one.   *1 John 5:19*

And the influence of hell's dark powers on all our minds is often more pronounced than we'd like to think. World-mindedness tends to taint our worship as well.

And do not be conformed to this world, but be transformed by the renewing of your mind. . .   *Romans 12:2*

The "sway of the wicked one," mentioned above, denotes the ceaseless efforts of hellish forces to suppress the advancement of God's Kingdom any way they can. As a result, the world is a hostile environment for people committed to worshiping the Living God in "truth and in spirit." Dynamic worship "goes against the grain" of this world's sway. Therefore, the dimensions of worship to which God has called men are—by their very nature—confrontive.

The attacks may be head-on: doubt sown in your mind; or criticism or anger against your worship patterns. Or, they may be subtle: a temptation to a cool reserve, a hesitation toward expressiveness, or a caution in commitment. But they'll be there—count on it. If hell's forces can't utterly silence the worship of God's people, they will try to pollute, weaken, or cripple its articulate expression. The spirit of the world has made these demands concerning worship:

• If you believe in God, then have *a quiet moment.*

(That's dignified.)

• If you believe in God, express it in *a theological thought.*

(That's respectable.)

• If you believe in God, *do a good deed* to display your worthiness.

(That's laudatory.)

. . . But *whatever* you do, DON'T be demonstrative in worshiping God! Don't act as if you believe the Creator of the Universe is capable of personally enjoying and welcoming your *audible* praise! Don't dare express before God even a fraction of

48

the *physical* enthusiasm, vigor and zeal that you do at a football game! After all, one activity is recreational and enjoyable, while the other is . . . well . . . religious!

So says the world. And that's the kind of thing it has always said. Listen to the voice of your world speaking against worship through the following historical incidents. These true stories all have one common denominator: the world will resist a man's physical expression of worship to God. The world doesn't care if you have silent meditation or cerebral affirmations about God—just as long as the physical, visible, audible realm isn't overtly penetrated. It's because the world insists on preserving its own comfort zones.

Cain's Assault Against Abel

Soiled hands placed the vegetables in a tidy arrangement on the rock altar. Cain felt proud of his display. His brother, Abel, had begun assembling his own offering hours ago and still wasn't done.

Cain was.

All Cain did was walk to his garden and pull up the fine specimens out of the ground. They had grown all by themselves. And the garden was close by. It all seemed so easy.

A smug smile curled Cain's lips. His brother—still searching out in the fields for an offering—was laboring for nothing, Cain mused. He looked again upon his grand, colorful altar.   There it was.

Vegetables.

On the altar.

Easy.

This being one of his first offerings, Cain wondered what exactly was to happen next. Pondering this, he sat on a nearby stone and waited. He looked over at his brother's altar just as Abel came through the bushes carrying several ewe lambs. It wasn't long before the lambs were mounted on Abel's altar and slain.

Cain noticed that Abel's altar was smaller than his. Good.

Having sacrificed the animals on the altar, Abel walked several paces back and knelt in prayer. Cain felt uneasy. He hadn't done that. But he comforted himself by observing that Abel's altar was blood-stained and dirty, while his was neat, tidy and colorful: orange and red and yellow and green and—just then: Whoosh! Brilliant flames from out of nowhere—from another realm—licked up all of Abel's sacrifice! All of it! Cain jumped to his feet. A few ashes drifted in the breeze. The colorful harvest on Cain's altar remained defiantly the same—unchanged. Nothing happened to his.

Cain stormed off, angered and pouting. And it was later, as his tormented mind seethed with hatred and jealousy, that the Lord met him near a tall palm tree: "Why are you angry? And why has your countenance fallen? If you do well, will you not be accepted? And if you do not do well, sin lies at the door. And its desire is for you, but you should rule over it" (Genesis 4:6, 7).

Shortly, Cain's competitive jealousy grew to such intolerable levels that he rose in fury to kill his brother, Abel. And thus, the record teaches us: the first murder was born in the heart of a man who resisted God's ways of worship. The first victim of violence was a man who worshiped God physically, openly, and freely.

Conclusion: the world will violently persecute those who worship the Lord in childlike obedience, even while they themselves exalt their own pretense of religious piety.

From that point in history, open worship of the Most High God has always been challenged and scorned.

• Israel's physical expression of worship through the rite of circumcision—an act of obedience which cut human flesh in the process of identifying with the God of Abraham—was mocked by pagan societies. Circumcision would never cut the world's flesh. But besides refusing the blade themselves, in anger the ancient society scorned those who did circumcise; those whose commitment was so physically expressed, they openly declared their intimate commitment to the true God. Exodus 4:24, 26 demonstrates this world-mind rejection. The anger of Moses' Midianite wife is the evidence of the stance the world held toward circumcision; a reflection of the world's mindset toward those who commit themselves to overtly express their praise and commitment to the Lord.

• Moses begged Pharoah to let God's people go to worship in the wilderness. Although this would not harm the Egyptians in any way, still witnessing the consecration of the Jews to the true God chaffed at heathen flesh. Pharoah could not stand to allow such devotion go unbridled, free from imprisonment—even though the Egyptians were beginning to feel threatened by the great multitude of the Jewish nation within their borders. Pharoah would risk it to punish true spirituality.

• Daniel and his friends revealed an impressive devotion to the Lord, at the same time as they were serving high political offices in a secular kingdom. The price was a death sentence. Yet on two occasions they refused to discontinue worshiping the Lord even though immutable decrees had been contrived by jealous men seeking to unseat them. The famous lion's den and fiery furnace stories (Daniel 3, 6) demonstrate the world's resistance to men who worship God. But they also reveal how the constancy of these men occasioned their dramatic witness of God's saving power to a heathen nation. And it was all by worship!

Perhaps one of the most remarkable case studies of a man's manliness being challenged because of his commitment to praise God openly and joyously, is wrapped in the episode of King David's being confronted by his wife, Michal.

Michal's Mockery

It was a balmy day and Michal was home—irritated again at David's preoccupation with the Ark of the Covenant. He seemed more interested in that wooden box than anything else—constantly talking about his desire for the Presence of God, which, he claimed, resided wherever that box was. His spiritual interests rankled her. After all, it was a triumphant warrior in battle she had married, not a worshiper of an invisible God. And then she heard it. At first, it was the sound of trumpets, and then as it drew nearer, Michal thought she heard yelling, or was it singing?

And there was clapping outside, too!

She hurried to the window and, looking out, saw the large crowd of people advancing toward the city. And then she saw the Ark of God, which she knew David was bent on bringing to Jerusalem to be housed in the special tabernacle he had built for it.

She had to admit, the procession was an interesting sight, but certainly not of any great importance to anybody who knew anything about anything. At least, that was Michal's assessment.

Her gaze had just begun to leave the window, but her attention sprang back instantly—something had caught her eye. She suddenly stiffened, a mixture of amazement, anger, and embarrassment sending surges of adrenaline into her whole system. Her face reddened.

It couldn't be! But it *was*!!

Her husband—this is impossible!!—the king, dancing before the Ark. And look—look what he's wearing! Her emotions churned as she spoke a curse under her breath, looking at David who had shed his regal garments and who was now wearing only a light linen ephod—a humble priestly smock. Michal's wrath wrenched her lips tight. Her hand trembled as she held back the window lace, then—almost tearing the covering from off the window as she slapped the curtain closed, she stormed off to the inner chamber, slamming the door behind her.

It was later that evening when David, having completed his worshipful placement of the Ark in the Jerusalem Tabernacle, entered his home. He was instantly greeted by Michal's enraged countenance and sneering accusation:

> *. . . How glorious was the king of Israel today, uncovering himself today in the eyes of the maids of his servants, as one of the base fellows shamelessly uncovers himself!* 2 Samuel 6:20

David's partial disrobing before all his subjects, as he stripped his royal outer garment to allow freedom for dancing his praise to the Lord God of Israel was, in her opinion, inexcusable. However, David had hardly been guilty of stark nudity or an obscene display that day. He had only danced in joyous praise to God. He had been "leaping and whirling before the Lord." The biblical record says that as she watched him, "she despised him in her heart."

2 Samuel 6 records David's response to Michal's confrontation, not only contextualizing the whole episode with spiritual sensitivity, but describing the unique childlikeness of David's heart toward God:

> *(My dancing) was before the Lord, who chose me instead of your father and all his house, to appoint me ruler over the people of the Lord, over Israel. Therefore I will play music before the Lord, and I will be even more undignified than this, and will be humble in my own sight . . .*   2 Samuel 6:21, 22

Here, yet again, there's a glimpse of the world-spirit's offense when the worship of the Most High God does not suit its cultural tastes or calculated reserve. There is a great deal of truth for us to distill as men who today would answer God's call to worship; drawn to answer it in the conviction that to do so is to see more than praise offered to God, but to see spiritual breakthrough unto fruitful witness and the overthrow of dark powers.

If we, like David, will commit to being men of powerful worship, we can be certain we'll be going against the grain of a cynical world. But such humility resisting the "grain" is destined to make a *gain*! The tragic consequences of a soul resistant to that order of humility which governed David's worship of the Lord, is seen in Michal, who despised her husband for openly praising the Lord. The Bible records the sad consequences of her embittered, socially sophisticated mockery: Barrenness.

Unfruitfulness.

Unproductivity.

Unfulfillment.

For Michal's part, from the moment her wrath burned at the sight of her husband's open worship until she eventually laid in her grave, she had no children—the direct result of her unrepentant hatred of her husband's worship.

There's a message, brother. If I resist worship, I restrict life.

And while being cautious to avoid that attitude, I need to be equally cautious to not feel critical or impatient with anyone who, like Michal, opposes worship. If we're honest, we'll probably find that we have at least a tinge of the same tendency buried somewhere in our own hearts. Or at least the potential for such failure.

Case in point: The "Michal" I found seeking a place in my heart.

"Dance for Me"

I have grown unable to read that story without thinking about our human preoccupation with dignity, and being reminded of a brutal confrontation when God brought me to deal with this problem in my own heart. Let me relate the story as recorded in my book, *Worship His Majesty*:

One is hard put at times to know the best way to tell of personal encounters with the Lord. To many people, the mere suggestion of someone's saying, "The Lord spoke to me," is roughly equivalent to claiming they had tea that afternoon on the Planet Venus with alien beings. To others, opinions about the relative validity of your report vary—from the notion you concocted the conversation yourself, to the cautious venturing of the possibility that God just *might* have spoken.

To whatever category my testimony may relegate me in your judgment, I cannot describe one of my most important experiences in Christ without telling you it began with a specific set of words from Him. There were actually only three words—following which neither the Lord nor I spoke. I did argue, debating mentally in my best forensic style as I recoiled from what He had spoken. But each argument was instantly deflated by so irrefutable a rebuttal that my debate was silenced. It hadn't been He who returned my argument. Simple honesty had me cornered. I simply and intuitively knew that to remain honest with God's dealings in my own heart, I had to obey the command of that quiet internal Voice I recognized so well.

"Dance for Me," the Voice said.

That's right. God told me to dance.

I had been at prayer for an extended period of time one morning, using the church sanctuary as my prayer room. No one was there, except for a few staff people in several of the offices. Thus, you can possibly appreciate my dilemma. Even if I did respond to the Voice and perform some holy jig (after all, who can say "No" to God!), what were the chances it would remain between Him and me? What I felt I certainly *didn't* need was for someone to step in and witness the pastor cavorting about like a rank fanatic!

All the thoughts racing through my mind are difficult to summarize, as I futilely attempted to negotiate the situation with the Most High. I could instantly think of innumerable reasons for *not* dancing: it was *impractical, unnecessary, undesirable* and entirely *unreasonable*! And yet none of the reasons was convincing, because deep down I knew the *real* issue. What God was dealing with was not dancing, but dignity, *false* dignity. Raw, carnal, fear-filled, self-centered *pride*.

I was the victim of Michal's Syndrome—that not-so-rare affliction that characterizes those of us who are more preoccupied with our style, sophistication or dignity than we are with being childlike in praising God. Michal's Syndrome is subject to a wide variety of "expert" opinions. Like competing physicians trying to be first to identify a new virus, there are religious analysts who hasten to advance their varied opinions lest a contagion of simplicity rampage through the Church. Their opinions span the spectrum of tastes so much so that if you simply, frankly, flatly *don't* want expressive worship, you can always find a spiritual expert whose "second opinion" will justify yours:

• "Well, some people just *need* a lot of exuberance. Others of us don't." (The implication is that *mature* people don't.)

• "It's all a matter of a person's cultural background. You and I are culturally reserved." (The implication is that "reserved" is socially superior or culturally advanced.)

• "You must watch out for emotionalism; it becomes *so* subjective and worship loses its objectivity in worshiping God and starts to center on man." (The theological concern for "God's glory" obviously makes this righteously unchallengeable.)

• "I believe—don't you?—that everyone should worship God in his own way, and according to his own beliefs. After all, to do otherwise is. . .well, it's. . .it's un-civil." (You know, each of us should worship God according to the dictates of his own heart.)

59

- (Smiling smugly) "I wouldn't let it worry me. After all, what difference can it make? God looks on the heart, anyway. All this activity doesn't add a thing!" (The ease with which the leader/counselor/observer dismisses it all as irrelevant consoles our quest for an escape from accountability as to our own responsiveness.)

The issue is expressiveness: openness, forthrightness—any assertive display of praise in worship settings beyond socially acceptable, cooperative singing. It begets a bevy of opinions from wild support to angered resistance. It has made me nervous many times, too.

Several of the above arguments had registered with me over the years, and I could think of the others and more. Having had a broad mixture of church background, running the gamut from Presbyterianism and Methodistism to Pentecostalism, I knew the "do's" and "don'ts" of every circle in evangelical Christianity. When it came to acceptable and unacceptable worship practices, I knew dancing wasn't one that *any* of them smiled on. So I didn't like the idea at *all*, and felt that God Himself was bullying me to the wall on an issue we all had the right to differ over.

I had my theology to stand upon, too.

After all, I knew as I stood there—"Dance for Me" still reverberating through my brain—that God's acceptance of me wasn't based on my antics at praise. I knew He didn't measure anyone by a set of calisthen-ics! But just as all these thoughts ran through my mind, I became aware of one stark fact: I could win this argument with *myself*, but I would risk losing something with God. I recognized that my potential "loss" was a hard lesson in humility—

in remaining as a child before the Father;
in keeping small in my own eyes;
in refusing the encrustation of religious sophistry which can inevitably cal-cify the bones of anyone's soul and grip them with a spiritual arthritis.

So, I danced.

I didn't do it well; but then, only God was looking. And within my heart I felt the warm, contented witness that Abba Father was pleased.

I knew His pleasure wasn't because He had won an argument, but because I had won a victory. I knew He wasn't happy because He had managed to exploit my vulnerability, but because I had chosen to *remain* vulnerable. I knew He wasn't dan-gling me as a pawnlike toy because He needed my dancing, but because I needed to respond that way. He knew it was essential to insure my future flexibility, my availabil-ity for learning the pathway of worship-unto-fruitfulness. The last point is so important—*fruitfulness*. Because the Michal Syndrome can lead anyone to a rationalized sense of superiority, it can come at the expense of a deadly, spiritual fruitlessness.

Barrenness is a high price to pay for one's dignity.*

The Michal Mentality. It's how the world feels about worship, hence, the confrontive nature of worship. Thus, each man will likely face a struggle within himself when the Holy Spirit beckons him to become a committed man of worship.

Brother, it's not an issue of your or my being received or loved any more by our Heavenly Father if we worship according to biblical patterns. The issue at hand isn't our relationship with Him, it's the opening of the doors to new dimensions of kingship—of rulership through the power of the Holy Spirit at work in the broken vessel of a man willing to be humble before His God.

And more. It's an issue of our full recognition and response to such great matters as:

• God's worthiness to be praised;
• His Word's directives for worship; and consequently,
• Our allowing God's Spirit to lead us into deeper expressions of adoration.

And so, Sir, God calls you and me to become men of worship, to do so wholeheartedly not mechanically, responsively not reticently, physically but not fanatically, dynamically but not foolishly.

---

* *Worship His Majesty*, Word Books, pages 127-129. Used by permission.

Foremost in our thinking, let us remember that God is not looking for a parade of noise-makers exercising a set of calisthenics for their own sake. Jesus said, "The Father is seeking those who will worship Him in spirit and in truth." The spirit to which He refers is not only that of a man born again through His Blood, but that begotten in a man who has welcomed the fullness of His Holy Spirit. And the "truth" to which He refers is not only that worship which is settled in Him—The Truth, but which is forthrightly aligned with all the biblical patterns of worship which show how, throughout history, true worshipers have timelessly worshiped the true and living God.

• Such is the worship that the world resists with a vengeance. But God rewards our obedience with supernatural boldness. The Lord says to us as He did to Jeremiah:

"Do not be afraid of their faces, for I am with you to deliver you," says the Lord.
                                   Jeremiah 1:8

• Such is the worship which causes hell to tremble in fear, for it is the power of their undoing.

Now when they began to sing and to praise, the Lord set ambushes against the people of Ammon, Moab, and Mount Seir, who had come against Judah; and

they were defeated.
                    2 Chronicles 20:22

That's victorious worship, my brother.
Let's go for it!
Together.

**TALK ABOUT IT! Chapter questions
to discuss with a friend.**

1. How do you feel about "dancing
before the Lord"? Have you ever tried it in
your personal worship times—not just when
the worship leader tells you to? Confess
any difficulties with this to another brother,
and invite the Holy Spirit to work a David-
like worship experience in your own life.

2. Pause a moment to take a spiritual
inventory. How did you act at the last
sports event you attended? How does this
compare with your stance in worship?
Discuss ways you can display more zeal in
your personal prayer and praise times
(without being fanatical!).

3. Do you know any other Christians
where you work? Partner with someone to
pray for your company and your co-work-
ers. Ask the Lord to develop Daniel-like
boldness in prayer concerning your workplace.

Chapter Four
The Invasion of Worship

Invasion: A Weapon of War

For the weapons of our warfare are not carnal but mighty in God for pulling down strongholds, casting down arguments and every high thing that exalts itself against the knowledge of God, bringing every thought into captivity to the obedience of Christ.

2 Corinthians 10:4-5

A hymnal and a rifle.

A worshiping choir and a fighting company of Marines.

A majestic cathedral organ and a Patriot Missile.

. . . Each of these may seem like dichotomous pairs with unrelated partners. At first glance, worship and warfare don't seem to have anything in common except the letter "w". But worship *is* a spiritual weapon.

Consider with me, Sir, the possibility of a man's intertwining worship and warfare. In this passage from Isaiah, observe the relationship between violent spiritual conquest and praise-filled music:

You shall have a song as in the night when a holy festival is kept, and gladness of heart as when one goes with a flute, to come into the mountain of the Lord, to the Mighty One of Israel. The

Lord will cause His glorious voice to be heard, and show the descent of His arm, with the indignation of His anger and the flame of a devouring fire, with scattering, tempest, and hailstones. For through the voice of the Lord, Assyria will be beaten down, who struck with a rod. And in every place where the staff of punishment passes, which the Lord lays on him, it will be with tambourines and harps; and in battles of brandishing He will fight with it.   *Isaiah 30:29-32*

Isaiah gives us a behind-the-scenes look into the spiritual realm wherein God fights enemy hosts with the accompaniment of musical praise and worship from His people—but look at yet another episode. Perhaps the most dramatic biblical account of the warfare aspect of worship is seen when King Jehoshaphat led his people to military victory by putting the choir in front of the army!

And they rose early in the morning and went out into the Wilderness of Tekoa; and as they went out, Jehoshaphat stood and said, "Hear me, O Judah and you inhabitants of Jerusalem: Believe in the Lord your God, and you shall be established; believe His prophets, and you shall prosper." And when he had consulted with the people, he appointed those who should sing to

*the Lord, and who should praise the
beauty of holiness, as they went out
before the army and were saying:
"Praise the Lord, for His mercy endures
forever."*

2 Chronicles 20:20, 21

The enemy was destroyed as the worshipers went first into battle.

Invading the Promised Land

Worship is highly significant to any form
of spiritual battle and it played a key role in
God's people taking possession of the Promised Land. Remember, Israel's preparation
in the wilderness—readying to enter the
Promised Land—was twofold. First, they
received the Law; second, they were instructed to build the Tabernacle. It's significant to see how receiving the Word of the
Commandments took about 40 days, but
the preparation of the Tabernacle, and their
learning God's way to worship there, took
about a year. As men, we might well ask
ourselves, "Is it easier for me to listen to and
intellectually assimilate the Bible than it is
to spiritually and practically commit myself
to vital expressions of worship?!"

It's an important consideration, because
Israel's victorious invasion of the land required a people ready to trust in the Presence of God as well as His Promise. Crucial
to the tearing down of enemy strongholds,
gaining military victory, and forging new

paths into a God-given, promised-land destiny was the worship of God via the tabernacle. His Presence, released by worship, spearheaded the invasion into enemy territory.

Invading Darkness: Songs in the Night

What are the potential implications of these insights for you and me as men living on the edge of the 21st Century? The answer is that while times change, the pathways to power do not. Worship is still the way for invading and winning.

Maybe it's not a promised land you see laying before you.

Maybe it's darkness. Inky black hopelessness that presses in to suffocate you. Silently, it speaks. It denies any hope for the future. It seeks to crush the words God has spoken to you in times past. It strains to erase every memory of joy and light you ever knew.

Darkness speaks. And it must be answered.

In song.

As we'll see, the Lord makes clear that worshiping in song—*even* in, *especially* in, dark times—is a believer's "nuclear arsenal" provided by God to obliterate the enemy and his works.

Now by "song" I'm not referring to our parroting the latest "easy listening" pop tune that has a cheerful message. I'm talking about placing the Word of God on your lips with heart-embraced melody—maybe from a chorus you remember from church, or scriptural truth paraphrased in your own words and melody—that's just as potent. Don't worry about *sounding* good. To sing truth with any degree of sincerity and the motive of lifting up the Lord—*that's* what detonates the nuclear explosion against the forces of hell! The Lord wants to teach men, all of us, the awesome power of song.

Six in the morning, a hidden corner of the house, nobody listening, face still unshaven; nevertheless—a gentle song rises simply from the lips of a man gutsy enough to defy his own fragile ego which clamors for protection against change—and fights to keep a self-perceived dignity intact, a dignity that loves nothing but itself.

Yes, it cuts. Like circumcision, growing in worship can cut—but it cuts away fear, doubt, and pride.

And worship in song also cuts right through the wall of darkness, shredding, with hurricane violence, the clouds of blackness trying to engulf your tomorrows with doom. Such worship comes with a price, but it buys so much more than you can imagine! God eagerly awaits for the moment you part your lips in song. For by it, you are tuning up to the symphony of Heaven, where the Song is being sung eternally, and by tuning up to Heaven's frequency, you usher in the dominion of God whose praises you sing!

You have nothing to sing about?—only futility, despair, and hopelessness? Then you're the *perfect candidate* to launch forth in song . . . according to the reasoning of the Lord:

*"**Sing, O barren,** you who have not borne! Break forth into singing, and cry aloud, you who have not labored with child! For more are the children of the desolate than the children of the married woman," says the Lord.*
Isaiah 54:1

How Lord? How could you ask us to do the *opposite* of what we feel like doing? Answer: if you do what you *feel* like doing, you'll just continue to despair. Right? When you're despairing, you don't *feel* like rejoicing before God. But how potent a spiritual weapon this is!

*For this cause everyone who is godly shall pray to You in a time when You may be found; surely in a flood of great waters they shall not come near him. You are my hiding place; You shall preserve me from trouble; You shall surround me with **songs of deliverance.** Selah*   *Psalm 32:6-7*

Why in the world would singing result in our deliverance? Because the oppressive works of hell cannot tolerate the singing of saints who refuse to be overtaken by circumstances and spiritual oppression, but instead lift their voices heavenward in song!

*Let the word of Christ dwell in you
richly in all wisdom, teaching and ad-
monishing one another in psalms and
hymns and **spiritual songs**, singing
with grace in your hearts to the Lord.*
Colossians 3:16

*And do not be drunk with wine, in
which is dissipation; but be filled with
the Spirit, speaking to one another in
psalms and hymns and **spiritual
songs**, singing and making melody in
your heart to the Lord.*

Ephesians 5:18-19

The above words from two of Paul's letters
merge together to teach us the power of song
to (1) keep you filled with the Holy Spirit, and
(2) make the Word of God alive and powerful
in your spirit and soul. It almost seems that
worshiping in song provides the spiritual
enzymes by which the "meat of the Word" is
digested and assimilated into our lives.

*Where were you when I laid the founda-
tions of the earth? Tell Me, if you have
understanding. Who determined its
measurements? Surely you know! Or
who stretched the line upon it? To what
were its foundations fastened? Or who
laid its cornerstone, when **the morning stars sang together,** and all the
sons of God shouted for joy?*
Job 38:4-7

In this passage, God describes to Job a
behind-the-scenes view of creation when

God's majestic art and wisdom hurled the universe into existence amid angelic song.

Think with me a moment about that. Creation. Accompanied by song. Could there be a connection? Of course there was at the time of Creation eons ago, but what about *now*? Could there be a universal spiritual dynamic still in force today?

I believe the Lord would have us understand that if we would enter into worshipful song more freely, more often, it would release Him to work far more creatively in life's circumstances. And whatever blessing or goodness the Lord wants to work in our lives—even if it doesn't exist yet—He can create it. Out of nothing . . . nothing but your song.

Paul knows what he's talking about when he says, "I will sing with the spirit, and I will also sing with the understanding" (1 Cor. 14:15b). His dramatic firsthand experience with the power of song is recorded in Acts 16:25-34. When he sang in worship, the bondage of a Philippian dungeon was shattered; and as a result, salvation came to the jailer's household.

Paul's song broke chains and flung open prison doors. The same power of song waits to be born on your lips, too.

Not long ago, in one of our men's meetings, hundreds of men were praising God with a holy boldness. It was a glorious time. At the conclusion of this "high worship" time, the Holy Spirit spoke through a word of prophecy. He said: "Against many of you the enemy of your souls has suppressed the childlike freedom to sing. He has kept you from singing ever since your adolescence when your voices changed. You felt embarrassed at the awkward irregularity of your voice. It sounded neither like a man nor a boy, but rather hovered in a transitional 'no man's land' of indecisiveness. Therefore, many of you no longer sing." But God declared that evening, "I'm bringing you to have a man's voice—a voice of authority and freedom to sing. For you have seen how a clear, powerful voice can literally shatter glass. And so there are obstacles that the Adversary has put before you in your life. But if you use your voice of worship—moving into boldness, confidence, and clarity of focus on Me—I will shatter, with your voice of praise, those barriers in your life that have seemed so impenetrable! So praise Me, My sons, worship with a bold, new voice!"

Let's pick up the theme, brother!

Sing!! And watch God break through in creative power and with shattering deliverance from bondage.

TALK ABOUT IT! Chapter questions to discuss with a friend.

1. Consider how you might wage spiritual warfare through praise and worship, followed by intercessory prayer, for a situation you're facing in your life right now. Share your prayer burden with another brother and plan your battle strategy.

2. Is it easier for you to play "Bible Trivia"—intellectually assimilating biblical teachings—than to spiritually and practically commit yourself to expressions of worship? If so, confess your tendency to trust in your own understanding instead of leaning on Him (Prov. 3:5, 6) and begin to open up to the Holy Spirit's leading in this vital area.

3. Do you make a regular practice of "singing in the spirit"? Pray together with another brother about any perceived inadequacies you feel about your voice and receive the promise of the word of prophecy written above. Practice singing bold praises to the Lord: in your car, in the shower, wherever you can!

Chapter Five
Worship:
Key to Evangelism

It was like being hit in the head with a five-pound sledge hammer!

Seated in the 8,000-seat convention center, I was listening to a man present *The First Ministry of Evangelism* to the massive group of pastors with whom I was seated in the giant arena. The thing he just said had stunned me: "The foundational pathway to evangelism is the cultivation of a people who will worship God."

I'd never heard anything like that.

Everything in my thoroughly evangelical background had been rooted in methods, training programs, witnessing campaigns, soul-winning approaches, altar workers guidelines, crusades and outreaches, etc. But worship?

Well, I believed in worship all right. And I knew that it wasn't unimportant. But it did seem like something remote to evangelism. To my mind "worship" was something Christians did *after* they were saved, *not* something they did in order to *see* people saved. I was puzzled by the speaker's proposition.

He went on: "Look at Acts 13," he exclaimed. And turning there, my attention was drawn to one of the most pivotal places and times in the history of the Early Church.

The place: Antioch, the new center of revival, where the Holy Spirit was moving in power.

The time: A season of waiting on the Lord for His purposes in the midst of this revival blessing.

I sat forward in my seat, looking around at the other 8,000 in the room, to see if they were feeling the awakening that was occurring in my soul. The speaker continued:

"Notice that 'as they ministered to the Lord and fasted,' the Word says that the Holy Spirit began to speak and to direct activities which became the most historic strategy for global evangelism since Jesus gave the great commission."

I knew what he was talking about. It's right after this time of "ministry to the Lord" (which is a biblical expression for worshiping) that Paul and Barnabas set forth on their first world-shaking missionary journey. I was starting to see it: *WORSHIP PRECEDES EVANGELISM*. The case was expanded from earlier events as I began to capture the principle:

• At Pentecost, the outpouring of the Holy Spirit produced supernatural *worship*: "We hear them speaking in our own tongues the wonderful works of God" (Acts 2:11). While Peter's preaching brought 3,000 decisions, it was praise and worship which drew the crowd and impressed the onlookers that they were seeing a miracle manifestation of God's Presence.

• I suddenly saw also how God had delivered Israel from Egypt to bring His nation to be (1) a people of blessed purpose (Ex. 3:15-17), and (2) a witness to the nations (Ex. 19:6). BUT . . . but the *key* to this realization would be *worship*, and the *pathway* to their purpose and victory would be via Sinai's Law (God's Word) and Moses' Tabernacle (God's worship). The fruit of their learning to know and honor God in worship resulted eventually in a people who conquered the land of God's purposed possession for them.

So there it was: Worship paves the way to evangelism! Worship is the pathway to expanded boundaries! I could see it in the Word, though I never had before, and it immediately began to change my life.

The result was to introduce the small group of people at the new pastorate I accepted shortly thereafter, to a priority of *"ministering to the Lord."* Taking that phrase from the Acts 13 record, and noting its repetition in the OT record of the priestly ministry of Aaron and his sons (Ex. 28:41; 29:1, 44; 30:30; et. al.) we committed to become a people of worship. These basic guidelines governed this pursuit:

• We would not apologize for biblical expressions of worship, but we would consistently explain them with graciousness, in a way that would invite but not coerce participation. *Discovery: People wanted to be free to worship expressively, and did—but for a reason.* The reason—

• We refused to be either mystical, unseemly, or fanatical in our expressiveness. In other words, we contended that spiritual worship would also logically be as sensitive, sensible, and scriptural as it was open, free, and joyous. *Discovery: Biblical controls prohibited foolishness, and spiritual sensitivity brought unity and a choir-like joining together in a loving worship of the Lord.*

Of course, expressiveness was the challenge. Most church worship forms don't present any problem (other than a possibility for deadness, dryness, or flesh-pampering caution) unless they are openly expressed. But by pursuing a biblical child-likeness, a joyous, gentle freedom filled the house whenever we came together.

But there was one key to it all which I've rarely mentioned.

Men who worship.

That is, cultivating men who would become *active* in worship.

I learned early on that if the men don't move into worship leadership, a certain kind of tinniness and short-lived exuberance was the best we could manage. If the body was to rise as a worshiping assembly, the men of the congregation would need to lead the way.

Not necessarily as singers.

Not necessarily as musicians.

Not necessarily as public leaders.

But the release of worship awaited a cadre of committed men who would lay aside male reserve and whatever vestige of pride would seek to find a haven in some secret corner of our souls—and worship!

Worship with full-bodied singing.

Worship with a ready understanding.

Worship with forthright joyousness.

Worship with "holy hands" upraised.

Worship and magnify the Savior as disciples who have answered His call to "Follow Me," and to follow Him right into the presence of the Father with praiseful song and biblically directed, soul-humbling, life-transforming worship.

The result was as had been predicted by the teacher who touched my heart with that transforming viewpoint—*Worship First!*

Evangelism followed. Marvelously, mightily, and continually.

As of the date of this writing, it is difficult to enumerate the whole of the record of God's grace in evangelistic results where worship was put in its biblical place—FIRST, and with MEN leading the way.

In the nearly 25 years since beginning, more than 40,000 decisions for Jesus Christ have been realized at our church services. More than 30 churches have been planted elsewhere, and over 100 pastors and church leaders have gone out from this one congregation to serve the Body of Christ. More than 100 nations are touched in some way each year by evangelistic enterprises reaching out from this worship center, and more than $20 million have been given away to serve human need and the spread of the Gospel of the Kingdom of God from Los Angeles to the far corners of the earth.

The Central Focus

But the central focus in this writing is to you, my brother. To you as a man who—like Abraham, Moses, David, Daniel, Peter, and Paul—God has called to worship Him "in spirit and in truth."

I have concluded with a testimony of God's dealing with me—one man. And the impact affected a whole "house"—the family of an entire congregation which grew and continues to do so as we worship the Lord today. But I began another way.

I began by sharing the story of another man named Jack. A roofing contractor who had a tough situation to deal with in his family, and who recognized that his role as a worshiping man might hold the key to the dominion of God's Kingdom over the situation. And it did. He worshiped God. God won the victory. Jack rejoiced in the aftermath. Hallelujah!

And so the "Hallelujahs!" are waiting to roll—

In heaven, as we join the angel
hosts in praise-filled worship;
On earth, as we take our place

shoulder-to-shoulder as men at
worship in our gatherings;
In the invisible, as hell's powers are
put to flight by our praises to the
Most High; and
In our homes and communities,
where transformed possibilities
are truly present if worshiping
men can be found.

The man who worships has already
begun his witness. But the man who worships will find his presence and his words
become welcomed by the needy and hungry
among whom he lives and with whom he
works. While the world may at times mock
the worshiping man, when that same
society's systems crumble, when the sick
suffer, when the homes collapse, when the
problems are pressing on people you
meet—it's to the worshiping man the world
turns.

And that's when the testimony of Jesus
the Savior is yours and mine to give. Our
witness of His power to save will find ready
entrance among those who have been watching a man like you.

A man of true worship, before the true
and living God.

TALK ABOUT IT! Chapter questions to discuss with a friend.

1. Take a moment to partner in prayer with a brother about your unsaved friends and family members. Begin with worship and thanksgiving, and ask the Lord to release pathways into their hearts and lives through the witness of your worshipful lifestyle.

2. Why is it important for men to move into worship leadership? Describe any reticence you may feel about your own participation in leading in worship and discuss ways you see how this temptation to timidity can be overcome.

3. You don't need to be on the church platform in order to be a worship leader: You can take more initiative when praying with friends or you can boldly lift your voice in praise during corporate worship and be an example to those around you in the congregation. Choose to be a worship leader in your arena of influence, whatever it may be!

DEVOTIONS
FROM SELECTED
PSALMS

Contributed by Bob Anderson

The Book of Psalms, written over a significant span of time from 1000—300 B.C., was authored by several men including King David, Solomon, Moses, Asaph, the Sons of Korah, and others. It contains a collection of hymns and prayers used for worship in Solomon's Temple as well as additional songs which were incorporated into the psalter later on.

The Psalms are rich in Hebrew poetry, a writing style primarily distinguished by the rhyming of thoughts instead of words.

It's interesting to note that about half of the references to the Messiah recorded by New Testament writers come directly from the Book of Psalms. Even Jesus confirms the Messianic prophecy of the Psalms in Luke 24:44.

The outstanding themes throughout this book are *prayer* and *praise* to the Most High God. The worship it instructs exceeds quiet devotional thoughts, encouraging active expressions of worship such as: clapping and shouting (47:1), bowing (95:6), lifting up of hands (141:2), and dancing (149:3).

(It is suggested that this devotional be used for stimulating discussion and prayer within a small group of men meeting regularly.)

☐ **Today's Text: Psalm 1** *(key vv. 2-3)*

1 **Today's Truth:** The Hebrew word for "meditate" transcends the idea of silent reflection upon the Word of God meaning "to mutter or make a quiet sound upon one's lips." That's the picture of a person *totally* immersed in God's Word! The promised results: prosperity in every area of life and upon all that we do!

Today's Thoughts:───────────

──────────────────────────

──────────────────────────

☐ **Today's Text: Psalm 4** *(key v. 7)*

2 **Today's Truth:** God gives us the power to enjoy what we have and to be glad in any situation—*more* than those people who have riches and good fortune but don't serve the Lord (Ecc. 5:10,19). Without God, life's blessings are meaningless and powerless to fill us with joy.

Today's Thoughts: ───────────

──────────────────────────

──────────────────────────

☐ **Today's Text: Psalm 8** *(key v.3)*

3 **Today's Truth:** David extols the One who constructed the Universe with His *fingers*. Certainly our personal problems can be borne by the *hands* of God whose mere *fingerwork* spans the greatest distances measured by man—more than 100 million light years of awesome craftsmanship!

Today's Thoughts: ───────────

──────────────────────────

──────────────────────────

☐ **Today's Text: Psalm 18** *(key vv. 11-14)*

4 **Today's Truth:** When we walk through the "valley of the shadow of death" or struggle through a season of personal darkness—not able to see "where God is" or what He is doing—we can rest in the knowledge that our darkness is God's hiding place. He is in there *with us* even though we can't see Him. And at the right moment, God will "thunder from heaven" and fight for us!

Today's Thoughts: _____
_____
_____

☐ **Today's Text: Psalm 20** *(key v. 7)*

5 **Today's Truth:** Some people trust in physical power to deliver them, but we have the Name of the Lord—a resource of help *far more solid* than earth's physical foundations. Though even the best of us may be tempted to look to the world for help when trials burn hot, time proves over and over that the Creator of everything is our security.

Today's Thoughts: _____
_____
_____

☐ **Today's Text: Psalm 22** *(key v. 1)*

6 **Today's Truth:** This psalm is rich in Messianic prophecy accurately predicting events in Jesus' life 1000 years before they happened! Only God could have fulfilled such prophetic complexity!

Today's Thoughts: _____
_____
_____

☐ **Today's Text: Psalm 23** *(key v. 6)*

7 **Today's Truth:** The scope of this psalm is precious and all-encompassing. <u>In this life</u>, goodness and mercy *shall pursue us!* . . . and throughout <u>all eternity</u> we'll *dwell with God* in His house! . . . if we'll only follow the Great Shepherd.

Today's Thoughts: ―――――――――

―――――――――――――――――――――

―――――――――――――――――――――

☐ **Today's Text: Psalm 25** *(key v. 1)*

8 **Today's Truth:** Sometimes the *gravity* of our trials or the *depth* of our pain occasions a *simple* posture: lifting up our souls to God. It's like a child lifting up a badly cut finger, "Owiee! Fix it, Daddy! Make it better!"

Today's Thoughts: ―――――――――

―――――――――――――――――――――

―――――――――――――――――――――

☐ **Today's Text: Psalm 32** *(key v. 1)*

9 **Today's Truth:** The condition of a person whose sins have been forgiven is "blessed," which literally means: "happy!" No one needs to be lost—no matter how vile his sins—if only he'll accept Jesus. God made salvation so simple that a child can understand and enter in, and yet so compelling that a scholar, if willing to come with simple faith as a child, can know the Lord.

Today's Thoughts: ―――――――――

―――――――――――――――――――――

―――――――――――――――――――――

☐ **Today's Text: Psalm 34** *(key v. 19)*

10 **Today's Truth:** Good! Just because I'm having an abundance of tough times, doesn't mean God is angry with me! Righteous people experience many afflictions, the Word says. 1 Pet. 5:9 encourages us that we're not alone in our sufferings. But we remain confident because of the promise: *God delivers the righteous out of them all!*

Today's Thoughts: _____

_____

_____

☐ **Today's Text: Psalm 45** *(key v. 1)*

11 **Today's Truth:** Our tongues should be like the pen of a ready writer—poised to lift up articulate praise to God. Here the psalmist uses his imagination to extol the Lord in fresh, powerful ways. What a talent to cultivate: finding *new ways* to tell the Lord how great He is!

Today's Thoughts: _____

_____

_____

☐ **Today's Text: Psalm 47** *(key v. 1)*

12 **Today's Truth:** For some of us, open and strong praise is difficult either because we were raised to be "quietly reverent" or because we feel that bold worship might turn us into fanatics. But should our cheers for our favorite sports team outdo our enthusiasm towards the Almighty? Selah.

Today's Thoughts: _____

_____

_____

☐ **Today's Text: Psalm 51** *(key v. 10)*

13 **Today's Truth:** David's heart-rending psalm of repentance has at its center the plea for a clean heart and a steadfast spirit. Forgiveness was not enough—David wanted strength to avoid future sin. But he knew he needed a redeemed nature from God's Spirit in order to continue to be victorious in the face of future temptation.

Today's Thoughts: _____

_____

_____

☐ **Today's Text: Psalm 55** *(key v. 22)*

14 **Today's Truth:** Reminiscent of 1 Peter 5:7, this verse affirms that if we cast our cares on God, He will sustain us. *Sustain* is a "power" word, meaning: to support, protect, provide food, nourish, defend, and give all means needed for living.

Today's Thoughts: _____

_____

_____

☐ **Today's Text: Psalm 62** *(key v. 11)*

15 **Today's Truth:** The human mind boggles. It isn't that "lots of power" belongs to God. Rather, *POWER* belongs to God. Period. When we worship Jesus, we are in touch with ALL POWER . . . available to flow into any of life's situations!

Today's Thoughts: _____

_____

_____

☐ **Today's Text: Psalm 63** *(key v. 1)*

16 **Today's Truth:** David set himself to seek God *early*. With pressurized schedules the way they are nowadays, often the only time left to carve from is the tail end of sleep! But the sacrifice of early worship is rewarded by God's rulership throughout the day. For God is "enthroned in the praises of His people" (Ps. 22:3).

Today's Thoughts: _____

_____

_____

☐ **Today's Text: Psalm 71** *(key vv. 20-21)*

17 **Today's Truth:** Although God allows troubles in our lives, He is quick and desirious to lift us out of our "pit" of despair, "bundle us up" in comfort, and enlarge the dimensions of our destinies!

Today's Thoughts: _____

_____

_____

☐ **Today's Text: Psalm 91** *(key vv. 11-12)*

18 **Today's Truth:** The Lord has given His angels as guardians over us. Apparently, *more* than one angel has been personally assigned to each of us as evidenced by the plural text. In heaven we may discover the myriad of ways they protected us!

Today's Thoughts: _____

_____

_____

☐ **Today's Text: Psalm 100** *(key v. 4)*

19 **Today's Truth:** This verse indicates that it's always good to approach the Lord with thanksgiving and praise on our lips—as opposed to popping into His presence with prayer requests and leaving just as quickly, devoid of any worship or gratitude.

Today's Thoughts: _____

_____

_____

☐ **Today's Text: Psalm 103** *(key v. 2)*

20 **Today's Truth:** David commands his own soul not to forget all of God's benefits, and then he proceeds to enumerate scores of them. At times when we are most downcast, it is all the more critical to speak aloud all that God has done for us throughout our lives.

Today's Thoughts: _____

_____

_____

☐ **Today's Text: Psalm 107** *(key v. 31)*

21 **Today's Truth:** The psalmist almost groans while expressing his wish for men to give thanks to God. Obviously, God's unceasing work throughout the world far outnumbers the people who thank Him.

Today's Thoughts: _____

_____

_____

☐ **Today's Text: Psalm 112** *(key vv. 1-3)*

22 **Today's Truth:** With such promises of God's spectacular and all-encompassing blessing upon those who diligently cleave to Him, it's amazing we don't worship Him more freely, more diligently, more often. People who do will find their hearts transformed by the nearness of His presence. Such are the people in whom God can trust with prosperity—because of the selfless love that's born in their hearts through praise.

Today's Thoughts: _____

_____

_____

☐ **Today's Text: Psalm 121** *(key vv. 7-8)*

23 **Today's Truth:** God's preservation of our souls from all evil during "our going out and coming in" is predicated on our eyes being lifted to Him in confident faith that He—Maker of Heaven and Earth—is our only true help.

Today's Thoughts: _____

_____

_____

☐ **Today's Text: Psalm 122** *(key v. 1)*

24 **Today's Truth:** David loved worshiping the Lord so much, the mere mention of going to the house of the Lord brought joy!

Today's Thoughts: _____

_____

_____

☐ **Today's Text: Psalm 126** *(key v. 1)*

25 **Today's Truth:** When the Lord brings full redemption and freedom to His saints, it can almost seem like a wonderful dream—too good to be true. But that's God's goal for us: abundant life, wherein He causes us to inherit beauty for ashes, and wherein He makes our former darkness to shine as the noonday sun (Isaiah 58:10; 61:3).

Today's Thoughts: _____

_____

_____

☐ **Today's Text: Psalm 127** *(key v. 1)*

26 **Today's Truth:** Our best effort without the Lord's blessing is an exercise in *futility*. Our expecting God to do everything without our obedient participation is *presumption*. This verse speaks of balance between human endeavor and Omnipotent *involvement*.

Today's Thoughts: _____

_____

_____

☐ **Today's Text: Psalm 139** *(key vv. 23-24)*

27 **Today's Truth:** David's quickness to seek the Lord's righteousness and lay his heart bare before Him helped cause him to be known as ''a man after God's own heart'' (1 Sam. 13:14).

Today's Thoughts: _____

_____

_____

☐ **Today's Text: Psalm 141** *(key v. 2)*

28 Today's Truth: What personal sacrifices do we make by raising our hands in worship to God?—Fleshly pride. Independence. Arrogance. False dignity. And what beautiful things does such a sacrifice of worship work within us? Humility. Grace. Power. A child-like spirit.

Today's Thoughts: _____

_____

_____

☐ **Today's Text: Psalm 145** *(key v. 4)*

29 Today's Truth: It is critical for us parents to instill within our kids a vital, personal faith—one in which they have a vested ownership. As the Book of Judges shows us, God's blessing and revelation can be lost in just one quick generation.

Today's Thoughts: _____

_____

_____

☐ **Today's Text: Psalm 149** *(key v. 3)*

30 Today's Truth: For most of us, the idea of dancing before the Lord induces embarrassment. Who among us can dance with skill, confidence, or precision? Very few. Yet a praiseful swaying of upraised hands with a simple step of the feet in worship—and in God's eyes—you're beyond Baryshnikov!

Today's Thoughts: _____

_____

_____

☐ **Today's Text: Psalm 150** *(key v. 6)*

31 **Today's Truth:** A fitting conclusion to the psalter is this repetitive exhortation to let all who have breath ''praise Him, praise Him, praise Him . . . '' (ad infinitum, amen, and hallelujah!). In other words, if you are still breathing, worship the Lord!

Today's Thoughts: _____

_____

_____

Additional Resources for Biblical Manhood

Available from Jack Hayford and
Living Way Ministries

AUDIO CASSETTE MINI-ALBUMS (2 tapes)

Honest to God	SC122	$8
Redeeming Relationships for Men & Women	SC177	$8
Why Sex Sins Are Worse Than Others	SC179	$8
How God Uses Men	SC223	$8
A Father's Approval	SC225	$8
Resisting the Devil	SC231	$8
How to Recession-Proof Your Home	SC369	$8
Safe Sex!	SC448	$8
The Leader Jesus Trusts	SC461	$8

AUDIO CASSETTE ALBUMS (# of tapes)

Cleansed for the Master's Use (3)	SC377	$13
Becoming God's Man (4)	SC457	$17
Fixing Family Fractures (4)	SC217	$17
The Power of Blessing (4)	SC395	$17
Men's Seminars 1990-91 (10)	MSEM	$42
Premarital Series (12)	PM02	$50
A Family Encyclopedia (24)	SC233	$99

VHS VIDEO ALBUMS

Why Sex Sins Are Worse Than Others	WSSV	$19
Divorce and the People of God	DIVV	$19
Earthly Search for a Heavenly Father	ESFV	$19

Add 15% for shipping and handling.
California residents add 8.25% sales tax.

Request your free Resource Catalog.

Living Way Ministries Resources
14820 Sherman Way • Van Nuys, CA 91405-2233
(818) 779-8480 or (800) 776-8180